Anoara
Mughal

THINK!

Metacognition-powered

PRIMARY
TEACHING

CORWIN

A SAGE company
2455 Teller Road
Thousand Oaks, California 91320
(0800)233-9936
www.corwin.com

SAGE Publications Ltd
1 Oliver's Yard
55 City Road
London EC1Y 1SP

SAGE Publications Inc.
2455 Teller Road
Thousand Oaks, California 91320

SAGE Publications India Pvt Ltd
B 1/I 1 Mohan Cooperative Industrial Area
Mathura Road
New Delhi 110 044

SAGE Publications Asia-Pacific Pte Ltd
3 Church Street
#10-04 Samsung Hub
Singapore 049483

Editor: James Clark
Assistant editor: Diana Alves
Production editor: Tanya Szwarnowska
Proofreader: Derek Markham
Indexer: Adam Pozner
Marketing manager: Dilhara Attygalle
Cover design: Wendy Scott
Typeset by: C&M Digitals (P) Ltd, Chennai, India
Printed in the UK

Library of Congress Control Number: 2021932460

British Library Cataloguing in Publication data

A catalogue record for this book is available from the British Library

ISBN 978-1-5297-1358-9
ISBN 978-1-5297-1357-2 (pbk)

At SAGE we take sustainability seriously. Most of our products are printed in the UK using responsibly sourced papers and boards. When we print overseas we ensure sustainable papers are used as measured by the PREPS grading system. We undertake an annual audit to monitor our sustainability.

CONTENTS

ABOUT THE AUTHOR

Anoara Mughal is an experienced Year 6 teacher and an Assistant Headteacher, who is passionate about language acquisition, closing the disadvantage gap and promoting social justice.

She has been teaching for fifteen years and currently teaches in a primary school in East London leading English, Attendance and Punctuality, Remote Learning and Challenge. She has also recently led CPD, Pupil Premium, metacognition, P4C, PPA cover, PGCE mentor and curriculum. Anoara has led Year 6 across two schools, English across three schools, developed two school libraries and designed and implemented the primary curriculum from scratch in two schools. She has also served as a parent governor at a local secondary school. As part of her initial degree course, she studied neurology, which first sparked her interest in how the brain works. During teaching she discovered a new found interest in the area of cognitive psychology. A former writing moderator, Anoara also served as a parent governor for a local secondary school. She is renowned for raising standards and school improvement. She has supported teachers and school leaders across the UK and delivered CPD nationally.

She serves on the Steering Group @HealthyToolkit and is a Network Leader @WomenEdLondon. Anoara is passionate about promoting equality, equity and diversity in education and has arranged two unconferences for @WomenEd. She has also delivered presentations about educational leadership at WomenEd conferences. She has written a number of online articles including for the TES, the Chartered College of Teaching and Learnus UK.

Her article entitled: 'Metacognition: Books, resources and teaching tips to help students know themselves as learners', was published online, by the Chartered College of Teaching, in January 2018.

In 2020, she founded @IMetacognition and currently hosts monthly chats.

Anoara is a founding fellow at the Chartered College of Teaching and passed the NPQH in 2020. Anoara is a skilled practitioner, who is committed to driving social change. She has helped children to maximise their learning potential enabling them to achieve academic and pastoral success. You can follow her @anoara_a.

ACKNOWLEDGEMENTS

There are so many people I would like to thank for this book. Thank you to Aidan Severs @thatboycanteach Chris Dyson @ChrisDysonHT, Keranjit Kaur @kerran77, Charles Wilson @chicanddot for encouraging me to blog.

#WomenEd @WomenEd and and in particular Vivienne Porritt @ViviennePorritt, Christalla Jamil @ChristallaJ, Alison Kriel @AlisonKriel, Hannah Wilson and @Ethical_leader thank you for helping me to become #10percentbraver and for finding my voice.

Melissa Create @melissacreate, Kathryn Morgan @KLMorgan_2 and Dr Jennifer A Hawkins @jenhawk6248, thank you for sending research papers my way. Mark Barker @mrb_sheff and Helen Akbary @helenakbary, thank you for taking the time to speak on the telephone.

Michael Walsh @mikefnw at the Let's Think Programme (which helps primary and secondary pupils develop the higher-order skills needed for success in English), thank you for putting me in touch with one of your Compass schools. Karen Baldwin Deansfield Primary School @Deansfield and Dr Kulvarn Atwal @Thethinkingschool2 at Highlands Primary School thank you for the visits to your amazing schools. Chris Parkhouse @chrisparkhouse, Jonny Davies @JonnyDavies16 and Christopher Harrison @MrHtheteacher at Grove Road Community Primary School, thank you for the visit to your amazing school and for including you as a case study.

There is no doubt that this book would not have been possible without James Clark and Diana Alves at SAGE, for having faith in the idea and for transforming the book. Thank you also to the whole editorial, marketing and production team, at SAGE, who have turned a dream into a reality- I hope I have lived up to expectations. Particular thanks go to Diana Alves, for being a source of inspiration, encouragement, comfort and support throughout the lockdown and the pandemic.

A huge thank you goes to @HealthyToolkit crew and in particular to Andrew Cowley @andew_cowley23 and Helen Dlamini @Artology for their continued support and Samira Ash @mindfulmiss1 for all the conversations about metacognition. Without you Matt Young @MattGovernor, this book would not exist; thank you for asking me to write a blog four years ago which kick-started my journey into research.

This book would also not have been possible without the love and support of my family and friends in particular Lee and my sister for the many conversations about metacognition. This book is dedicated to my mum beloved mum Banecha, and has been written in honour and in loving memory of my late father, Shona, who set the wheels of metacognition in motion. Without the continued love, encouragement, support and patience of my amazing husband, Arif, and my three children, this book would not have been possible; thank you all!

TEACHERS' STANDARDS

The following table shows how chapter coverage links to the Teachers' Standards.

Table 0.1 Teachers' Standards

Teachers' Standards	Relevant chapters
1. Set high expectations which inspire, motivate and challenge pupils	2, 3, 4, 6, 7, 8, 9, 10, 11, 12, 13, 14
2. Promote good progress and outcomes by pupils	1, 2, 3, 5, 6, 7, 8, 9, 10, 11, 12, 13, 14
3. Demonstrate good subject and curriculum knowledge	2, 5, 6, 7, 9, 10, 11, 13
4. Plan and teach well-structured lessons	2, 3, 4, 6, 7, 8, 9, 10, 13
5. Adapt teaching to respond to the strengths and needs of all pupils	2, 4, 5, 6, 7, 9, 10, 11, 14
6. Make accurate and productive use of assessment	2, 3, 4, 5, 6, 7, 8, 9, 11, 12, 13, 14
7. Manage behaviour effectively to ensure a good and safe learning environment	3, 4, 5, 6, 7, 9, 11, 14
8. Fulfil wider professional responsibilities	1, 2, 3, 4, 5, 6, 7, 8, 9, 10, 11, 12, 13, 14

EARLY CAREER FRAMEWORK

The following table shows how chapter coverage links to the Early Career Framework.

Table 0.2 Early Career Framework

Early Career Framework	Relevant chapters
Standard 1 – Set high expectations	2, 3, 4, 6, 7, 8, 9, 10, 11, 12, 13, 14
Standard 2 – Promote good progress	2, 3, 5, 7, 8, 9, 10, 11, 12, 13, 14
Standard 3 – Demonstrate good subject and curriculum knowledge	2, 3, 4, 6, 7, 8, 9, 10, 11, 12, 13
Standard 4 – Plan and teach well-structured lessons	2, 3, 4, 5, 6, 7, 8, 9, 10, 11, 12, 13
Standard 5 – Adapt teaching	2, 3, 4, 5, 6, 7, 9, 10, 11, 13, 14
Standard 6 – Make accurate and productive use of assessment	2, 3, 4, 5, 6, 7, 9, 10, 11, 13, 14
Standard 7 – Manage behaviour effectively	3, 4, 6, 7, 8, 9, 11, 12, 14
Standard 8 – Fulfil wider professional responsibilities	1, 2, 3, 4, 5, 6, 7, 8, 9, 10, 11, 12, 13, 14

THE USE OF RESEARCH IN TEACHING

Contents

In this chapter we will explore

- the potential of using external research and evidence-informed research in the classroom
- our understanding of intuition in teaching compared to what we know about cognitive psychology
- the phenomena of confirmation bias
- reasons why seeking out contradictory evidence is required
- ideas around why our intuition cannot always be relied upon and can be misleading
- what teachers think about using research in the classroom
- how to use evidence base to drive teaching and learning forward.

The problems with using research directly in the classroom

Over the last fifty years our understanding about what works in education has developed rapidly. Researchers have conducted studies around the world and distilled what works and what does not work when improving learning. But the question is: can research always be taken off the peg and implemented successfully? The answer is no.

The research is not always 'a recipe' (Coe, 2017) for successful implementation. Research does not tell us exactly how to implement a particular intervention in the classroom and schools are required to translate the research into classroom practice. In order to do this effectively, schools require a certain 'depth of evidence-informed' (Coe, 2017) understanding. Lofthouse (2015) agrees that 'on a simple level it is not classroom practice we should consider but classroom practices (plural)' and that there should be 'ongoing development of diverse classroom practices'. In 1976, Travers stated in the 'Impact of research on classroom teaching' that in his experience, 'teachers show considerable sense in deciding whether particular areas of scientific inquiry do or do not have implications for classroom use' (Travers, 1976: 501). He expands this idea by stating that teachers' scientific knowledge, which has been assimilated over the years, is something 'which has stood the test of time, even with fads coming and going'.

Coe (2017) confirms that schools require 'practical wisdom' in order to do this effectively. Lofthouse (2015) calls this 'practical wisdom' used 'widely in context', 'phronesis'. Being able to work in this way may lead to 'knowing what to do in the circumstances' (Lofthouse, 2015) and this is something that research could definitely enable. Both types of research are valid in their own way but together they could be an even more powerful and could be a way to improve our understanding of learning in different contexts.

Classroom research and collation of findings could be useful and it is certainly something that organisations such as the Education Endowment Foundation (EEF), the Sutton Trust, as well as John Hattie and Carol Dweck have been working on for a number of years.

Let us consider the two types of research which could be useful: those who conduct research not based in the classroom and classroom teachers conducting research in their own classrooms. This is called evidence-based practice or 'evidence-informed practice' (Stoll, 2017). Thinking of it in terms of being evidence-informed means that teachers have autonomy. Just like pupils, teachers also have prior knowledge and experience to bring to the classroom, which could be developed further (Stoll, 2017).

Although not always the case, sometimes the prior knowledge and experiences could be based on intuition only and this can cause some problems, particularly in deciding upon implementing interventions.

The problem with intuition

'Understanding how, when and where learning takes place is an extremely complex issue. It encompasses everything from the composition of our DNA, our neural processes, the environment we develop in, the social dynamics of the classroom, and the pedagogical practices that teachers and children engage in' (Slocombe and Bell, 2020) and our own intuition. Classroom teachers are required to expertly balance everything from behaviour management, to balancing of the emotional needs of approximately thirty pupils all with varying learning needs, improving outcomes for all the pupils in their care.

On top of that teachers are also required to implement the latest government policies, which have been changing at an alarming rate more recently. Not only that, but teachers have hundreds of interactions every day.

No wonder educators view voices from the top with scepticism. Unfortunately, experts are not trusted and are also viewed in this way. Due to this and various other factors, educators (teachers, parents and students) tend to rely on their intuition instead (Weinstein, Sumeracki and Caviglioli, 2019). Another reason for mistrust may be that nearly every single person has had years of educational experience as a pupil, which leads us to trust our instincts more.

In addition to this, if you are a primary school or secondary school teacher you would have a bachelor's degree and would have spent at least seventeen years in education (Weinstein, Sumeracki and Caviglioli, 2019).

According to Weinstein, Sumeracki and Caviglioli (2019: 23), although our teaching philosophy is based on how 'we were taught in school', this 'may not be the best or most efficient way to learn'. Using our own intuition for teaching and learning is a complex issue and mistakes can be made if this is the only way we teach, which 'can lead us to pick up the wrong learning strategies,' Weinstein, Sumeracki and Caviglioli (2019: 23). 'The problem with these faulty intuitions and biases is that they are notoriously difficult to correct,' Weinstein, Sumeracki and Caviglioli (2019: 27).

Our perception about how much we learned could also be incorrect and can often misinform our classroom practice. Solely relying on intuition can lead to two main issues: choosing incorrect learning strategies and once a learning strategy is chosen, searching for evidence to back that up. This approach seems to be favoured over seeking contradictory evidence and is known as confirmation bias.

Confirmation bias and why contradictory evidence is required

In *Understanding How We Learn*, Weinstein, Sumeracki and Caviglioli (2019) highlight re-reading as an example of how our intuition can impact on what we think about how we learn effectively. One of the reasons given is that it feels good to re-read notes over and over again, which was explored by Karpicke, J.D., Butler, A.C. and Roediger, H.L. (2009). There have been many comparisons about the effect of reading once, to re-reading the same text twice in a row. These studies show that the use of time re-reading is not effective for developing long-term memory (Callendar and McDaniel, 2009; Weinstein, Sumeracki and Caviglioli, 2009).

Although re-reading something increases reading fluency, this does not translate to deeper level thinking or being able to recall the information at a later date. However, 'this feeling of fluency is seductive' (Weinstein, Sumeracki and Caviglioli, 2009: 23) and it is this feeling that prompts us to continue with this strategy even though it is not the most effective way to learn something. While 're-reading text and massed practice of a skill or new knowledge are by far the preferred study strategies by learners of all stripes, but they're also among the least productive,' according to Brown, Roediger and McDaniel (2014: 23).

Confirmation bias is the second issue when there is an over reliance on intuition. 'Confirmation bias is the tendency for us to search out information that confirms our own beliefs, or interpret information in a way that confirms them' (Weinstein, Sumeracki and Caviglioli, 2019: 26).

It is human nature to make biased choices, then search for evidence to confirm them as opposed to refuting them. If we believe that a particular strategy works to produce a large amount of learning, we will look for examples to confirm this.

Case study: Beliefs and how they can shape teaching

In a conversation between a teacher and a non-teacher friend about how to teach writing, the non-teacher friend expressed firm beliefs about how it should be taught. The non-teacher friend believed that writing should be an entirely creative process with very little or no guidance. The teacher explained that although there are times when this would be the case, writing skills would also need to be taught explicitly. The non-teacher friend explained that they had never been taught this way and they did well. The teacher, who questioned the non-teacher friend about how to teach writing to the pupils who were not picking up the writing skills required. Although this made the non-teacher friend pause for thought and reflect for a few moments, they

(Continued)

were still adamant that writing is not a subject that required explicit teaching.

- Why did the non-teacher friend have such strong beliefs?
- Why was it so difficult to change the mind of the non-teacher friend?

Our memory or how much we remember is affected by what we believe in. We tend 'to notice and remember examples that support our belief than to notice and remember examples that do not' (Weinstein, Sumeracki and Caviglioli, 2019: 27). An example would be Brain Gym. If we believe in Brain Gym, we would recognise the time when we think it has worked, rather than when it didn't. For example, when we notice a pupil, who was concentrating better after a session of Brain Gym, we may assume that this was due the 'brain buttons' being activated in 'specific areas of the brain to enhance learning' (Simmonds, 2014). Was this really the case or was it that merely having a break from learning for five minutes that helped refocus the pupil?

Our beliefs also affect our intuition. If we believe that learning styles works, we tend to remember the times that it did work as opposed to the times it did not work (Weinstein, Sumeracki and Caviglioli, 2019).

Not only is 'the problem with faulty intuitions ... that they are no-toriously difficult to correct' (Weinstein, Sumeracki and Caviglioli, 2019: 27) but also believing that biases exist is a challenging concept for people to accept (Weinstein, Sumeracki and Caviglioli, 2019). Even those who research this area of cognitive psychology have faulty biases. It is human nature to make mistakes and assumptions, have faulty biases and to judge. There is nothing wrong with relying on intuition and in fact this appears to be a protective mechanism in human beings which has evolved over millions of years. However, children only get one chance at education and for that reason we need to make sure that we are being reflective and critical about our practice and build upon it.

According to Weinstein, Sumeracki and Caviglioli (2019: 27), the role 'of science is to disprove ideas not prove them'. When someone tries to prove something to us, our first question is usually 'what are they trying to sell us?' In trying to disprove something, scientists discover a lot of useful information.

Contradictory evidence is required for two reasons: firstly, to enable the reflective process to occur to correct faulty intuition and secondly, to develop critical thinking, which may lead to innovative thinking.

One way perhaps to correct faulty biases would be through the use of evidence-informed practice (more on this later in this chapter). Another way could be through feedback and evaluation. Just as we expect pupils to plan, monitor and evaluate their learning, surely as educators we need to be equally as reflective in our teaching practice. Coe (2017) argues for 'high-quality, local evaluation'. Simmonds (2014) states that 'real-time feedback' or 'biofeedback' about how exactly to implement a certain intervention is crucial to the evaluation process.

Teachers' views on the potential of using research in the classroom

In order to gauge what teachers and parents think of research, it may be beneficial to look at some studies which have carried this out. The report called *How Neuroscience Is Affecting Education: Report of Teacher and Parent Surveys* (Simmonds, 2014), carried out by the Wellcome Trust, is a collection of representative data from a number of surveys exploring the impact of neuroscience on teaching and learning, from both teachers and parents.

The findings of the surveys were very positive with more than 90 per cent saying that 'their understanding of neuroscience influences their practice' and approximately 80 per cent saying 'they would collaborate with neuroscientists doing research in education' (Simmonds, 2014).

Although the findings were very positive, many teachers stated that it was challenging to measure the impact of interventions used in the classroom. However, they were aware that academic progress had been made.

Another interesting finding from the report was that teachers tend to learn about interventions from colleagues, other teachers. However, schools were less likely to learn from scientific papers which is very interesting. Teachers also preferred to have evidence as in evidence-based or evidence-informed practice as suggested by both Lofthouse (2015) and Coe (2017). These are some of the reasons why the Wellcome Trust have teamed up with the EEF to produce the evidence base 'and application of neuroscience in education' (Simmonds, 2014) something which has been lacking in education.

In medicine, neuroscience seems to have been effectively translated into practice but the reality of doing this in classrooms seems to be more difficult. However, cognitive psychologists realise the potential of improving learning through research but lack the 'educational or methodological expertise to translate their findings into practical education interventions' (Simmonds, 2014).

Similarly, teachers would like to learn about improving their practice through neuroscience but are not necessarily aware where to start or how to approach it (Simmonds, 2014).

Slocombe and Bell (2020) have similar views on closing the researcher–practitioner gap by bringing academics and teachers together to learn from each other. Both bring 'depth of knowledge and expertise' 'to our understanding of learning'. Both researchers and teachers are experts in their own areas, with cognitive scientists understanding the structure of how learning happens in the mind, however, teachers' understanding is compiled from years of experience 'teaching thousands of pupils building an implicit and explicit understanding of how learning takes place in the highly varied social dynamics of a school classroom'. Cognitive scientists do not have knowledge of the complexity of teaching practice and it is a luxury that they are not privy to.

Teachers understand learning in the broader sense but less so the mechanics of cognition and how it works in the brain; however, cognitive scientists understand about the mechanics of learning in the brain but have very little understanding of the social context for learning.

Although increased researcher-practitioner collaboration had been suggested many years ago, little progress has been made. More recently though, there have been some advances made with it 'many exciting initiatives already working to develop links between basic science and educational practice, including research reviews, collaborative projects, conferences, and research schools' (Slocombe and Bell, 2020). At present both researchers and practitioners are still very disconnected from the one goal they are trying to improve and much needed work needs to continue in this area. Perhaps now is the time to move towards practice-informed research instead.

Using evidence base to drive learning forwards

Although it is a huge challenge conducting fair testing in schools – as we don't really know if a particular intervention has worked due to so many other interventions taking place all at the same time and the fact that it is a huge risk to get rid of some interventions – fair testing could be a way forward to getting closer to the truth about what works and what does not work.

Although there are many differences between medicine and education, there are some similarities and the disciplin of education can learn so much from medicine:

> Both involve craft and personal expertise, learnt over years of experience. Both work best when we learn from the experiences of others, and what worked best for them. Every child is different, of course, and every patient is different too; but we are all similar enough that research can help. (Goldacre, 2013)

Ben Goldacre (2013), a hospital doctor, suggests that this could be a way forward for education. Evidence-based practice has allowed the medical profession to make huge strides in knowing what works for patients 'by conducting randomised trials – fair tests, comparing one treatment against another', and it is due to this that patient outcomes have improved. In addition to this, there was a shift in the culture of medicine.

Culture is something that manifests itself 'in the day-to-day operation of schools' (Kime, 2017). 'Once the beliefs and expectations' of routinely using evidence base is in place, where decisions are made at all levels 'from Newly qualified Teachers (NQTs) to Secretaries of State', then the value of evidence base can be recognised and the culture can become embedded. In addition to this, time must be allocated, training must be provided and permission must be given by all stakeholders, and changes must be made to policies and procedures (Kime, 2017).

In medicine, 'whole new systems' were put into place to 'run trials as a matter of routine' (Goldacre, 2013). The process involved identifying questions which were important to medics, gathering 'evidence on what worked best, get it read, understood and put into practice' (Goldacre, 2013).

In medicine every patient is different and similarly in education every child is different. However, the similarities appear to outweigh the differences and there is a case for research being used to 'help find out which interventions will work best', the strategies that could be tried and the order in which the strategies should be tried in order to 'achieve the best outcome' possible (Goldacre, 2013).

Some may think that using evidence base could be a stick to beat teachers with and it is a way of telling teachers what to do but it is far from this. Goldacre (2013) suggests that it could be a way of 'empowering teachers, and setting the profession free from governments, ministers and civil servants'. It may also be a way of taking ownership of the profession where teachers can make 'informed decisions' (Goldacre, 2013) and advise on what works best for their pupils, using the best evidence currently in place. Nobody in government would dream of telling doctors what to prescribe for their patients and perhaps one day teachers could also be in a similar position.

The other thing to be aware of is that only 'a few decades ago, best medical practice was driven by things like eminence, charisma and personal experience' (Goldacre, 2013) and many medics challenged the use of evidence base as a way forward. They saw it 'as a challenge to their authority' (Goldacre, 2013). With hindsight, it was eventually realised that advances in medicine could not be made in this way but rather by listening to people on the ground through an intelligible set of systems, by identifying where the qualms were and ultimately deciding 'the ideas worth testing' (Goldacre, 2013) were the very elements which would improve understanding of medicine and lead to better outcomes for patients.

This also involved collaboration between 'statisticians, epidemiologists, information librarians, and experts in trial design to move forwards' (Goldacre, 2013). This shift in culture took time to change. This is not to say that we all become experts in research and evidence-based practice, but using these resources and learning from them about what works and what does not work may be an opportunity to remove barriers to learning, making advances in education, thereby leading to better outcomes for all pupils. There are, however, some challenges that are worth exploring.

Challenges of using evidence-informed practice

In this section, we are moving away from using the term evidence-based to evidence-informed practice as suggested by Stoll (2017) in her article, 'Five challenges in moving towards evidence-informed practice'.

Even though the teaching profession is moving towards a more evidence-informed profession, (Stoll, 2017) there are five main challenges that educators may be faced with when thinking about using such practices. These are as follows:

1. Views about what is classed as evidence

Since evidence can come from a wide range of sources, such as your own classroom, colleagues' classrooms, data from internal and external assessments, it is important to clarify what constitutes as evidence. Stoll (2017) suggests a 'thoughtful blend' to understanding what should be included in evidence-informed practice. These are: 'external research, different kinds of data and collaborative enquiry and research and development (R&D)'.

At first glance, external research may be interpreted as solely relying on academic research, however, it involves a multitude of factors. Although we cannot underestimate the use of academic research and effect-size, there is so much more evidence which needs to be included in external research (Stoll, 2017), for teachers to become evidence-informed. In doing so, we must include how to foster broader outcomes such as creativity and resilience, which this kind of research does not usually highlight. We must also include evidence about how pupils learn, how motivation develops, the impact of social and emotional issues on learning and how to create the conditions required to facilitate all these other crucial aspects of learning.

Bringing about change in schools is a highly complex process. 'Research on professional learning', leadership of change management and 'schools as learning communities' must also be considered as part of the evidence (Stoll, 2017).

The second aspect to consider is data. Not only do we include pupil assessments as part of this but we also need to consider including assessments on 'critical thinking, entrepreneurship and wellbeing'. Data can be created from 'different forms of assessment', including pupil and teacher interviews, from learning walks, from surveys, and so on. In evidence-informed practice, data is used from beginning to end, starting with 'baseline' assessment, then evaluating throughout the process, and at the end of the process to 'evaluate' the 'impact' (Stoll, 2017).

And thirdly, 'collaborative enquiry and research and development (R&D)' are usually a combination of the two aspects mentioned above but incorporate the 'cycles of investigating practice, exploring, trialling and carefully evaluating new practices' (Stoll, 2017).

2. Thinking of evidence as evidence-based

Stoll (2017) suggests that our choice of language is a crucial factor when distinguishing 'who' (teachers) rather than 'what' (evidence) is driving the change forward. As mentioned earlier in the chapter, being evidence-informed as opposed to evidence-based means that teachers are in the driving seat and have autonomy over the changes being made.

3. Taking risks in your own practice

It can be very risky engaging in something different such as being evidence-informed rather than continuing with your own practice. In fact it may be easier to continue doing the same thing, to ignore what is not working, rather than embracing challenges and trying something different. It is the way that evidence-informed practice is seen which is important here. If evidence-informed practice is viewed as a 'professional learning' opportunity to test our conventions instead of being an obstacle, then it would enable educators to test their assumptions about how pupils learn best. 'Coming out of your comfort zone' and the willingness to be open and keep exploring and evaluating are the best ways to support pupils' learning. It requires a teacher-led, dynamic approach to development; with the keenness, drive and resilience for 'learning new skills, developing new teaching strategies and practising them deliberately to develop expertise' (Stoll, 2017).

4. Persuading others about the value of evidence-informed practice

Taking risks with your own practice can be challenging, but it can be even more challenging to persuade others to take risks, especially when it comes to evidence-informed practice. Stoll (2017) states that the language used here is important. Carefully selecting vocabulary can be beneficial when convincing colleagues. Stoll also suggests using the term 'evidence-enriched', particularly when introducing new projects, so that skills and knowledge already there can be built upon. Engagement may seem a long process but buying in at all levels is important. One way is to start off 'designing small projects with other interested volunteers and then sharing the findings', sharing 'quick wins and other successes but also what you have learnt not to do' is a good way to get the engagement process started.

There is also a suggestion that head teachers should buy into evidence-informed practice, must understand and use evidence, support colleagues and try to develop a culture of trust and action. Stoll (2017) goes on to suggest that senior leaders must be on board in order to provide support, develop and embed evidence-informed practice into the culture of the school. Head teachers must ensure that the correct conditions are set for growth of evidence-informed practice in schools by becoming fully engaged, enabling colleagues to develop their practice by allocating sufficient time, giving access to research articles, creating occasions for 'knowledge-exchange', modelling a passion for being evidence-informed and 'testing out their own theories of action about what they expect from particular interventions, nurturing evidence champions, networking and con-necting with critical friends and research partners (Stoll, 2015)' (Stoll, 2017).

5. Doing it on your own

Although it is great to see individual teachers want to try out projects and interventions in their own classrooms, there is a staggering amount of research which points to reasons why collaborative, social and collective learning are crucial for teacher development. Having teacher 'autonomy' is much more about 'peer networking – collaborating with colleagues across schools' (Stoll, 2017), collective agency (can do) and responsibility (accountability to peers) than anything else.

Summary

- Intuition can play a huge role in how we teach and in our views about how children learn.
- Our intuition can also be misguided and may mislead us.
- We may be able to overcome issues that result solely on intuition by becoming more reflective and by becoming more evidence-informed.

(Continued)

- Using evidence can be challenging but also rewarding.
- Researchers and teachers should work collaboratively in identifying questions and issues which arise in the classroom.
- A combination of research, evidence-informed practice and collective agency can be very powerful at driving teacher development and ultimately pupil outcomes.
- Senior leaders should create a climate and culture for evidence-informed practice.

Think!

- Teachers have limited time and although research does not tell us how to implement the findings in classroom, what can be done to make sure such vital findings are not lost in the ether?
- How can we, as a profession, move away from relying solely on our intuition to guide us?
- Why should we seek contradictory evidence when it comes to confirmation bias?
- Why is it better to be evidence-informed rather than evidence-based?

Teacher metacognition

- How do you feel about trying new ideas?
- If it is challenging, how do you overcome the challenges?
- What keeps you motivated to continue with an idea that does not appear to be working?
- What new idea have you tried implementing?
- How did you overcome your own biases towards a new idea?

Pupil metacognition

- How do pupils feel about new challenges and ideas?
- Which pupils in your class find new learning a challenge?
- What are the challenges?
- How can you help pupils overcome their own biases and embrace new learning?

References

Brown, P.C., Roediger III, H.L., and McDaniel, M.A. (2014) Make it Stick: The Science of Successful Learning.

Callendar, A.A., and Mcdaniel, M.A. (2009) The limited benefits of rereading educational texts. *Contemporary Educational Psychology*, 34, 30–41.

Coe, R. (2017) Evaluation: Why, what and how. *Impact: Journal of the Chartered College of Teaching* [online]. Available at: https://impact.chartered.college/article/coe-evaluation-why-what-how/ (accessed 3 February 2021).

Goldacre, B. (2013) *Building Evidence into Education*. Department for Education [online]. Available at: www.gov.uk/government/news/building-evidence-into-education (accessed 16 March 2021).

Karpicke, J.D., Butler, A.C., and Roediger, H.L. (2009) Metacognitive strategies in student learning: Do students practice retrieval when they study on their own? *Memory*, 17, 471–479.

Kime, S. (2017) From intentions to implementation: Establishing a culture of evidence-informed education. *Impact: Journal of the Chartered College of Teaching* [online]. Available at: https://impact.chartered.college/article/kime-culture-evidence-informed-education/ (accessed 3 February 2021).

Lofthouse, R. (2015) Is research-based classroom practice realistic and is it desirable? [online]. Available at: https://blogs.ncl.ac.uk/education/2015/09/01/is-research-based-classroom-practice-realistic-and-is-it-desirable/ (accessed 3 February 2021).

Simmonds, A. (2014) *How Neuroscience Is Affecting Education: Report of Teacher and Parent Surveys* [online]. Available at: https://wellcome.org/sites/default/files/wtp055240.pdf (accessed 3 February 2021).

Slocombe, M. and Bell, D. (2020) Closing the gap between science and practice in education: From metaphorical bridges to concrete common ground [online]. Available at: www.positiveproof.co.uk/articles.php?page=1 (accessed 3 February 2021).

Stoll, L. (2017) Five challenges in moving towards evidence-informed practice. *Impact: Journal of the Chartered College of Teaching* [online].

Available at: https://impact.chartered.college/article/stoll-five-challenges-evidence-informed-practice/ (accessed 3 February 2021).

Travers, R. (1976) Impact of research on classroom teaching. *Educational Leadership*, 33 (7), 498–501.

Weinstein, Y., Sumeracki, M., and Caviglioli, O. (2019) *Understanding How We Learn*. Abingdon: Routledge.

2

WHAT IS METACOGNITION AND SELF-REGULATED LEARNING?

Contents

In this chapter we will explore

- the differences between self-regulation and self-regulated learning
- the three components of self-regulation: cognition, metacognition and motivation
- metacognitive knowledge and metacognitive regulation
- what explicit metacognition looks like and how educators can recognise what it is and how much of it they already do
- what metacognition could look like in everyday classroom teaching
- the importance of explicit metacognition training and lessons; how much educators already do in their everyday practice and how to close the gap.

What is metacognition?

Metacognition is nothing new and has been around since the 1970s, first described by Flavell in 1976. As our learning has evolved and become more complex, in recent years, so has its definition. Researched for over thirty years, metacognition is one of those concepts that is described as being 'fuzzy' and 'really hard to grasp' (Akturk and Sahin, 2011: 3731). Some still define it as being nothing more than 'thinking about thinking'. However, metacognition is so much more than thinking about thinking. Metacognition encompasses motivation, cognition, emotional awareness and intelligence, managing behaviours, improved well-being, the development of human connections and relationships and so much more. Everything is interrelated.

Although metacognition itself is not a higher order thinking skill, teachers find it difficult to recognise it and see the links between their teaching and metacognition as a theme. There are many reasons for this, one could be that thinking about how to teach it is a higher order thinking skill.

Although Piaget (1886–1980) was concerned with the study of cognition and realised that the old-fashioned view of children being and thinking like mini-adults was flawed and that there were four stages to the learning of children, he was the first to discover that children learnt by social construction and interaction with the environment. This discovery was not known as metacognition back then but it was certainly the beginning of it.

The significance of metacognition to improve student outcomes has been well publicised by educational psychologists and interest in this has grown rapidly in recent years. In the 1970s, an American developmental psychologist, John Flavell, conducted research into how children knew and controlled their memory processes. Due to this research he was recognised as introducing the word 'metacognition' (Flavell, 1976). Flavell described metacognition as being something that you struggle with: 'I am engaging in metacognition if I notice that I am having more trouble learning A than B; if it strikes me that I should double check C before accepting it as fact' (Huntington School of Research).

Although Flavell (1976) coined the term 'metacognition', he was not the first to study the processes of metacognition. The importance of controlling and monitoring reading comprehension processes has been researched since the beginning of 1901. During the 1960s, researchers focused their investigations on how we monitor and keep track of our thinking processes. This was further developed in the 1970s, when theoretical models were created, describing how we process knowledge. The findings illustrated that our basic cognitive processes were controlled by a 'central executive'. A central executive or 'executive functioning' describes 'a variety of cognitive processes that are required to attain a goal, including working memory, inhibitory control, attention control and attention shifting' (cambridge-community.org.uk, n.d.).

Lev Vygotsky (1896–1934), a Soviet psychologist, developed the idea of the Zone of Proximal Development. This includes the theories of what is now regarded as metacognition. It explains the developmental process of pupils learning with and without guided support by an expert. At first the educator takes responsibility for goal setting, planning tasks, monitoring progress and allocating attention, with the view that eventually these obligations will be handed over to the pupils. By the time they are ready to take on such responsibilities, they would have become more capable of monitoring their own cognition, which is the basis for metacognition.

One of the challenges for educators is to be able to assess how well pupils recognise and understand their own internal thinking and learning processes, for some of whom it remains at a subconscious level. David Perkins (1992), as mentioned in Getting started with Metacognition (cambridge-community.org.uk), named the four stages of metacognition as: tacit, aware, strategic and reflective (more on this later). This gives teachers a useful framework within which to assess where pupils are along their metacognitive journey, which we will discuss now.

What is self-regulated learning?

Self-regulation is having an awareness of your strengths and awareness of areas for development and the strategies used to learn. It is also about how the learner motivates themselves to engage in learning and in developing strategies to enhance their learning and to improve. Self-regulated learning includes cognition, metacognition, motivation, emotional control and the kindness factor (see more about self-regulation in Chapter 14). However, self-regulation can be broken down into three essential components: cognition, metacognition and motivation. These can help pupils develop into successful learners.

Cognition is the mental processes involved in learning, understanding and knowing as described in the EEF guidance on *Metacognition and Self-regulated Learning* (2018). It is about acquiring cognitive strategies to complete tasks and learn knowledge. Cognitive strategies are the skills to facilitate learning. Some examples are: subject to specific strategies such as using different methods to solve mathematical calculations, learning how to throw a ball in different ways or and techniques to improve memory. Metacognition or metacognitive strategies are the strategies used to control and monitor our cognition. During this process of thinking we select the most appropriate cognitive strategy for the task we are completing and check that our technique of memorisation is accurate. It is a way of monitoring and directing learning in a purposeful way. Pupils should monitor if a particular memorisation technique has been successful or not. They can then deliberately change this, if required, based on the evidence of how successful it had been.

Motivation is about how willing we are to engage our metacognitive and cognitive skills and apply them to learning. Convincing yourself to carry out a tricky revision task now, which affects your current well-being, is a way of improving your well-being for a test tomorrow (EEF, 2018) (see Chapter 3).

There is a complex interaction between the three strands of self-regulation: cognition, metacognition and motivation. However, a feeling of success can be used to motivate pupils. It can also help them to recognise themselves as learners. The following case study looks at how this might look like in practice.

Case study: The metacognitive journey of Grove Road Community Primary School

I was honoured and delighted to visit Grove Road Community Primary School, Harrogate, in January 2020. The Headteacher Chris Parkhouse, Deputy Headteacher, Jonny Davies and the Assistant Headteacher, Chris Harrison have worked tirelessly to implement metacognition as a whole community approach to teaching and learning.

Chris Harrison took me on a tour of the school and set up pupil interviews to hear all about their metacognitive journey. Not only had they implemented aspects of metacognition but a year after implementation were already thinking about innovating and moving their practice forward.

They began their journey implementing a programme called ReflectED from Rosendale Research School in London and were a hub school. The curriculum is steeped in reflection, providing opportunities to record learning moments and strategies. Evidence from ReflectED suggests that pupils will make accelerated progress.

The programme starts off with lessons on metacognition, where pupils are put through their paces, learning new skills such as juggling or how to use chopsticks. These lessons provide enough challenge for pupils to be able to reflect upon.

After that, lessons on the growth mindset are delivered where pupils explore what a successful learner looks and feels like. Pupils recognise that in order to be a successful learner, they require the skills of grit, resilience and determination.

Opportunities are built into the school day to reflect about their learning, where pupils are encouraged to discuss what has helped them to be successful in their learning, how they are feeling and how confident they are:

Red means they feel stuck and need to be resilient and find strategies to help them.

Yellow means they are getting there, but need to continue to be determined in order to become more confident.

(Continued)

Green means they feel confident, and by working smarter, to uti-lise different strategies to improve, children will become masters of a particular task.

Blue means that the children feel so confident about a task that they can 'coach' and support a partner to learn.

Blue learners are ready to seek additional challenge so that they are stretching themselves to achieve more. (Grove Road Community Primary School, n.d.)

A platform called Seesaw is used for pupils to share new learning with their parents. Pupils are encouraged to share their 'marvellous mistakes' and their reflections with their parents, and parents are encouraged to 'like' and 'comment' on their children's work (Grove Road Community Primary School, n.d.).

The three pupils who had been chosen to speak to me were very articulate and were able to express their own metacognitive journey and how their learning had improved through the colour coded system. They spoke enthusiastically about how they were going to move through the colour coded system. They were also able to articulate what they knew about themselves as learners and what their learning goals were.

The school has developed 'flow charts' in each subject. The flow charts outline prior knowledge required, opportunities for reflections, teacher modelling and misconceptions pupils may have. They have also developed a Self-Evaluation Record Form or SERF for teachers to reflect on their practice before conducting learning walks. This has removed the need for formal lesson observations and has reduced stress on staff significantly. The teachers whom I had the privilege to speak to were excited and enthused about the learning journey they were on.

- How has this metacognitive programme led to improving the lan-guage of metacognition throughout the community?
- How is teacher metacognition being developed?
- What has led to pupils being able to start setting their own learning goals?

Although we will be focusing on metacognition, it is important to recognise that cognition and motivation are equally as important in self-regulated learning. Let us imagine making a snowball. We know that no two snowflakes are the same and that snowflakes need other snowflakes to stick to make a snowball. However, all snowflakes are different, hence the different metacognitive strategies needed.

According to the Education Endowment Foundation guidance, 'It is impossible to be metacognitive without having different cognitive strategies to hand' (EEF, 2018). Metacognition needs something to stick to and that is cognition. Using the example of making a snowball, cognition is knowing how to form a snowball and how much pressure to apply. Metacognition is about knowing what to do when you are challenged with plummeting temperatures and when your hands get icy cold. The motivation is the desire to make a snowball to get your friends with. What do you do? You put gloves on to overcome the challenge of feeling cold and you still achieve your goal. Figure 2.1 shows what a model of self-regulation could look like.

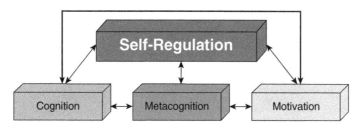

Figure 2.1   A model of self-regulation

Metacognition is an essential component of self-regulated learning. It can be further broken down into two parts: metacognitive knowledge and metacognitive regulation. Metacognitive knowledge can be split into three strands: knowledge of task, knowledge of self, knowledge of strategies.

With the knowledge of task, learners are required to recognise how challenging the task is for them, what the most difficult aspects are, the time required to get the task done and prioritising the easy parts of the task.

When pupils display knowledge of themselves as learners, they should demonstrate whether they can recognise if the task requires them to retrieve knowledge they can recall, whether they understand the underpinning concepts, if they are motivated to complete the task and how they can remain focused.

Understanding the knowledge of strategies requires pupils to work out whether their notes are effective for understanding the task, whether they need help, which strategies to use if they find the task challenging and how they can take responsibility for developing their own memory.

Although this chapter is about metacognition and self-regulated learning, it is important to include what a model of self-regulated learning could look like. See Figure 2.2 for a possible model.

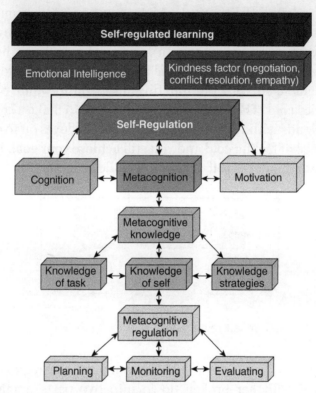

Figure 2.2 A model of self-regulated learning

Metacognitive knowledge

In the book *Metacognition in Science Education* by Zohar and Dori (2012), they refer to metacognition being about 'one's declarative knowledge' and the 'interplay between person, task and strategy characteristics', as described by Flavell (1979). The three strands of metacognitive knowledge require certain thinking processes to be developed in the classroom, to enable pupils to understand who they are as learners and how they learn. These questions are nothing new and educators are using these already as part of daily classroom practice. However, when it comes to metacognition, some pupils will have well-developed knowledge about themselves but others will need it to be explicitly taught.

Having the knowledge of task requires pupils to work out whether a task is too challenging for them. This could be where explicit teaching about recognising what is challenging and how we recognise challenge could be useful. Pupils should be taught a thinking pattern of prioritising, reprioritising and evaluating as they complete the task. We use metacognitive strategies in our everyday lives, carrying out quite complex levels of thinking. Metacognition becomes more of a general skill with age and we pay less attention to explicitly thinking through strategies.

Let us take the example of travelling to a new place to illustrate how we use metacognition to achieve that goal. Our knowledge of this task is to be at a particular place by a certain time. We may be emotionally aware that we may need to get there before the time stated on our invitation so we would work out what we need to do in order to achieve this goal. We would come up with a route to get there and know some strategies to get to the destination, for example we may use a satellite navigation system. We would also know how to travel to our destination, such as catching a bus or train, or driving. We are not likely to think about this in separate steps or stages but in a complex way. However, for pupils we need to clarify this thinking process to help them carefully understand their own emotions and motivations towards it. The metacognitive regulation kicks in when you have started that journey. See Figure 2.3 on questions which could be asked to develop metacognitive knowledge.

Metacognitive regulation

Metacognitive regulation kicks in after the task has been commenced. There is a complex interaction between all of the components that lead to self-regulation, in which metacognitive knowledge and regulation play a crucial and equally complex role too. However, in order to improve our understanding of metacognitive regulation we have broken it down into smaller separate steps. In reality and in the classroom, our questioning and prompting of pupils to develop metacognitive thoughts and processes would require us to use a combination of questions from each section together.

Metacognitive regulation is the planning, motoring and evaluating process, which is subject or task specific. Effective learners are able to subconsciously think about the stages of planning, monitoring and

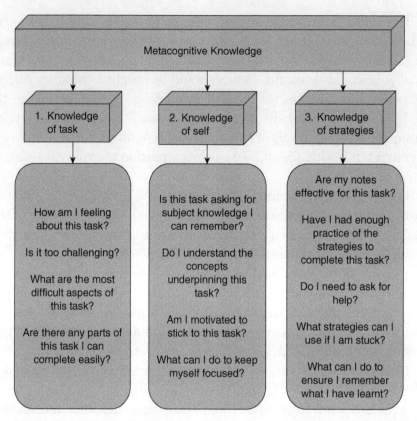

Figure 2.3 Question development in pupils (based on Huntington RSN/EEF guidance)

evaluating implicitly. However, less effective learners cannot. Pupils struggle with transferring metacognitive knowledge between subjects and this is something that needs to be taught explicitly. 'While transfer can and does happen, to varying degrees, it certainly does not always happen automatically, and thus requires careful planning and monitoring' (Mannion and Mercer, 2016: 6).

For example, for maths pupils must have good number sense and ask themselves what they know about the relationship between numbers subconsciously. For reading, good comprehenders ask themselves a series of questions to monitor their comprehension subconsciously. How well a pupil develops metacognitive strategies depends on how explicitly it is modelled by the teacher and applied to specific tasks.

Consider the following mathematical question: Mason and Jasmine have £5 between them. Mason has 90p more than Jasmine. How much money does Jasmine have?

As soon as the pupil has identified their metacognitive knowledge of the task, self and strategies, metacognitive regulation begins, with the complex interaction of cognition. The question for educators is how do we develop the metacognitive regulation required for pupils to be able to complete a task such as this independently?

Figure 2.4 shows a visual representation of the planning, monitoring and evaluating cycle, which can be used to plan questions to develop metacognitive thinking.

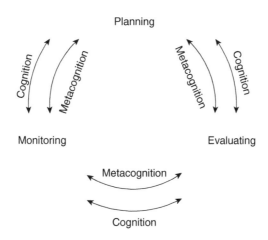

Figure 2.4 A simple representation of the cycle of metacognitive regulation

Now we are going to use this cycle to start answering a mathematical calculation. For example:

> On Saturday, Ali spent 84 minutes on maths homework and 37 minutes on reading homework. On Wednesday he spent 45 minutes completing an art project. How much longer did he spend on homework on Saturday compared to Wednesday?

Figure 2.5 shows an example of the thought processes which pupils could go through.

All educators are aware that having high expectations is crucial for all pupils and metacognition offers a framework for breaking down the learning into smaller steps. When metacognition is taught explicitly, in a structured and cumulative way, it can have a huge impact on pupil outcomes (EEF, 2018). In schools there is usually a common focus on approaches to planning. However, due to a number of factors such as time constraints and the variation of knowledge of metacognition amongst teachers, sometimes the evaluating part of a lesson falls away. Pupils require the language of metacognition and

1. Planning	2. Monitoring	3. Evaluating
What is the question asking me to do? How many steps do I need to work out? What is the first thing I need to do? Which number operation do I need to work out the first part? Which number operation do I need to do to work out the second part? How can I record my calculation and answers?	Did underlining the keywords and writing out the calculation help me to understand the question? I can see that the first step is to add the first two numbers. I will record that first. I know that the third number in the question is smaller than the answer after adding the first two numbers. My next step will be to subtract the answer from the third number.	I learned that writing out the calculation helped me to work out what I need to do next.

Figure 2.5   An example of thought processes of metacognitive regulation whilst performing a mathematical calculation

time for evaluation. Metacognition provides us with a framework to develop thinking and self-regulated learning and offers a structure to close the gap. It is therefore important for teachers to be given high quality training and time to become deeply trained in metacognition (EEF, 2018).

How can you recognise metacognition in the classroom?

As mentioned, David Perkins (1992) named the four stages of meta-cognition as tacit, aware, strategic and reflective. This gives teachers a useful framework against which to assess levels of metacognition development. The tacit stage is where pupils are not aware of meta-cognitive strategies. They accept what they know and do not know, and are not yet able to think about particular strategies. At this stage, pupils may exhibit behaviours such as being disengaged with learning or going off task because they have no strategies to draw upon to scaffold their learning themselves. Disengagement may be due to other external factors but what can we do as educators to overcome this?

The second stage is the aware learner, who knows about some thinking processes. Although their thinking is not deliberate or planned, they can come up with some ideas and find evidence. How would we need to tailor our teaching to develop thinking further at this stage? How can we get pupils to start applying what they know and developing further?

When pupils reach the strategic learner stage, they are quite well developed in their thinking processes. They understand how strategies work, and can organise and apply strategies but are not able to reflect yet. What can we do to enable the process of reflection?

The final and highest stage of learning is reflective learning, when pupils are able to reflect upon their own thinking and adjust their thoughts and strategies as they are learning.

Figure 2.6 shows the hierarchical structural stages of metacognition in relation to cognition.

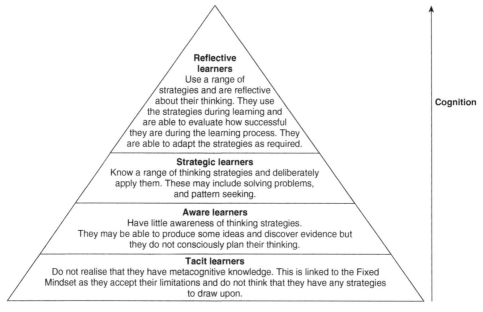

Figure 2.6 Hierarchical structure of the stages of metacognitive development (adapted from Cambridge-community.org.uk, n.d.)

How does motivation interplay with metacognition and cognition?

Motivation is defined as 'the attribute that moves us to do or not do something' (Gredler, M.E., Broussard, S.C. and Garrison, M.E.B., 2004: 106). It is about our willingness to engage both our cognitive and metacognitive skills and apply them to learning. There are two types of motivation: intrinsic and extrinsic. When we are intrinsically motivated, we feel a sense of pleasure and personal enjoyment. However, extrinsic motivation is something which needs continuous reinforcement and requires rewards to be given. The most desirable type of motivation is intrinsic motivation. In comparison to extrinsic motivation, educators around the world think that intrinsic motivation results in better educational outcomes than motivation based on rewarding pupils extrinsically (Deci, Koestner and Ryan, 1999).

Table 2.1 What the research could look like in the classroom (adapted from Lai, 2001)

Motivation	Classroom climate	Implications for behaviour management	Implications for teaching	Implications for learning
What the research says	'Create a warm and nurturing environment which is child-centred' (Lai, 2001)	'Negative effects of tangible rewards were more dramatic for children' (Lai, 2001)	'Extrinsic rewards have no effect on motivation for participating in boring tasks' (Lai, 2001)	'Intrinsic motivation may depend on the length of involvement and complexity of the task. A combination of intrinsic motivation and extrinsic rewards in the form of performance feedback may be most effective' (Lai, 2001)
Classroom practice	Focus on positive praise as opposed to negative reinforcement Calm positive learning environment, where pupils will rate their own abilities as being significantly higher and have high expectations of themselves They will take more pride in their academic achievements and display fewer signs of academic anxiety	Limit use of rewards Focus on what the child can do as opposed to what they cannot do Use extrinsic rewards sparingly a small minority of individual pupils who may require them on a short-term basis	Plan an appropriate challenge Design tasks which are collaborative and cooperative	Focus on skills Immediate feedback Performance feedback on longer tasks and for groups

Motivational strategies will include, for example, convincing oneself to undertake a tricky revision task now, affecting our current well-being as well as improving our future well-being in the test tomorrow.

An important element which usually proceeds motivation is achievement and success. By ensuring that pupils understand what achievement feels like and the success that comes with it, they are likely to continue to be motivated by the feeling of success. You will notice that motivation is one of the elements of self-regulation and it interplays with metacognitive knowledge of self.

The motivation to learn declines as pupils move through school. When eight-to-eleven-year-old pupils are asked what their favourite subject is, they will always choose the one that they feel they are the most successful at.

Summary

- Success precedes motivation.
- The planning, monitoring and evaluating cycle can help with the breakdown of the thinking process and form a scaffold.
- Some pupils require the temporary use of extrinsic rewards.
- Allocate time within lessons for pupils to evaluate their learning.
- Provide and allocate time for high-quality training on metacognition.

Think!

- What are the differences between self-regulation and self-regulated learning?
- Motivation can be a complex element to include in teaching. How can you make sure that all pupils are motivated to learn?
- At what stage can extrinsic rewards be removed?
- How can the language of metacognition be developed alongside cognition?
- How can the learning environment be developed to be inclusive of all pupils?
- How can educators enable all pupils to feel included in their own learning process?

Teacher metacognition

- Which metacognitive strategies do you explicitly teach to help pupils plan, monitor and evaluate already?
- Are there any areas of metacognitive knowledge or regulation that you find challenging to teach?
- How can you develop my knowledge and understanding?
- How can you support my pupils to develop their understanding with support and eventually move on to independent thinking?
- Are the following behaviours more subject specific and what would they look like in the classroom: tacit, aware, strategic, reflective?

Pupil metacognition

- Which pupils are highly metacognitive?
- Which pupils need more support to develop their metacognitive skills?
- To what degree are my pupils aware about metacognitive knowledge and metacognitive regulation?

References

Akturk Ahmet Oguz and Shain (2011) Literature Review on Metacognition and its Measurement, Ermenek Community College, Karamanoglu Mehmetbey University, Karaman, 70400, Turkey b Ahmet Kelesoglu Education Faculty, Selcuk University, Konya, 42090, Turkey, P. 3731.

Cambridge-community.org.uk (n.d.) *Getting Started With Metacognition* [online]. Available at: https://cambridge-community.org.uk/professional-development/gswmeta/index.html (accessed 9 November 2020).

Deci, E.L., Koestner, R. and Ryan, R.M. (1999) A meta-analytic review of experiments examining the effects of extrinsic rewards on intrinsic motivation. *Psychological Bulletin*, 125 (6): 627–700. https://doi.org/10.1037/0033-2909.125.6.627

EEF (2018) *Metacognition and Self-regulated Learning: Guidance Report* [online]. Available at: https://educationendowmentfoundation.org.uk/public/files/Publications/Metacognition/EEF_Metacognition_and_self-regulated_learning.pdf (accessed 9 November 2020).

Flavell, J.H. (1976) Metacognitive aspects of problem solving. In L.B. Resnick (ed.), *The nature of intelligence* (pp. 231–236). Hillsdale, NJ: Erlbaum.

Flavell, J. (1979) Metacognition and cognitive monitoring: A new area of cognitive-developmental inquiry. *American Psychologist*, 34: 906–911.

Gredler, M.E., Broussard, S.C. and Garrison, M.E.B. (2004) The Relationship between Classroom Motivation and Academic Achievement in Elementary School Aged Children. *Family and Consumer Sciences Research Journal*, 33: 106–120. https://doi.org/10.1177/1077727X04269573

Grove Road Community Primary School (n.d.) *Metacognition* [online]. Available at: www.groveroad.n-yorks.sch.uk/teaching-and-learning/metacognition (accessed 16 March 2021).

Lai, E.R. (2011) *Motivation: A Literature Review*. Pearson Research Report [online]. Available at: https://images.pearsonassessments.com/images/tmrs/Motivation_Review_final.pdf (accessed 12 January 2020).

Mannion, J. and Mercer, N. (2016) Learning to learn: improving attainment, closing the gap at Key Stage 3, http://dx.doi.org/10.1080/09585176.2015.1137778

Zohar, A. and Dori, Y.J. (2012) *Metacognition in Science Education*. Dordrecht: Springer Netherlands.

3

THE IMPACT OF METACOGNITION

Contents

- Teacher beliefs and attitudes
- Building self-efficacy
- High expectations and challenge
- Using reflection and mistakes made to effectively move learning forward
- Developing trust
- Social construction
- Teachers investing in their own training and development
- References

In this chapter we will explore

- the importance of teacher's beliefs and commitments
- what the impact could look like in the classroom in terms of pupil engagement, behaviour and attitude
- how the impact of having high expectations on pupils helps us to make necessary adjustments to our teaching, to allow for progression
- how being increasingly reflective of the impact you are having on your pupils, and using mistakes to move learning on, can influence pupil achievement
- the idea of self-efficacy coined by Hattie, 2012
- how teachers demonstrating that they are learners has a huge impact on how pupils see themselves as learners (Hattie, 2012)
- the benefits of social construct
- the benefits of developing trust between pupil and teacher
- how teachers who invest time and effort in their own training and development can improve their impact.

Teacher beliefs and attitudes

Rita Pierson, who was an educator for forty years and whose parents and maternal grandparents were educators, presented a Ted Talk in 2013 called 'Every kid needs a champion'. She gives reasons why some pupils may not do well at school, ranging from 'poverty, low attendance and negative peer influences', but there is one thing that is constant and very powerful and that is 'human connection'. Pierson goes on to say that everyone would have somehow been 'affected by a teacher or an adult' and that the most important thing is 'human connection and relationship'. Drawing examples from her mother's career as a teacher and judging by the sheer attendance at her mother's funeral by her former students, Rita states that after everything, what remains is a 'legacy of relationships' (Pierson, 2013).

Watching the video, the passion can be seen oozing out of every pore as Rita speaks about how she inherited a very low achieving class and agonised over how to raise attainment in nine months. This philosophical view is the basis on which the journey to building self-belief begins. The impact at the end of the journey is used as a goal to work towards. Although the journey was a long and arduous one, Rita is brutally honest about how hard a teacher's job is, but her speech is filled with so much humour that the challenges go relatively un-noticed, as the focus turns to only what needs to be done to 'make a difference' (Pierson, 2013). Rita emphasises how teachers have to become great actors and actresses to deflect the effects of pupil disappointment and failure. She really has a way of making you believe that you can do it. Perhaps this is the passion that Hattie (2012, 2017) talks about.

Hattie's work spans over fifteen years and includes a meta-analysis of over 1,200 which show the impact on achievement in school-aged students. 'It presents the largest ever collection of evidence-based research into what actually works in schools to improve learning (and what doesn't)' (Hattie, 2012). A meta-analysis is a combination of numerous scientific studies and it is usually carried out when seeking answers for a similar question. It gives an estimated answer with a small degree of error. Meta-analysis can identify patterns of both agreement and disagreement. Hattie's 2012 findings are interesting, with the top three being: collective teacher efficacy, self-reported grades and teacher estimates of achievement. Some of the least effective strategies are: teacher performance related pay, student control over learning, and parental employment.

However, some of Hattie's findings are very similar to that of the EEF guidance (2018) and Rosenshine (2012) (see Table 3.1).

There are many similarities in the three works listed in Table 3.1, with a few exceptions. According to Hattie (2012, 2017), belief and impact also form part of effective teaching, and these are also mentioned in Rita Pierson's TED Talk (2013).

All three works agree that activating prior knowledge always precedes a lesson, for two purposes: to retrieve prior learning and to build new concepts upon. The rest of the criteria, in Table 3.1, could be used as a guide when planning lessons, interweaving elements into lessons where required, and could be planned in any order, depending on the learning and the tasks involved. The table is not intended to be used as a tick list for each lesson.

Table 3.1 Comparing the EEF *Metacognition and Self-regulated Learning: Guidance Report* (2018), Hattie's findings (2012, 2018) and Rosenshine's 'Principles of instruction' (2012)

	Recommendations from EEF **Metacognition and Self-regulated learning 2018**	Hattie 2012 and 2018	Rosenshine 2012
Belief		Teachers should 'believe all students can improve' (Hattie, 2018)	
Impact		Teachers should 'know their impact' Set goals	
Activate prior knowledge	Strand 2 Activate prior knowledge (explicit instruction)	Activate knowledge	'Begin a lesson with a short review of previous learning: Daily review can strengthen previous learning and can lead to fluent recall
Success and motivation	Strand 6 Teachers should also support pupils' motivation to undertake the learning tasks.	Support pupils to achieve success by utilising formative assessments and continue to guide if necessary Set goals to help pupils control own motivations and improve outcomes (Hattie, 2018)	Ensure that success is built into the lesson and that all pupils achieve this Teach in small steps
Answering questions and checking for understanding	Strand 2 Plan in a range of questions.	Have a range of questions from 'surface level' to deeper questioning so that connections can be made to prior learning and ideas can be related (Hattie, 2018)	Involve all pupils in answering questioning to check understanding Ask a lot of questions and check responses given
Misconceptions		'Build relationships and trust so that learning can occur in a place where it is safe to make mistakes and learn from others' (Hattie, 2018)	Check regularly for misconceptions by asking questions – also a way to move learning to the long-term memory

(Continued)

Table 3.1 (Continued)

	Recommendations from EEF Metacognition and Self-regulated learning 2018	Hattie 2012 and 2018	Rosenshine 2012
Challenge	**Strand 4** 'Challenge is crucial to allow pupils to develop and progress their knowledge of tasks, strategies, and of themselves as learners. • However, challenge needs to be at an appropriate level. • Pupils must have the motivation to accept the challenge. • Tasks should not overload pupils' cognitive processes, particularly when they are expected to apply new strategies.'	'Design lessons with challenging goals' so that pupils can make an effort (2018) Give even more feedback (purposeful and considered) when learning becomes challenging	Provide scaffolds and checklists, adopt teacher thinking out loud strategies and anticipate errors when teaching challenging concepts
Social construction	**Strand 5** 'As well as explicit instruction and modelling, classroom dialogue can be used to develop metacognitive skills. • Pupil-to-pupil and pupil teacher talk can help to build knowledge and understanding of cognitive and metacognitive strategies. • However, dialogue needs to be purposeful, with teachers guiding and supporting the conversation to ensure it is challenging and builds on prior subject knowledge.'	Teach co-operative learning strategies explicitly	Provide opportunities for pupil-pupil talk
Cognitive strategies	**Strand 2** Plan in questions not to initiate and develop cognitive strategies and to evaluate them.	Teach pupils a range of cognitive strategies which they can draw upon	Use models to provide cognitive support
Schema		Build layers of knowledge-schema development	We learn by attaching new learning to pre-existing learning and knowledge, 'constructing a mental summary'
Feedback	**Strand 6** Give timely feedback and help with planning, monitoring and evaluating for self-regulation to develop.	Give feedback to all pupils but give even more feedback when the task is challenging (Hattie 2012) 'Give and help students understand feedback and interpret and act on feedback given to me' (Hattie 2018)	Give pupils lots of opportunities to rehearse new material and provide feedback

	Recommendations from EEF Metacognition and Self-regulated learning 2018	Hattie 2012 and 2018	Rosenshine 2012
Models and guided practice	Strand 2 Structured Practice (explicit instruction)	Provide guidance on instruction	Ensure there is lots of opportunity for independent practice and that it is the same as the guided practice
	Strand 3 'Modelling by the teacher is a cornerstone of effective teaching; revealing the thought processes of an expert learner helps to develop pupils' metacognitive skills.'		Guide pupils through new learning and breaking it down into the tiniest pieces possible Model thought processes
Scaffolds	Strand 3 'Scaffolded tasks, like worked examples, allow pupils to develop their metacognitive and cognitive skills without placing too many demands on their mental resources.' Strand 4 'Make sure that learning activities don't overburden working memory; we need to teach strategies to cope with demanding tasks – for example, using diagrams, notes, and other external aids, talking through the problem out loud, or breaking the task down into simpler steps.' Strand 6 'Carefully designed guided practice, with support gradually withdrawn as the pupil becomes proficient, can allow pupils to develop skills and strategies before applying them in independent practice.'	Remove the scaffolds when pupils are making progress and guidance is no longer needed	'Provide scaffold for challenging tasks'
Evaluation	Strand 2 Structured Reflection (explicit instruction)	Ensure that time is planned in for evaluating the impact of teaching on pupil learning	Ensure that weekly and monthly evaluations are part of the teaching cycle

For Rosenshine (2012), guiding pupils through new learning and breaking it down into the tiniest pieces possible is recommended. Rosenshine highlights how overloading pupils' working memory with too much information at the same time could lead to confusion. This is where teaching metacognition alongside the cognition would provide a structure or framework to aid the breaking down of cognition into the minute pieces of information or building blocks.

John Hattie (2012), who has conducted the largest 'ever research project on teaching strategies to practical classroom implementation', describes effective teaching as being a complex and intricately interwoven series of stages but with the golden thread of passion running through it. He describes the passion as being a 'particular form of passion'. This particular type of passion stems from 'having a positive impact on all students in the classroom', but that the most important aspect is realising the impact that passion will have on all pupils. Hattie argues that a teacher's beliefs and commitments are the greatest influence on student achievement. Passion drives teacher performance and acts as a motivating factor (Mart, 2013: 473). There is a strong correlation between pupil achievement and passionate teachers (Fried, 1995). If teaching is not weakened and diluted by school systems, then every teacher can be a passionate one (Fried, 1995, p. 24).

Hattie (2017) suggests that one way of improving student achievement is by evaluating the impact you are having. This must be carried out regularly in order to be effective, and to help fine-tune teaching methods consequently. When teachers make the learning explicit, pupils are made aware about what they have to do. Teachers should also be aware if pupils are meeting their learning goals. 'Teaching and learning are visible when the learning goal is not only challenging but is explicit' Hattie (2012: 14).

Hattie (2012: VIII) calls for such mindsets 'to be developed in teacher education programs'. He emphasises that in order to develop effective teachers and school leaders CPD should be designed not only to provide the right resources but also to incorporate nurturing. He also states that there are three main ways teachers can have a larger impact on pupil outcomes. Firstly, realising the impact teachers have on their pupils helps them to make necessary adjustments to their teaching, to allow for pupil progression. Secondly, being increasingly reflective of the impact teachers are having on their pupils has a significant influence on pupil achievement. Thirdly, Hattie goes on to say that 'teachers demonstrating that they are learners has a huge impact in how pupils see themselves as learners' (Hattie, 2019: 126).

Case study: How modelling learning can impact positively on pupil outcomes

Sharmilla's parents arrived in England during the 1960s knowing very little English. As a child, Sharmilla watched her father trying to decipher English in letters but to no avail. He would need to pay interpreters to translate letters written in English. When she was five years old, her father decided that enough was enough and started to learn English himself. Her father would read books in Bengali to her and in return she would read books in English to him. She taught him how to sound out letters and put sentences together. His understanding and comprehension of English began to improve. Watching her father learn a new language had a profound effect on her. It helped her to work out how she learned. At the age of seven, amongst many dreams, she set herself a goal to improve her handwriting. She realised that the way she learnt was to watch others, so she requested to watch a BBC programme on handwriting.

- How did watching her father learn English have a profound effect on Sharmilla?
- Which strategies did Sharmilla pick up, when observing her father learn something new?
- What made Sharmilla realise that setting herself a goal would help her to achieve that dream?

Building self-efficacy

How do we create an environment where teachers can flourish to make the most impact on our pupils?

Both Hattie and the EEF suggest self-efficacy as a high impact strategy. The EEF (2018) states that when 'motivating pupils to persevere at challenging tasks, it is important to reward effort rather than absolute levels of achievement; to give feedback about personal progress, and to avoid social comparison'.

This can be compared to Maslow's hierarchy of needs. In 1943, Abraham Maslow had a set of papers published titled *A Theory of Human Motivation*. Here he suggests a way of explaining how to live a happy life and the layers of motivation which humans experience. This has been represented in a pyramid structure and split into five categories: physiological, safety and security, love and belonging, self-esteem, self-actualisation.

Maslow's theory suggests that humans start at the bottom of the pyramid and require the most basic human needs to be met before proceeding through the other levels. He argues that if the physiological needs of breathing, food, shelter, sleep and clothing are not met, humans will not be able to reach the next level of realisation, which are safety and security. There is truth in that: if you cannot feed yourself, how can you go on to have a family and provide a roof over their heads and provide social stability? The next stage of the pyramid is love and belonging, where you develop friendship, have a family, intimacy and develop a sense of connection. This is where you will notice that the pyramid does not quite work in the way it was intended, as a way of understanding human motivation, and some would argue that intimacy is a physiological need. The fourth rung is self-esteem. Once you have met your physiological, safety and security, and love and belonging criteria, you can then move on to the self-esteem category. This is where your confidence really begins to develop, you start to achieve and have the respect of others and realise that you need to be a unique individual. Once you have reached this stage, you are ready to achieve your ultimate goal: self-actualisation. Here you can be creative and spontaneous. You can fulfil your potenital and live with moral purpose and seek meaning. It is ultimate self-awareness where you stop seeking the approval of others and instead focus on reaching your true potential.

So how does this link to self-efficacy? Self-efficacy is when the child has self-confidence in their ability to complete a challenging task. The use of metacognitive strategies can be predicted by the amount of self-confidence a pupil has. The EEF guidance (2018) recommends that during difficult tasks, when motivating pupils, it is important to give feedback at timely intervals and to reward effort rather than outcome. Giving immediate feedback from time to time (Hattie, 2012) also helps with pupil motivation and helps develop accuracy of judgement which can lead to development of the growth mindset. Social comparisons are best avoided, however, personal and individual comparison could be beneficial.

High expectations and challenge

Educators have high expectations for pupils but not all pupils readily accept challenging tasks. This can depend on a range of factors from not having the cognitive or metacognitive strategies to having other barriers to learning, and those that are outside of the control of the teacher. People are more likely to abandon tasks that are deemed too difficult and will avoid tests at all costs (Kornell, 2009). This is one of the reasons why pupils need adults to provide the emotional support, which will enable them to persevere with challenge.

Along with metacognition and cognition, motivation is a key component of self-regulation. Being motivated helps pupils to maintain concentration and put effort into the right places (Kornell, N. and Bjork, R.A. (2007).

The challenge allows pupils to develop deep reflective skills, which helps them to understand themselves as learners. If pupils 'struggle' (EEF, 2018) with learning, recall from the long-term memory becomes more automatic later on (Bjork, 2011). This enabled the cycle of planning, monitoring and evaluating.

Whilst pupils who are aware of their learning will naturally use these thinking processes, when facing challenging tasks, lower attaining pupils will need to be taught the skills of metacognitive knowledge and strategies explicitly (see Chapter 2). Careful consideration must be given when setting challenging tasks; if it is too challenging there will be cognitive overload and pupils will give up, thus not accepting the challenge. The challenge must be difficult enough to ignite the motivation to strive towards it. During this stage of decision-making about the best possible approaches to study for a challenging tasks, whilst keeping the effort going, metacognition becomes paramount (Kornell and Bjork, 2007) (see Chapter 6 for more on challenge).

Educators are aware that creating challenges in lessons helps develop deeper critical thinking skills as it creates the conditions for deeper internal reflection. What is clear is that in order to develop metacognition, challenge is required (Adey, 2008). There is a misconception that in order to develop self-esteem teachers should plan easy activities. However, this can lead to all sorts of problems from switching off and becoming withdrawn in lessons to displaying both low levels and extreme behavioural issues. The benefits of cognitive challenge cannot be underestimated. With the right amount of challenge or 'The Goldilocks Effect' (EEF, 2018), challenging a child brings a number of benefits such as increased pupil engagement, decreased behavioural issues, better problem-solving skills, improved social and emotional skills, improved teamwork, increased motivation to complete the task, improvement in speaking and listening skills, improved language progression, increased confidence in learning, increased self-knowledge about how pupils learn, increased understanding of teachers about how pupils learn and ultimately improved memory and recall.

Adey (2008) suggests that a way to develop cognitive acceleration is to plan challenging activities and create cognitive conflict. Hattie (2019), Rosenshine (2012) and the EEF (2018) all agree about providing pupils with challenge but Adey (2008) suggests that sometimes it is acceptable to plan sessions where there is no definitive answer. This is when pupils' thinking is challenged but where they do not necessarily solve a problem with a definite answer.

Using reflection and mistakes made to effectively move learning forward

When it comes to using reflections and mistakes to move learning on, there are many parallels which can be drawn between the work of the EEF (2018). Hattie (2017) and Rosenshine (2012). The EEF guidance (2018) and Rosenshine (2012) talk about pupil evaluations and reflections. Hattie (2012) mentions the impact of teacher reflections as being equally important, stating that teachers evaluating their impact is 'the most important factor of all mindframes' and one that 'dominates the major message from the Visible Learning research,' (Hattie and Zierer, 2017) It involves a cycle of repeatedly fine-tuning and filtering teachers' work 'to maximise the impact' for every pupil. He calls for teachers to make their 'impact visible' by 'listening out for it'. One way of doing this is through measuring both summative and formative progress, which is closely linked to feedback. However, there is a clear distinction between each, for example, summative assessment is for the teacher whereas formative assessment is for the pupils. Whilst measuring progress teachers need clarity about what they are measuring.

Hattie (2012) also has found that when pupils are faced with challenging work, they require more feedback, which is important for learning. The main issue with this is that the teacher is required to be there to enable the pupil to achieve the challenges. He goes on to say that not only do teachers have to be 'vigilant to what is working and what is not' but that this information or formative assessment should be used to plan the next steps for pupils whereby the teacher decides the 'cognitive supports' (Rosenshine, 2012) required. This is something which cannot be left to chance but must be part of a teacher's conscious repertoire of thought (Hattie, 2012). Teachers must also think about how the learning environment creates impact on pupils' learning. It is a teacher's moral imperative to make 'the teaching and learning visible'.

Rosenshine (2012) states that rectifying mistakes at the point of learning is the quickest way for pupils to make progress.

According to Hattie (2012), the teacher needs to 'provide direction and redirection' in terms of content being understood. However, a teacher should recognise when to 'move out of the way' or remove scaffolds. Rosenshine (2012) makes a pertinent point about ensuring that 'pupils achieve high success rates' and providing feedback to rectify mistakes in the classroom is a way of achieving this.

If pupils are allowed to continue making mistakes, where there is very little guidance to learn from the mistake and rectify it, then they will continue practising misconceptions. Once misconceptions are practised over and over again, they become embedded into the long-term memory and pupils master misconceptions. It is therefore important that although there must be room for making errors, these mistakes require swift guidance to resolve.

Developing trust

Hattie's findings indicate two ways to develop trust, by developing positive relationships and by creating a classroom of mistake-making. In *10 Mindframes for Visible Learning*, Hattie and Zierer (2017) talks about ways of alleviating teacher anxiety, increasing teacher expectations and building relationships with pupils. In this book, Hattie and Zierer give an example of a pupil who may fear giving a presentation and state that 'the child needs an atmosphere of confidence and trust, an atmosphere that gives him or her a feeling of security so that the child can make the presentation' (Hattie and Zierer, 2017: 129). They state that 'positive relationships are the precursors to learning,'

(Hattie and Zierer, 2017: 129). These 'positive relationships' between pupils and teachers and between peers are crucial to learning. Pupils need to know that they can trust adults in order to seek support, look for possibilities, maintain effort and not give up. It is this trust that leads to developing the growth mindset.

An example where high levels of metacognition knowledge and strategies are required is homework. When carrying out homework there is an absence of teacher support and pupils are required to motivate themselves to complete tasks. In the absence of face-to-face teaching and support it is important that the challenge set is appropriately. Pupils will evaluate the difficulty of the task and if they judge that the task is too difficult, it will either be partially completed or not completed at all.

Only those who can 'delay gratification' (EEF, 2018) will be able to persevere (see more on delayed gratification in Chapter 6). Although rewarding effort is usually viewed negatively, it can be a way to alleviate feelings of failure and disappointment. Another way to avoid feelings of failure, depending on the level of metacognition knowledge and strategies developed by pupils, is to give careful consideration as to the purpose of setting the homework. Perhaps challenging homework cannot be set for some pupils, especially if there is no parental or carer support available at home. In such cases homework can be set for consolidation instead of challenge (see more on homework in Chapter 7).

In addition to this, another way to develop trust is to allow pupils to make mistakes. Whilst challenging pupils' thinking and learning, it is imperative that a classroom culture of trust is developed (Hattie, 2012) by allowing pupils to make mistakes. Pupils must realise that making mistakes is part of learning. This is a real challenge in itself for teachers, balancing challenge whilst creating classroom conditions where it is acceptable to make mistakes. Educators require a repertoire of strategies to help pupils accept that they have made a mistake.

A visual image which has been associated with challenge recently is known as being 'in the learning pit', with associated classroom displays springing up all over the country. Although the intention is clear, to enable pupils to see that it is perfectly acceptable to be in this pit, there is a danger that pupils may dwell in it for longer than necessary.

In addition, some images suggest that a friend can help you out of the pit. If we are to develop true independence, having friends helping us should not be the first port of call. Without trainings pupils may see this as an opportunity to avoid thinking and merely asking friends for answers.

Only once all possibilities have been exhausted should we seek help from our friends. The emphasis should be on realising our own strengths, identifying areas to improve on and realising strategies that we can draw upon. The aim for practitioners is to ensure that pupils do not feel too disappointed when they make a mistake. Mathematical success partly depends on confidence. Using mistakes to learn from is not recommended or lower attaining pupils in maths as this may decrease confidence further.

Social construction

One way to develop confidence in our learners is to build on existing knowledge and 'create something new' through social construction (Adey, 2008). In his book *Dialogic Inquiry Toward a Sociocultural Practice and Theory of Education*, Wells (1999) discusses how to develop pupils' thinking about their own learning through focused activities which promote dialogic talk. This type of talk should be carefully constructed. Ensuring that all pupils in small groups make a contribution to the discussion is a dilemma faced by many educators and this is something that requires careful consideration. Some pupils will feel vulnerable about opening up and sharing their ideas for fear of being rejected or questioned. Creating a classroom climate which is a safe space for speaking about one's ideas is crucial not only in whole class but also in small group discussions.

So, how do we ensure that all pupils are included in group discussions? We need to consider: How are the tables arranged in the classroom? Do they facilitate discussions? Do the resources given hinder or progress the discussion? Can the pupils work collaboratively in a group? If not, what social and emotional support do they need? Can pupils see and hear each other from where they are sitting?

Teachers investing in their own training and development

We are all too aware that teaching thinking skills is a very complex matter. Some teachers can take new pedagogical ideas and incorporate into their teaching effortlessly. The majority of teachers need high quality professional development and training to help them make the changes (Adey, 2008; Weston and Clay, 2018).

Strand 3 from the EEF guidance (2018) has put together a seven-step strategy to be incorporated into teaching practice. The seven steps, decreasing in teacher input, are: activating in prior knowledge, explicit strategy instruction, modelling learned strategy, memorisation of strategy, guided practice, independent practice and structured reflection. The recommendation suggests that during this teaching process, pupils who are new to metacognition should evaluate their efforts and successes at the end of the lesson as opposed to during the lesson. The reason for this is when learning, for example, a particular skill, reflection may 'interfere with completing the skill'. There is much evidence to indicate that teachers who invest time and effort in their own development have greater impact on their pupils (Hattie, 2012). Fried (1995) suggests that a willingness for reflection on pupil outcome is just as important as modelling the learning process:

> Great teachers reflect on their commitment to student achievement through seeking an opportunity to share the things they have learnt. (Fried, 1995)

Peer trio observations is a way teachers can develop their practice further. This is where teachers, usually from different year groups, plan a lesson together with a particular focus and observe each other, with a view to providing constructive (Headteacher Update, 2013) feedback to each other. This form of peer review can have a great impact on teacher development. Some schools use IRIS Connect, which is time consuming but overall does have a moderate impact on pupil outcomes (EEF, 2020), where teachers are filmed and constructive feedback is given. Teachers also watch the video back as a way of 'seeing' how they teach. The idea is that this form of self-reflection and evaluation can help teachers 'see' their practice in the classroom and can reflect and change.

Summary

- Teaching is a complex process.
- Focus on what pupils can achieve and what the intended outcome (impact) is.
- Build connections to new learning through prior knowledge.
- Use feedback to provide timely direction and redirection.
- Remove scaffolds when pupils are making progress towards learning independently.
- Know how to develop conceptual understanding from surface and deep knowledge.
- Use findings from research and interpretations not as a tick box exercise for each lesson but as a guide for school policy development.
- Powerful impact on pupil achievement can be achieved when teacher self-belief is combined with belief in pupils.
- Success-led practice is crucial to develop self-esteem and to motivate.

Think!

- What is your intended impact on your pupils?
- What are your beliefs about your lowest achieving, most hard to reach pupils?
- How can you continue developing your passion given the constraints of systemic pressures and continuing political changes in the educational landscape?
- How can you ensure that there is good coverage across your planning to include all of the recommendations or principles?

Teacher metacognition

- What strategies do you use for your own learning?
- How can you model how you learn to your pupils?

(Continued)

- Is the way you learn different in different subjects?
- What are your views about using rewards in the classroom?
- How do you use rewards in the classroom?
- How do you provide opportunities to develop pupil reflection and evaluation?
- How often do you get the opportunity to reflect upon and evaluate your own practice?

Pupil metacognition

- How do pupils reflect on their learning?
- How do they evaluate their learning?
- How often are pupils given the opportunity to reflect and evaluate their learning?

References

Adey, P. (2008) Let's Think Handbook: A Guide to Cognitive Acceleration in the Primary School. London: GL Assessment Limited.

Bjork, R. (2011) On the symbiosis of learning, remembering, and forgetting. In A.S. Benjamin (ed.), *Successful Remembering and Successful Forgetting: A Festschrift in Honor of Robert A. Bjork*. New York: Psychology Press, pp. 1–22.

EEF (2018) *Metacognition and Self-Regulated Learning: Guidance Report* [online]. Available at: https://educationendowmentfoundation.org.uk/public/files/Publications/Metacognition/EEF_Metacognition_and_self-regulated_learning.pdf (accessed 3 February 2021).

EEF (2020) IRIS Connect: Developing classroom dialogue and feedback through collective video reflection [online]. https://educationendowmentfoundation.org.uk/projects-and-evaluation/projects/iris-connect/ (accessed 16 March 2021).

Fried, Robert L. (1995), The Passionate Teacher. Beacon Press.

Gredler, M.E., Broussard, S.C. and Garrison, M.E.B. (2004) The Relationship between Classroom Motivation and Academic Achievement in Elementary School Aged Children. *Family and Consumer Sciences Research Journal*, 33, 106–120. https://doi.org/10.1177/1077727X04269573

Hattie, J. (2012) Visible Learning for Teachers: Maximising Impact on Learning. London: Routledge.

Hattie, J. and Zierer, K. (2017) *10 Mindframes for Visible Learning.* Abingdon: Routledge.

Hattie, J. (2018) Visible Learning: Feedback. London: Routledge.

Kornell, N. and Bjork, R.A. (2007) The promise and perils of self-regulated study', *Psychonomic Bulletin and Review*, 14, p. 219.

Kornell, N. (2009) 'Metacognition in animals and humans', *Current Directions in Psychological Science*, 18(1), University of California, Los Angeles.

Mart, C.T. (2013) A Passionate Teacher: Teacher Commitment and Dedication to Student Learning. *International Journal of Academic Research in Progressive Education and Development*, 2(1).

Maslow, A. ([1943] 2013) A Theory of Human Motivation. Start Publishing.

Pierson, R. (2020) Every kid needs a champion. Ted Talks Education [online]. Ted.com. Available at: www.ted.com/talks/rita_pierson_every_kid_needs_a_champion (accessed 16 March 2021).

Rosenshine, B. (2012) Principles of instruction: Research-based strategies that all teachers should know. *The American Educator*, 36 (1): 12–19.

Wells, G. (1999) Dialogic Inquiry Toward a Sociocultural Practice and Theory of Education. Cambridge: Cambridge University Press.

Weston, D. and Clay, B. (2018) Unleashing Great Teaching: The Secrets to the Most Effective Teacher. London: Routledge.

4

METACOGNITION AND MINDSETS

Contents

- What is mindset?
- Mindframes and the growth mindset
- Perseverance
- Why growth mindset is important
- How social and emotional well-being link to the growth mindset and metacognition
- Resilience
- References

In this chapter we will explore

- what mindsets are
- the importance of developing a growth mindset
- links between well-being, mindfulness, the growth mindset and metacognition
- what a growth mindset classroom could look like
- perseverance, grit and the growth mindset.

What is mindset?

Walk into any primary school playground and observe those playing sports in the playground. Observing football is a good start. The game usually starts off quite amicably, with players warming up into the game. You will hear players discuss tactics before the start of the game and see them strive to work as a team to score goals. The high stakes nature of the game and adrenaline running high may sometimes, inevitably, lead to arguments. However, those same pupils may lose that passion upon entering the classroom and when it comes to academic subjects. What is the reason for this? What is the difference between football and, for example, mathematics? Why do some pupils have a passion for football and not for maths? Is it something to do with not enjoying the subject itself? Is it to do with mindset? Is it something to do with not feeling as successful in maths as in football?

In recent years, the growth mindset has become increasingly popular, with posters and stickers springing up everywhere, and 'I can't do it yet!' becoming a required mantra in a teacher's language toolkit.

The growth mindset was developed by psychologist Carol Dweck after years of study and research into how people's beliefs 'can affect their motivation, achievement and well-being' (Dweck and Yeager, 2019). It is centred around the differences between belief and ability, where your ability does not necessarily lead to success but rather 'your beliefs about your ability' do (Hymer and Gershon, 2014). If you believe you can succeed at something, you will probably be able to do it. But it is more than that and there are many strategies which educators could implement in their classrooms to help develop pupils' mindsets.

The growth mindset is based on beliefs about intelligence: that intelligence is not something which is fixed at birth but is malleable and can change and grow. Dweck discovered that there are two mindsets humans have when thinking about intelligence and learning: the growth mindset and the fixed mindset. People who have the fixed mindset think that humans are born with fixed intelligence and that this cannot be changed. However, those who have the growth mindset believe that intelligence is something that, given the right conditions, can grow and change (Dweck, 2017).

Mindframes and the growth mindset

There are some similarities between Hattie and Zierer's *Mindframes* (2018) and Carol Dweck's growth mindset. These include that those with a growth mindset are more likely to take on challenges readily, learn from their mistakes, see failing as an opportunity for learning and growth, put in effort, readily accept feedback and evaluate it. In addition to this, Hattie has always advocated that educators should be aware of their impact, balance dialogue and listening, and build positive relationships by working collaboratively, whereas Dweck's focus has mainly been on the growth mindset.

Table 4.1 shows some features of growth and fixed mindsets.

Table 4.1 Growth mindset vs fixed mindset

	Growth Mindset	Fixed Mindset
Beliefs	Intelligence is malleable and can grow/believes that effort leads to mastery	Intelligence is fixed at birth and cannot change/ believes that effort is fruitless
Failure	Views failure as an opportunity for learning	Believes failure defines who they are
Success	Views others' successes as inspirational	Feels threatened by others' successes
Attitude	Embraces challenge	Does not enjoy challenges
Feedback	Views feedback as a form of learning/ responds to feedback positively	Sees feedback as a form of criticism/ignores feedback

These findings indicate that intelligence is malleable and it is something which can be grown through practice and effort. The brain is organised with a series of neurons (nerve cells), which 'send and receive chemical and electrical signals to each other across a gap called a synapse' (Taylor, Caviglioli and Dibner, 2019: 220).

The more you practise a particular skill or repeat knowledge, the stronger the neural pathways become, 'the signals can travel faster' and more neural networks are created (Taylor, Caviglioli and Dibner, 2019: 220).

Neurons or nerve cells consist of four parts: a cell body, which has long narrow projections, called dendrites (looks a bit like an octopus) and a long string-like structure called an axon, which is protected by insulation called a myelin sheath (a bit like electrical wires being protected by a rubber covering). Nerve cells are positioned so that there is a gap (called the synapse) from the axon of one cell to the dendrite of another cell (Taylor, Caviglioli and Dibner, 2019).

When learning something new, neurons become activated and signals are transmitted from the dendrites of one neuron down the axon, this is carried across the synaptic gap and continues through the dendrite of the next nerve cell or neuron, 'creating a pathway across the brain' (Taylor, Caviglioli and Dibner, 2019: 220).

It is when the myelin sheath becomes destroyed that conditions such as multiple sclerosis (MS) can develop, where nerve signals are either interrupted, slowed down, misdirected or completely prevented from travelling. Although the symptoms of MS are similar to that of other neurological conditions, they can interfere with thinking, learning and planning (NHS.uk, n.d.). There can be problems associated with reduced attention span, issues with how information entering the eyes is translated in the brain and challenges with planning, solving problems and mathematical reasoning. Although long-term memory is unaffected, MS affects learning and remembering new things.

During the learning process as neurons fire repeatedly over time, the myelin sheath around the axon becomes thicker, enabling faster transmission of the electrical signal. The trail between two neurons becomes stronger when the regularity of the signals increases (Taylor, Caviglioli and Dibner, 2019). This suggests that classroom strategies can result in physiological change in the axon as it thickens with repeated practice.

An example would be repeated retrieval practice where pupils who have practiced regularly, can recall information quickly from the long-term memory due to the pathway being strengthened over time. Let us think about a particular type of pupil. Imagine a pupil who is high achieving in sports – any sport but usually football – but when it comes to academic study, they struggle. We have all taught such pupils and perhaps at some point wondered what makes them persevere with the sport but not with academic study. Would this pupil be classified as having a growth mindset or not?

A study refuting some of the claims of growth mindset were published in 2020 by Burgoyne, Hambrick and Macnamara. They discovered that 'self-efficacy' and the need for 'achievement' led to motivation and ultimately achievement. They claim that there are weaknesses in the growth mindset theory and 'that bold claims about mindset appear to be overstated' (Burgoyne, Hambrick and Macnamara, 2020: 258).

They studied six characteristics of growth mindset theory in 438 participants and they discovered that those with a growth mindset and those with a fixed mindset did not automatically hold learning goals; those with a fixed mindset did not hold performance-avoidance goals; people with a fixed mindset did not believe that talent alone, without effort, creates success; people with a growth mindset did not persist to overcome challenges; those with a growth mindset are not resilient following failure. These findings suggest that there appear to be misunderstandings about what a growth mindset actually is and how to develop it in the classroom. Dweck herself has stated that her research has been misinterpreted and it requires deeper thought for successful implementation to have impact in the classroom. Do these findings indicate that we may in fact have both mindsets? Perhaps we have a choice about the mindset we use depending on our passions? Surely we cannot be passionate about everything, otherwise we would burn out. And how do we help our pupils to become passionate about school and academic study?

Perseverance

Three years ago, I had a conversation about perseverance with the well-known children's author SF Said, who has written three children's books: *Varjak Paw*, *The Outlaw Varjak Paw* and *Phoenix*. I first met him in 2017, when I invited him to our school for World Book Day. He told us his story about resilience. He had forty rejections at his very first attempt to publish a book, which has never been published. SF had another forty rejections for his second attempt at publishing a second book, which again was never published. For *Varjak Paw*, he had ten rejections before finding a publisher. It was a total of ninety rejections over three books.

Most people would have given up at the first hurdle but something pushed him forward. I was intrigued by his resilience and determination so I asked him what his views were on the matter. SF stated that he thought it was a choice, and the motivation to persevere was borne out of really wanting to do something. He explained that there were lots of things he did not persevere with because they did not mean that much to him and because he did not value them. SF loved stories as a child and they meant so much to him. He thinks that maybe that was why he persevered and could not give up and had to write his own stories. SF explained that perseverance is a choice, not a talent. Anyone can do it, if they want to.

This suggests that perhaps we have both fixed and growth mindsets and adopt a growth mindset attitude for that which motivates or drives us. Or perhaps our mindset is on a continuum like the shades on a colour pallet? Perhaps where we place ourselves on this continuum depends on how motivated we are to achieve the task in hand.

Returning to the playground, we can see that one motivation could be the feeling of success – for example, when pupils score a goal. But what happens when children lose? What strategies do they draw upon? The first thing you'll notice is that they talk through the game and what went wrong. They begin to reflect about what they should have done and then this moves on to what they would do if the situation arose again and figure out further failsafe tactics and strategies. This process of learning from mistakes drives them forward and they get better and better at it. It is this process of learning from mistakes that helps to develop the growth mindset. During this process, the emotional toil of failure is cushioned by the team. The team are the shock absorbers, who provide the emotional, social support and strength to continue forward. How many times have we allowed children to truly fail in a task in the classroom? Often high stakes accountability prevents us from allowing this to happen. However, in order to boost a growth mindset and manufacture some cognitive conflict, we plan for this in our curricula and are ready with emotional support, with mindfulness strategies and with nurture for those who require them.

In 2018, Sisk, Burgoyne, Sun, Butler and Macnamara found that although there was little evidence to suggest that 'overall' pupil achievement improves with interventions in growth mindset, there was a possibility that disadvantaged pupils may benefit from mindset interventions. They set about testing the theory of mindset and studied the 'relationship between mind-sets and academic achievement' and the conditions under which the relationship strengthens or weakens (Sisk et al., 1918: 2).

They also studied whether mindset interventions 'positively impact academic achievement', and under which situations that impact increased or decreased it (Sisk et al., 1918: 2). In order to understand the theories, Sisk et al. (2018) thought it crucial to explain the difference between implicit theories of intelligence and personality.

Their overall findings indicated that developing mindset alone may not lead to improved outcomes but that academic achievement is a complex issue. There may be other factors contributing to improved outcomes.

How social and emotional well-being link to the growth mindset and metacognition

Dweck has been under fire about her claims regarding mindset and states that she has been misunderstood and that improving outcomes is not just about telling pupils to try harder or about having a growth mindset (Dweck, 2015).

Although there have been recent claims that the growth mindset is a fad, which has seen mindset reduced from a very complex area of study into posters, stickers and chants of 'I can do it', and an increased focus on overturning Dweck's claims, the real message appears to have been lost in translation.

Dweck states that she did not anticipate the problems associated with the idea of the growth mindset when she shared it with the world (Severs, 2020). She explains that researchers have conducted their research under such conditions as they could not possibly test every situation or context available and that they provide indication about what transpires under certain situations. Dweck calls for more collaboration between teachers and researchers as it is teacher trial and feedback that moves the learning and research on.

There are two areas which have been misinterpreted; explaining what the growth mindset and fixed mindset are will lead to improved results and that the growth mindset is not just about praising effort. The growth mindset involves working collaboratively to identify what is working and not working given the contexts in which this is happening. It is something which needs to be broken down even further.

There appear to be similarities between Dweck's findings and metacognition, which seems to have been overlooked. Both Dweck's findings and Whitbread and Colman's findings indicate that the most important aspect, when it comes to closing the disadvantage gap, is the planning, monitoring and evaluating process of the learning journey (Whitbread and Colman, 2010) and that this does not just happen without explicit teaching. In the same way it is clear that a growth mindset does not just happen – well, not for all children. It appears that a growth mindset is also something that needs to be explained and explicitly developed. This seems to be linked to self-efficacy (Burgoyne, Hambrick and Macnamara, 2020) which is explored further in Chapter 3 on the impact of metacognition. In Dweck's TED Talk on 'The power of believing you can improve', she states that when pupils with a growth mindset were given challenging tasks, she heard a pupil exclaim that 'I love a challenge' (Dweck, 2014). When they observed brain activity, there was more brain activity in these pupils compared to the pupils with a fixed mindset.

Certain aspects of the growth mindset, mindfulness, well-being and metacognition seem to be closely related. The main one being about our own belief about being able to change. Change is a challenge for most of us; we become used to being comfortable with ourselves and do not always seek out challenges. Motivation is required in order for pupils to accept challenges and where this is lacking, emotional support, mindfulness and nurture could be beneficial.

Table 4.2 shows some similarities between the growth mindset, well-being and mindfulness and metacognition.

Table 4.2 Similarities between the growth mindset, well-being and mindfulness, and metacognition

	Growth mindset	Mindfulness and well-being	Metacognition
Attitude	Solutions focused mindset	Positive mental health	Solutions focused leading to independent thinking
Belief about change	Belief that you and others can change (intelligence is not fixed and can change over time)	Believe that everything is changing all the time	Believe that by thinking about how you learn it can improve your learning
Effort	Positive praise about effort rather than outcome leading to learning helps develop a growth mindset	Making an effort to look after your well-being leads to better understanding of yourself which leads to being able to better cope in challenging circumstances	The more cognitive conflict there is the more effort is required to reflect on your learning
Challenge	Well-motivated to accept challenges	Seeking support builds resilience Use mindfulness strategies to overcome feelings of failure from challenge including seeking support	Support the development of pupil motivation to readily accept challenges Scaffolds should be provided when learning becomes challenging Peer support and teacher support in terms of increased feedback should be given
Learning	The more you practice the more the neural pathways are used and get stronger More neural connections are made thereby increasing intelligence	Mindfulness and well-being strategies help attention to stay focused in the moment (in the present) This leads to improved concentration	Using metacognitive strategies helps to direct attention to the task in hand
Mistakes	Find mistakes motivating	See mistakes as learning opportunities	Learn to use mistakes to learn about themselves as learners

Having a growth mindset requires you to be in the present and in the moment. The same goes for metacognition. If you are dwelling on the past and focusing on the future, your attention becomes diverted and you cannot think in the moment about what knowledge you have not yet acquired or what skill you cannot do yet.

Mindfulness helps you to realise that everything is changing and growth mindset helps you to realise that you and others are capable of change.

That is not to say that fixed mindsets are necessarily bad either. There may be times when being fixed in your thinking is necessary, for instance when you believe in something so much.

In *Fifty Fantastic Ideas for Mindfulness*, Tammie Prince (2019) states that many of our pupils currently lack the 'skills necessary to cope with the stresses that life presents to them' in an increasingly fast-paced life. Mindfulness can be seen as a coping strategy which can lead to resilience. Prince explains that children, from a very young age, are naturally mindful. They concentrate intently on things which they are drawn into. Being able to focus your sole attention on a given task is very easy for a very young child, particularly those in Early Years. Prince (2019) states that being mindful is not just about meditating and stillness. When our minds shift from the past to the future, this can have a negative impact on our sense of well-being. It's about being present in the moment, recognising our emotions and changing them if necessary.

Resilience

Having a growth mindset is believed to lead to the development of resilience. Let us explore what resilience is. In his book, *Ten Traits of Resilience*, James Hilton (2018) has compiled a list of qualities which enable the development of resilience. They are: a sense of purpose, optimism, trust, courage, decisiveness, asking for help, a sense of fun, curiosity, taking care of yourself and others and turning adversity into opportunity (Hilton, 2018). Although the book is aimed at school leadership at all levels, it could be beneficial in the classroom for pupils too.

How do we develop a sense of purpose in the classroom? Teachers are required to be great actors and even when things are falling apart, they put on a brave smile and are optimistic at all times. Part of being optimistic is recognising our feelings and using strategies to overcome these feelings and change them. How do we teach our pupils to overcome challenges and failure? How do we teach pupils to become courageous and accept challenges in the face of adversity, whether or not they are in the classroom? In addition to this, in order for pupils to learn, classroom relationships need to be based on mutual trust and understanding. How do we develop the trust required for learning and therefore impact in the classroom? How do we ensure that pupils seek help and support when required to do so? Seeking help and support is crucial to developing our resilience. How do we create a safe environment where pupils feel they are able to do this?

Resilience is often thought of as having the ability to 'bounce back' in the face of adversity. Resilience is much more than whether people persevere when facing minor setbacks. Resilience is about whether individuals can adapt despite facing particular risks. Resilience is not something that an individual is born with or inherits. It is a process of internal development; it can be seen when pupils have achieved and succeeded despite exposure to significant risks such as bereavement, illness or poverty. Not all pupils are resilient in all areas of life or even all subject areas and some high flyers may not be resilient in all subjects.

Coping is when individuals have to deal with internal conflicts from managing outside stresses, which surpasses a person's limitations. Pupils may be dealing with a range of issues from serious ordeal to exploitation. For such issues they will require specialist interventions and coping strategies.

Although there are similarities between coping and resilience in terms of how people act towards pressures, there is a key difference. 'Resilience is the outcome of successful coping,' (What we mean by Resilience, 2020).

Individuals use certain coping skills depending on the challenge posed. However, resilience is a process, which is achieved as an end goal when the skills used are successfully utilised (Gutman and Schoon, 2013). In the same way, the growth mindset could be viewed as a similar end point or goal. Coping is an intervention and something that is flexible or adaptable, which protects against danger and is something that can be taught. 'Resilience is a process which follows the exercise of those' coping skills (Gutman and Schoon, 2013: 27). As resilience is not something that can be adapted, it is better to focus on coping strategies.

Wolchik and Sandler (1997) found that both academic and psychological outcomes are dependent on the coping strategies that pupils utilise in pressurised conditions. In other words, pupils who have better coping skills tend to have positive outcomes, including higher self-efficacy higher psychological well-being, less depression and less likelihood to partake in bad behaviour (Sawyer et al., 2009).

Let us explore which coping strategies pupils use and how these may develop with age. Younger pupils tend to seek help from their primary caregivers. This tends to progress to using cognitive means such as problem solving and distraction. Metacognitive strategies such as positive self-talk and cognitive reframing then begin to overtake. Although Skinner, E. A., Kindermann, T.A. and Carrie Furrer, C. (2007) state that the ability to use skills such as decision-making, planning and reflection may not adequately develop until adolescence or early adulthood, these self-regulation skills can be taught to much younger pupils as stated in the EEF guidance (2018).

According to Duckworth (2016) resilience is also known as grit. Grit and engagement are both part of perseverance and it is the

Table 4.3 Showing how perseverance is broken down (based on Gutman and Schoon, 2013)

Perseverance			
Engagement (meta-construct)			Grit/Resilience
Behavioural	Emotional	Cognitive	Non-cognitive
Academic, social, extra-curricular and community involvement			Passion
Behaviours: • Effort • Persistence • Concentration • Asking questions • Contribution to class discussion	• Strong relationships • Feeling safe • A sense of belonging- Emotional reactions to teachers, classmates, academics and school. • A sense of belonging – Opportunity to participate as valued members of the community • Hope • Coping	• High expectations • Accepting high expectations and difficult ideas • Reflection and inclination of effort to understand challenging and difficult ideas and to achieve	• Conscientiousness • Tirelessly works hard despite challenges • Resistant to failure • Works hard despite adverse conditions even when progress remains steady • Has plenty of stamina despite being disillusioned or jaded • Can keep stamina going for long periods of time (years)

two processes combined that leads to how much a person capitalises in achieving a goal. Engagement is to do with behaviour, feeling and thinking, which are all linked. Grit can also demonstrate how conscientious and passionate an individual is (Gutman and Schoon, 2013).

Table 4.3 shows how perseverance could be broken down and developed in the classroom.

Case study: Developing a growth mindset in academic subjects

Edward is the pupil who found it very difficult to concentrate in the classroom and had over the years fallen behind. When he entered Year 6 he was two years behind in all areas of learning and he hated maths. He was disengaged in learning in the classroom but had a passion for football. Every lunchtime and playtime would end in the same way, with arguments over football. He would return to class in a bad mood and found it very difficult to start lessons. He was not the only pupil who would return from playtime in this mood. His teacher decided to teach a one-off lesson on the growth mindset and neuroplasticity. Then, at the beginning of lessons after play and lunch, she would start with meditation and breathing exercises. These five-minute sessions would help Edward and his friends to be present in the moment and focus on classroom activities. Each session continued until anxieties about the playground had been left behind and calmness ensued. Once this had happened, the teacher taught them to recognise the emotion and taught strategies to deal with the feelings. These were all embedded into the lesson. Once Edward and his friends were in a calm state, the lesson would begin and the growth mindset would be built up through a combination of positive praise, giving immediate feedback, focusing on the moment, providing enough challenge to move the learning forward and developing self-belief through the lesson. Maths was also taught through other subjects, such as science, history, geography and PE. By the time Edward and his friends finished the academic year they were at the expected level for that year group in all subjects. For younger pupils it may be useful to read mindset stories, which they can relate to more easily.

- Which strategies were used to develop a growth mindset in the classroom?
- How was self-regulation developed in the classroom setting?
- Why was it important to embed the teaching of recognising and dealing with emotions in teaching in the classroom?

Summary

- Passion usually drives a growth mindset.
- At primary school level passion should drive the learning and subjects should be taught with passion.
- It is possible to develop a growth mindset in the classroom through lessons.
- Teaching a short series of one-off lessons on developing a growth mindset could be beneficial.
- Passion usually drives a growth mindset.
- Family, teacher and peer support are required for resilience to develop.

Think!

- How do you feel about dealing with problems?
- How do you think problems can be solved?
- How confident are you in your ability to achieve your goals?
- Do you think that you could easily handle any unexpected situations which could arise?
- After stressful events, are you able to bounce back quite quickly?
- How do you react when trying challenging things?
- How do you respond to pressure?
- Do you tend to get overwhelmed by pressure or are you able to see the progress you have made?
- What are your beliefs about working smarter?

Teacher metacognition

- Which aspects of life do you have a growth mindset in?
- Which subjects/topics do you have a growth mindset in?
- What do you find challenging and how do you overcome these challenges?
- What motivates you?
- What strategies do you use to keep going when all you want to do is give up?

Pupil metacognition

- Which pupils in your class have a generic growth mindset?
- Which pupils have a growth mindset in one or a few particular areas?
- What areas of learning do your pupils find challenging?
- How do they overcome these challenges?
- What motivates individual pupils in your class?
- Who are the pupils who need to be taught explicit strategies for developing a growth mindset?
- How do pupils feel about the learning process?

References

A resilience and coping framework for supporting transitions back to school Transition: resilience WHAT WE MEAN BY 'RESILIENCE,' (2020) The British Psychological Society.

Burgoyne, A.P., Hambrick, D.Z and Macnamara, B.N. (2020) How firm are the foundations of mind-set theory? The claims appear stronger than the evidence. *Psychological Science, 31* (3): 258–267. Doi: 10.1177/0956 797619897588

Duckworth, A. (2016) *Grit: The Power of Passion and Perseverance.* Ebury Digital.

Dweck, C. (2014) The power of believing that you can improve. TEDxNorrköping [online]. Available at: www.ted.com/talks/carol_dweck_the_power_of_believing_that_you_can_improve/ (accessed 16 March 2021).

Dweck, C.S. (2017) From needs to goals and representations: Foundations for a unified theory of motivation, personality, and development. *Psychological Review, 124* (6): 689–719. https://doi.org/10.1037/rev0000082

Dweck, C.S. and Yeager, D.S. (2019) Mindsets: A view from two eras. *Perspectives on Psychological Science, 14* (3): 481–496. Doi: 10.1177/1745691618804166

EEF (2018) *Metacognition and Self-regulated Learning: Guidance Report* [online]. Available at: https://educationendowmentfoundation.org.uk/public/files/Publications/Metacognition/EEF_Metacognition_and_self-regulated_learning.pdf (accessed 9 November 2020).

Gutman, L. and Schoon, I. (2013) The Impact of Noncognitive Skills on Outcomes for Young People: Literature Review. London: Education Endowment Foundation. Available at: https://educationendowment-foundation.org.uk/public/files/Presentations/Publications/Non-cognitive_skills_literature_review_1.pdf

Hattie, J. and Zierer, K. (2018) *10 Mindframes for Visible Learning.* Abingdon: Routledge.

Hilton, J. (2018) *Ten Traits of Resilience.* London: Bloomsbury Education.

Hymer, B. and Gershon, M. (2020) *Growth Mindset Pocketbook.* Teachers' Pocketbooks.

NHS.uk (n.d.) *Causes: Multiple sclerosis* [online]. Available at: www.nhs.uk/conditions/multiple-sclerosis/causes/ (accessed 4 February 2021).

Prince, T. (2019) *Fifty Fantastic Ideas for Mindfulness.* Featherstone: London.

Sawyer, M.G., Pfeiffer, S., Spence, S.H., Bond, L., Graetz, B., Kay, D., Patton, G. and Sheffield, J. (2010) School-based prevention of depression: A randomised controlled study of the beyondblue schools research initiative. *Journal of Child Psychology and Psychiatry, and Allied Disciplines, 51* (2): 199–209. https://doi.org/10.1111/j.1469-7610.2009.02136.x

Severs, J. (2020) *Growth mindset: Where did it go wrong?* [online]. Available at: www.tes.com/news/growth-mindset-where-did-it-go-wrong (accessed 4 February 2021).

Sisk, V.F., Burgoyne, A.P., Sun, J., Butler, J.L. and Macnamara, B.N. (2018) To what extent and under which circumstances are growth mind-sets important to academic achievement? Two meta-analyses. *Psychological Science, 29* (4): 549–571. Doi: 10.1177/0956797617739704

Skinner, E.A., Kindermann, T.A. and Furrer, C. (Draft: August 10, 2007) A Motivational Perspective on Engagement and Disaffection: Conceptualization and Assessment of Children's Behavioral and Emotional Participation in Academic Activities in the Classroom. Portland State University and NPC Research.

Taylor, T., Caviglioli, O. and Dibner, N. (2019) Connect the Dots: The Collective Power of Relationships, Memory and Mindset. John Catt.

Whitebread, D. and Coltman, P. (2010) Aspects of pedagogy supporting metacognition and self-regulation in mathematical learning of young children: evidence from an observational study, *ZDM Mathematics Education*, *42* (2): 163–178. https://doi.Org/10.1007/s11858-009-0233-1

Wolchik, S.A. and Sandler, I.N. (eds) (1997) *Handbook of Children's Coping: Linking Theory and Intervention.* New York: Plenum Press. https://doi.org/10.1007/978-1-4757-2677-0

Yeager, D.S. and Dweck, C. (2012) Mindsets that promote resilience: When students believe that personal characteristics can be developed. *Educational Psychologist, 47* (4): 302–314. DOI: 10.1080/004615 20.2012.722805

5

METACOGNITIVE MISCONCEPTIONS

Contents

In this chapter we will explore

- what neuromyths are in education
- the discovery of penicillin and what we can learn from this
- how solely relying on intuition can contribute to the creation of myths
- how the variance in teacher experience can create misunderstand-ings in education
- the role of intuition in creating misconceptions about how we learn to read
- EEF findings on metacognitive misconceptions.

Neuromyths in education

Myths about the brain, or neuromyths, coupled with our own intui-tions are a powerful combination. This can lead to the creation of misconceptions. This combination of beliefs about the brain and our own life experiences and assumptions have contributed to some mis-conceptions being implemented throughout schools.

Myths about education and learning have existed for decades weaving their way through schools and colleges, often used to justify ineffective approaches to teaching. Many myths are biased misinter-pretations of scientific facts. Although scientific communications have increased, the gap between neuroscience and education has also increased in recent years. Messages are often distorted by the same conditions and biases as those responsible for neuromyths. Our inherent intuitions also play a part in the development of misconcep-tions (Weinstein, Sumeracki and Caviglioli, 2019).

It is human nature to make mistakes and form misconceptions. These are usually based on our intuitions, life experiences and assumptions. Misconceptions occur in everyday life due to the power of intuition and the reasons for these intuition are wide and varied. Our intuition has become well-developed over millions of years. (Weinstein, Sumeracki and Caviglioli, 2019). Sometimes, miscon-ceptions result from using our intuition as a protective mechanism, or from lack of knowledge, or simply from misinformation or misinterpretation.

One of the reasons why misconceptions occur is because by the time we obtain a degree, we have been in the schooling system for approximately seventeen years and we tend to use our schooling experience to inform our teaching practice. When building teacher philosophy and practice, using our own experiences as students and teachers can be extremely valuable. However, solely relying on our own intuition and how we should teach is not always correct (Weinstein, Sumeracki and Caviglioli, 2019).

Educators find explanations about how the brain works fascinating. Programmes such as Brain Gym, founded by Paul and Gail Dennison in the 1980s, have utilised this to sell an ideology about how 'brain buttons can be deeply massaged with one hand while holding the navel with the other hand' (Maccabe and Castel, 2008). This supposedly improves your ability to send messages from the right hemisphere of your brain to the left side of your body. There are a number of problems with this. Firstly, there is very little research published in high-quality journals evidencing how an alluring ideology, such as Brain Gym, can proliferate in our practice and demonstrating a rise in achievement, and secondly, the theory is flawed (Howard-Jones, 2014). This is one example of how the alluring ideology of brain gym has proliferated teaching practice.

By solely relying on our intuition, not only can we mislead ourselves but also others.

'Relying upon intuition, rather than science, can also lead us to latch on to false positives' (Weinstein, Sumeracki and Caviglioli, 2019: 4). Sometimes we see positives due to luck or chance. But this positive result does not mean that a method will work consistently over time. There are two major problems that arise from a reliance on intuition. Firstly, we may 'pick the wrong learning strategies,' based on intuition. Secondly, 'once we land on a learning strategy, we tend to seek out "evidence" that favours the strategy we have picked, while ignoring evidence that refutes our intuitions' (Weinstein, Sumeracki and Caviglioli, 2019: 22, 23). This is called confirmation bias, which is when we seek out evidence to confirm our ideas. One way of reducing confirmation bias may be to carry out continuous evaluations.

The discovery of penicillin

The story about the discovery of penicillin is a great example where a drug was suggested for treating bacterial infections because it had better outcomes than the placebo it was then promoted and which was evaluated by science.

The gap between research and education has become immense mainly due to 'dubious sources of evidence such as untested theories' and 'educational fads' (Weinstein, Sumeracki and Caviglioli, 2019: 23). The example of the development of penicillin from discovery to clinical testing (Aldridge, Parascandola and Sturchio, 1999) can provide clues about the usefulness of rigorous testing, which could be applied in education before adopting new ideas or strategies.

The discovery and development of penicillin is one of the greatest advances in therapeutic medicine. Before the dawn of the antibiotic era there were no treatments available for infections such as gonorrhoea, pneumonia or rheumatic fever.

Bacteria and fungi produce compounds called antibiotics naturally. This is a protective process to kill or inhibit competing microbes. The understanding of this phenomena goes back to the time of the ancient Egyptians, who used to apply mouldy bread to treat infected wounds. However, the first 'true antibiotic' was discovered by Alexander Fleming, who was the Professor of Bacteriology at St Mary's Hospital in London.

As Alexander Fleming began sorting through petri dishes of staphylococcus, which causes boils, sore throats and abscesses, after a holiday on 3 September 1928, he noticed something unusual in one dish. There was a blob of mould growing amongst the colonies of staphylococcus. He discovered that this 'mould juice' was not only capable of killing staphylococcus but also other harmful bacteria such as streptococcus, meningococcus and diphtheria bacillus. Separating the pure penicillin from the mould juice proved to be a difficult task. His assistants, Stuart Craddock and Frederick Ridley, found it to be very unstable. When his findings were published in the *British Journal of Experimental Pathology*, only penicillin's potential therapeutic benefits were discussed.

This stage of explanation is often overlooked or surpassed in education, for many reasons, as educators are sold the final product as the holy grail in teaching.

Setbacks

Many others tried to purify penicillin but to no avail, including Harold Raistrick, Professor of Biochemistry at the London School of

Hygiene and Tropical Medicine. It was not until 1939, just when research was becoming increasingly difficult due to wartime conditions, that work resumed on purifying penicillin. At the Sir William Dunn School of Pathology, Oxford University, Howard Florey and Ernst Chain turned penicillin from a blob in a petri dish into a life-saving drug. At the same time, biochemists Norman Heatley and Edward Abraham helped step up production prior to clinical trials.

A year later, experimentation on mice showed that penicillin could protect them from the deadly streptococci. The first recipient of the Oxford penicillin was a forty-three-year-old police officer, Albert Alexander, on 12 February 1941. He had developed a life-threatening infection on the side of his face, after being scratched whilst pruning rose bushes. The huge abscess that developed was affecting his eyes, face and lungs. Within days of penicillin being injected, he made a remarkable recovery. However, he died a few days later, as a result of supplies running out. Results were better with other patients, so it was decided that penicillin would be made available for British troops out on the battlefield. Industrial production of penicillin proved difficult due to wartime conditions and British companies, including GlaxoSmithKline (formerly Glaxo) and Kemball Bishop later bought by Pfizer, stepped up to the challenge.

Challenges

However, the journey to saving millions of lives through the ingestion of a course of penicillin was not without obstacles. During the growth of penicillin on the surface of a nutrient medium, the Oxford group discovered that it was inefficient and did not produce a good yield. They decided that growing penicillin in a submerged culture, in large tanks, would be far more efficient and in amongst the traces of penicillin produced, there was one strain which produced acceptable levels of penicillin in submerged conditions and penicillin research continued. Collaboration was critical at this stage of developments and Merck and Squibb joined Pfizer in September 1942.

The story about the penicillin discovery highlights some important issues, which could be applied to the field of education. Penicillin was discovered by accident but its benefits were noticed and discussed within the medical community first. This was because scientists drew upon their prior knowledge, about the use of bread mould in ancient Egyptian therapies, and there was a clear possibility that penicillin would have a similar effect. This important stage is often missed in education and any research which can be beneficial is quickly commercialised. Another step that we frequently miss in education is conducting the equivalent of the clinical trial. To test the rigour of a new discovery in education, surely it would be beneficial to conduct a trial in order to perfect the models of change. During the discovery of penicillin, when the task of purifying penicillin became overwhelming, the huge medical companies stepped in to provide support. Although from an external point of view, there appears to be a lot of support for schools, the support is not always in line with up-to-date thinking and advances in education. The other important aspect to consider is: What was it about circumstances being difficult that led to this huge discovery? Although context is crucial when deciding on interventions or programmes which may help to narrow the disadvantage gap, perhaps educational trials could be carried out in challenging contexts before being applied further afield. Surely trialling in schools in more disadvantaged areas would give a clearer indication for a particular intervention or programme to work, than trialling in less disadvantaged areas.

More on neuromyths in education

There are many myths that exist, which are based loosely on scientific fact and have adverse effects on education. A huge experimental study was carried out in The Netherlands to observe how much knowledge teachers had of the brain. Due to the interest in neuroscience of the 242 primary and secondary teachers, they predicted that there would not be any neuromyths present in the group (Dekker, S., Lee, N., Howard-Jones, P. and Jolles, J., 2012).

After completing an online survey of thirty-two statements about the brain, fifteen of which were neuromyths, Dekker et al. found that teachers believed nearly half of the neuromyths presented (49 per cent) and that these beliefs were 'related to commercialized educational programs' (Dekker, S., Lee, N., Howard-Jones, P. and Jolles, J., 2012). They also found that those who were readers of the most favoured science magazines scored highly on general knowledge questions. There appeared to be a definite correlation between general knowledge and belief in neuromyths: an increased belief in neuromyths was evident in teachers who had higher levels of general knowledge. This finding that more general knowledge about the brain did not prevent teachers from believing in neuro-myths is surprising (Dekker, S., Lee, N., Howard-Jones, P. and Jolles, J., 2012).

One possible explanation is that teachers who are interested in learning about the brain may be exposed to more misinformation and may misunderstand the content, which may lead to more false beliefs (Macdonald, Germine, Anderson, Christodoulou and McGrath, 2017). As teachers become saturated with information, the lines of myth and neuroscience become increasingly blurred, with teachers finding it challenging to sift through the minefield of interpretations of research and ascertain what is myth and what is neuroscience.

'However, it is equally possible that teachers who believe neuromyths may seek out more information about the brain' (Macdonald, Germine, Anderson, Christodoulou and McGrath, 2017). Another potential explanation could be that there is little neuroscience training on initial teacher training courses (Dekker, S., Lee, N., Howard-Jones, P. and Jolles, J., 2012). According to them, teachers are not skilled enough to be able to be critical and filter out the gems of neuroscience.

There are, however, many factors which have contributed to the rapid increase of neuromyths. Firstly, teachers start the profession with wide ranging understanding of professional vocabulary of neuro-science and education and huge differences in training backgrounds (Howard-Jones, 2014). Secondly, there is a huge variance in inquiry to bridge the gap that exists between individual neurons and large-scale educational policies (Goswami, 2006). Thirdly, research is a challenge to access and this forces reliance on the media rather than original research (Ansari and Coch, 2006). Fourthly, there is a lack of professionals with expertise in bridging the gap between neuroscience and education. And finally, the willingness of teachers wishing to improve their practice is coupled with the allure of explanations which seem to be based on neuroscien-tific evidence (McCabe and Castel, 2008); (Weisberg, D.S., Keil, F.C., Goodstein, J., Rawson, E. and Gray, J.R., 2008).

A great example of a myth about reading is that most pupils learn to read naturally, by simply being exposed to reading texts. Reading is a complex skill of connecting speech, language, hearing, vision and cognition and much of it depends on how intrinsically motivated pupils are. However, having such strong beliefs about learning to read through absorption can be detrimental.

Only 30 per cent of the population in the 1600s could read (Hurst, 2013). Compared to speech, reading is a relatively new invention. Our brains are hard-wired for speech and babies are born with the ability to communicate through speech, however, we are not born with the ability to read. Dehaene (2019) suggests that there are three areas of the brain associated with reading. If the areas of the brain associated with speech are very well developed, the neural connections required for reading are created and strengthened. Even when children are exposed to text regularly, this may not be enough to learn how to read. Some children need to be taught phonics and graphemes explicitly, how sounds and letters can be broken down and then recombined to read words, and how those words then combine to make sentences and paragraphs. Stanovich (1993) found that children who had difficulties learning to read, with poor attitude and lack of achievement, had similar cognitive profiles to those who could read. He also discovered that 'exposure to print seems to be efficacious regardless of the level of the child's cognitive and reading abilities', Stanovich (1993: 282). A great predictor of verbal growth was exposing children to print, including disadvantaged children. Through immersion, children with limited reading skills and with a perception of low ability, 'will build vocabulary and cognitive structures through immersion in literacy activities just as his or her high-achieving counterpart does', Stanovich (1993: 282).

Intuition

Our intuition, beliefs and experiences play a crucial role in pupil progress. Educators who believe that reading happens naturally gravitate towards what they have always been doing and are less likely to be concerned with reading methods and strategies. Despite knowing that pupils only get one shot at education, and even if pupils are struggling, they believe that pupils will eventually learn to read. There tends to be a shift to focusing on less effective strategies and content, even if those strategies have been tried and tested and proven not to be effective previously. There is also the misconception that such pupils do not have any comprehension ability or enough life experience to link to reading complex texts. Pupils are more likely to struggle with words in context, which prevents them from reading with meaning. These beliefs can slow down the process of becoming fluent readers (Johnston and Watson, 2006), impacting on the overall learning outcomes of pupils in the long term, with progress and attainment which is not in line with higher achievers.

Our intuition is so strong that even when we are presented with research findings about strategies that have worked, we continue to follow our instincts. This suggests that the idea of reading could benefit from a mindset change in the beliefs of the educator.

With the focus on phonics since 2006, this has helped many children learn to read, however, there is a small percentage who still cannot read. As well as seeking strategies that work for them, we must ensure that intrinsic motivation is developed because reading is hard work.

According to Dehaene (2010), 'At first sight, reading seems close to magical: our gaze lands on a word and our brain effortlessly gives us access to its meaning and pronunciation'. However, even before we get to the stage of making meaning and feeling emotions from words simply written on a page, there is a complex series of processes that needs to happen. First of all, we need to recognise that readers are essentially two robots with cameras – two eyes and two retinas usually. Words are seen as fragments of light and dark. The information needs to be recoded and understood in recognisable spoken language. 'Then we can access the correct sounds, words and meanings. We have natural automatic character recognition software, which takes the pixels on a page as input and outputs them as words' (Dehaene, 2010). There are many more processes that occur in the brain, even before the affective and cognitive processes take place.

Being able to read largely depends on intrinsic motivation (Guthrie, J.T., Wigfield, A., Tonks, S. and Perencevich, K.C. (Eds.) (2004)). 'Children who are intrinsically motivated read more frequently than do other children' (Guthrie, Wigfield, Metsala and Cox, 1999). Extrinsic motivation, or those who read for the outcomes of reading, was negatively associated with reading. There are different relationships with the two forms of motivation. Guthrie, J.T., Wigfield, A., Tonks, S. and Perencevich, K.C. (2004) also found that pupils who are extrinsically motivated have a surface level understanding of text, such as guessing; however, those who are intrinsically motivated have a deeper understanding.

Yet the misconception of learning to read through absorption still persists, partly based on assumptions and our intuition. The problem with intuition is that it is very difficult to correct.

Whose responsibility is it to alleviate misunderstandings of neuroscientific findings? Some would argue that it is the role of neuroscientists to reduce complex information into smaller bitesize information which is easily accessible to teachers and relevant to the classroom setting. Others would say it is the role of the teacher to weed out neuro-myths and use what they know works in their context. One suggestion is that this gap can be closed by a scientist with an interest in learning and education (Rohrer and Pashler, 2012).

Misconceptions

Due to the variety of factors that contribute towards the creation of misconceptions, it is no wonder that misconceptions exist about a complex idea such as metacognition.

The EEF have identified a number of misconceptions concerning metacognitive which have manifested themselves in recent years (EEF, 2018). These misconceptions range from what metacognition actually is to whether it can be taught.

Misconception 1: Metacognition is 'thinking about thinking'

Teachers often say that metacognition is merely 'thinking about thinking'. One of the reasons this misconception exists could be because looking through search engines for definitions of metacognition, the answers range from: 'cognition about cognition', 'thinking about thinking' and 'knowing about knowing'. Although the longer definition may appear later on, not all teachers read on and accept these phrases as the ultimate definition. Even though metacognition is about thinking, it is so much more than just thinking about thinking. As mentioned in Chapter 2, metacognition encompasses motivation, cognition, emotional awareness, managing behaviours, improved well-being, the development of human connections and relationships and so much more. It's all linked.

Misconception 2: All strategies to do with cognition are metacognition

There seems to be some misunderstanding about strategies, as not all learning strategies are metacognitive. For example, using times table knowledge to solve a mathematical calculation is a cognitive strategy. *Knowing* that times table knowledge can be used to solve a mathematical calculation, is a metacognitive strategy. Flavell (1979) identified a useful distinction between the two: strategies used to *make* cognitive progress are 'cognitive strategies'; strategies used to *monitor* cognitive progress are 'metacognitive strategies' (Cambridge-community.org.uk., n.d.).

Misconception 3: Metacognition cannot be taught

Although pupils who find learning easy display metacognitive knowledge and strategies at a subconscious level, these are the pupils who have picked up the strategies along the way. However, pupils who are not at this stage of reflection need to be taught the strategies explicitly, in order to gain the same level of independence.

Misconception 4: Metacognition is only developed in older pupils

A common belief is that metacognition can only be developed in young adults and not children. Research (Whitebread and Colman, 2010) has shown that children as young as three can engage in self-regulation, such as setting goals and checking their understanding. With tasks young children (aged between 3 and 5) choose themselves, they tend to show greater accuracy (Bernard, Proust and Clément, 2015).

There is, however an over-inflation of knowledge levels in pupils up to the age of eight, with self-knowledge being inaccurate (Clark and Dumas, 2016). Even though older children display a broader range of metacognitive strategies, metacognitive understanding can be seen at an early age. Perhaps we need to carry out more studies in the Early Years settings to observe metacognition in action.

Misconception 5: Metacognition is a general skill that can be separated from subject knowledge

The word metacognition contains the word cognition within it. The strategies of metacognition become stronger when they are taught through subject knowledge. Metacognitive strategies require an anchor to become effectively grounded, as it is the basis of cognitive acceleration. It is virtually impossible to understand how you can learn something without having something to learn. For example, without having the subject knowledge about how a water cycle works, you cannot possibly describe all the factors which can lead to flooding.

Misconception 6: Metacognition represents 'higher order' thinking and is therefore more important than mere cognition or subject knowledge

As educators we use Bloom's taxonomy to help us distinguish what constitutes higher order thinking. However, it is a misconception to use this to place metacognition on a hierarchical platform. Evaluation is not on a higher level than remembering knowledge. Tangible subject knowledge is required as a medium through which metacognition is taught. It is very difficult to teach meta-cognitive knowledge about how you can best learn a subject without being taught the subject knowledge. For example, in order to write a newspaper article on a given topic, pupils need to first understand what a newspaper article is and what features they contain. Without this knowledge they are unable to use metacog-nitive strategies to observe whether or not they have been successful. Metacognition and cognition have a complex interac-tion, as pupils learn. We should develop both at the same time instead of creating hierarchies. See Figure 5.1 showing showing that there is no hierarchy between metacognition and cognition and that they need to be developed at the same time.

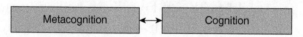

Figure 5.1   Non-heirarchical representation of metacognition and cognition

Misconception 7: You can easily teach metacognitive knowledge and strategies in discrete 'thinking skills' lessons

When metacognitive approaches are taught in discrete lessons, pupils find it harder to transfer these generic skills to specific tasks. Self-regulation and metacognition are context-driven. How you plan art is completely different from how you plan writing. Pupils who have very well-developed metacognitive strategies in art, may not have the same levels of expertise in writing. This suggests that some metacognitive strategies are subject specific and that teaching discrete lessons in metacognition can be ineffective. 'This does not, however, mean that metacognitive knowledge and skills will automatically develop through content knowledge teaching' (EEF, 2018: 24). As pupils mature and develop, over time, they can possess a range of strategies, which they can apply across a plethora of contexts and tasks. Their understanding develops further with knowing when to use what strategies and what may be missing in their repertoire of strategies.

Case study: Demonstrating metacognitive strategies

One day, as four-year-old Zeeshan was playing in the garden, I observed him move from looking for worms to learning how to ride a two-wheeled bicycle, without stabilisers. He propped up the bicycle against the garden table and mounted it carefully. When he realised that he was fully balanced, he let go of the garden table and rode the bicycle. After about a metre of riding he fell off his bicycle. I was transfixed by what he did next. He simply got back up and started the process again. He repeated this about twenty times and each time rode a little further.

- Did Zeeshan have a goal in mind?
- If so, how did he realise this goal?
- What kept him motivated to continue even though he fell off his bicycle repeatedly?
- How did he overcome challenges?
- How did he monitor his success?
- How did he evaluate how he was doing?

Summary

- It can be a challenge to embrace the findings of research but this can lead to an improvement in teaching and learning.
- Examples about how research and evidence are collated, from medicine, can be beneficial to education.
- The sole reliance on our intuitions can be detrimental to learners.
- Moving towards making informed decisions based on research and expertise could be beneficial to pupils.

Think!

- What can we learn about the discovery of penicillin?
- Why do neuromyths exist in education?

(Continued)

- What can we do to reduce the number of neuromyths in education?
- How do our intuition, beliefs and experiences affect how we think?
- Why do misconceptions exist?
- Why does metacognition need tangible subject knowledge to be taught through?
- How do metacognitive strategies differ in different subjects?

Teacher metacognition

- What are your own beliefs about metacognition?
- Do you have any misconceptions about metacognition?
- What steps can you take to alleviate misconceptions?
- How can you teach both metacognition and cognition concurrently?

Pupil metacognition

- What do your pupils have misconceptions about?
- How do you alleviate these misconceptions?
- How easy is it to challenge misconceptions, which pupils may have?
- How do pupils respond to having their misconceptions challenged?
- If pupils respond negatively, how can you support them through the process?

References

Aldridge, S., Parascandola, J. and Sturchio, J.L. (1999) *The Discovery and Development of Penicillin 1928–1945.* Washington and London: American Chemical Society and Royal Society of Chemistry.

Bernard, S., Proust, J. and Clément, F. (2015) Procedural metacognition and false belief understanding in 3- to 5-year-old children. *PLOS One, 10* (10): e0141321. doi:10.1371/journal.pone.0141321

Cambridge-community.org.uk (n.d.) *Getting Started With Metacognition* [online]. Available at: https://cambridge-community.org.uk/professional-development/gswmeta/index.html (accessed 4 February 2021).

Clark, I. and Dumas, G. (2016) The regulation of task performance: A trans-disciplinary review. *Frontiers in Psychology, 6.* https://doi.org/10.3389/fpsyg.2015.01862

Dehaene, S. (2010) *Reading in the Brain.* New York: Penguin Books.

Dekker, S., Lee, N., Howard-Jones, P. and Jolles, J. (2012) Neuromyths in education: Prevalence and predictors of misconceptions among teachers. *Frontiers in Psychology, 3.* https://doi.org/10.3389/fpsyg.2012.00429

EEF (2018) *Metacognition and Self-regulated Learning: Guidance Report* [online]. Available at: https://educationendowmentfoundation.org.uk/public/files/Publications/Metacognition/EEF_Metacognition_and_self-regulated_learning.pdf (accessed 4 February 2021).

Flavell, J. (1979) Metacognition and cognitive monitoring: A new area of cognitive-developmental inquiry. *American Psychologist, 34*: 906–911.

Goswami, U. (2006) Neuroscience and education: From research to practice? *Nature Reviews Neuroscience, 7*: 406–413. https://doi.org/10.1038/nrn1907

Guthrie, J.T., Wigfield, A., Tonks, S. and Perencevich, K.C. (2004) Children's Motivation for Reading: Domain Specificity and Instructional Influences. *The Journal of Educational Research.* University of Maryland.

Guthrie, J.T., Wigfield, A., Metsala, J. and Cox, K.E. (1999) Predicting text comprehension and reading activity with motivational and cognitive variables. *Scientific Studies of Reading, 3*: 231–256.

Howard-Jones, P. (2014) Neuroscience and education: myths and messages. *Nature Reviews Neuroscience, 15* (12), 817–824.

Hurst, S. (2013) *Misconceptions about phonics instruction – #1 – Most children learn to read naturally* [online]. Available at: www.readinghorizons.com/blog/misconceptions-about-phonics-instruction-most-children-learn-to-read-naturally (accessed 4 February 2021).

Macdonald, K., Germine, L., Anderson, A., Christodoulou, J. and McGrath, L.M. (2017) Dispelling the myth: Training in education or neuroscience decreases but does not eliminate beliefs in neuromyths. *Frontiers in Psychology, 8.* https://doi.org/10.3389/fpsyg.2017.01314

Rohrer, D. and Pashler, H. (2012) Learning styles: Where's the evidence? *Medical Education, 46* (7): 634–635. https://doi.org/10.1111/j.1365-2923.2012.04273.x

Stanovich, K.E. (1993) Romance and reality. *The Reading Teacher, 47* (4): 280–291. Available at: www.keithstanovich.com/Site/Research_on_Reading_files/RdTch93.pdf

Weinstein, Y., Sumeracki, M. and Caviglioli, O. (2019) *Understanding How We Learn.* Abingdon: Routledge.

Weisberg, D.S., Keil, F.C., Goodstein, J., Rawson, E. and Gray, J.R. (2008) The Seductive Allure of Neuroscience Explanations. *Journal of Cognitive*

Neuroscience 20: 3, pp. 470–477. Massachusetts Institute of Technology, Yale University. Available at: http://cogdevlab.yale.edu/sites/default/files/files/Weisbergetal2008.pdf

Whitebread, D. and Coltman, P. (2010) Aspects of pedagogy supporting metacognition and self-regulation in mathematical learning of young children: Evidence from an observational study. *ZDM, 42* (2): 163–178.

6

METACOGNITION AND THE LEARNING ENVIRONMENT

Contents

In this chapter we will explore

- what motivation is and what it could look like in the classroom
- the importance of feedback
- how rewards can be used to develop intrinsic motivation
- how to create the 'Goldilocks effect' and at the same time reduce the cognitive load
- how to create challenge in lessons and use Bloom's taxonomy effectively
- the role of social and emotional learning and progression of language.

The problem with thinking

According to Willingham (2009) 'the brain is not designed for thinking'. In fact, it is designed to prevent you from thinking because thinking is 'slow and unreliable'. Thinking becomes an enjoyable experience if it leads to success. If pupils are overloaded with challenge continuously to the point where they are unable to solve problems, it is highly likely that they will not enjoy learning and will give up easily.

At this rate, we may not be motivated to learn anything.

Although the link between metacognition and motivation is briefly mentioned in Chapter 2, it is important to explore how it contributes to the classroom environment in more detail.

What is motivation?

It has long been recognised that motivation is a crucial component for learning. However, there are many definitions for motivation ranging from, being that which drives us to achieving something or not, to being a characteristic or quality which helps us to achieve a task or goal. According to Adam Boxer (2019) it is important to clarify the definition of motivation, as this is something which is not always consistently defined and the current definitions do not apply to classroom teaching.

When motivation is considered within the context of metacognition, it is defined as 'beliefs and attitudes that affect the use and development of cognitive and metacognitive skills' (Schraw et al., 2006, cited in Lai, 2011: 18). For the purposes of this chapter, this is the definition that we will use as the foundation. But how does motivation develop? How can educators develop motivation in pupils and how can motivation be assessed?

Before these questions are answered it is important to distinguish between the two types of motivation, commonly known as intrinsic and extrinsic motivation.

Intrinsic motivation is a highly favoured quality and educators consider it to be crucial in leading to better pupil outcomes (Deci, E.L., Koestner, R. and Ryan, R.M., 1999; Lai, 2011). It is characterised by evoking 'personal enjoyment, interest, or pleasure' (Lai, 2011: 34). However, extrinsic motivation is doing something in order to gain external validation. Even though intrinsic motivation is highly sought after, there appears to be an inextricable link between the two in terms of behaviour. Intrinsic motivation appears as 'play, exploration, and challenge seeking that people often do for external rewards' (Deci, E.L., Koestner, R. and Ryan, R.M., 1999: 658, cited in Lai, 2011: 4). This suggests that in order to develop intrinsic motivation, tasks and activities in the classroom must be challenging.

The goal of metacognition is ultimately to reach a stage where pupils begin to take responsibility for their own learning through strategies such as setting goals, monitoring their own emotions and behaviour, realising, selecting and using metacognitive strategies, and controlling their own rewards.

If responsibility for learning is handed over too early to pupils, this may result in pupils setting low standards for themselves, cheating and rewarding themselves unnecessarily (Lai, 2011). This suggests that it is important to give this careful consideration in the classroom and continuous assessments need to be made about when the right time would be to hand over such a huge responsibility. Questions should be focused on whether pupils are able to accurately judge whether they can complete the task independently, exploring why they want to complete the task and realising what they have to do in order to be successful in the task (Lai, 2011) are all important factors when transferring responsibility to pupils.

Self-efficacy and self-concept

Gutman and Schoon (2013) make a distinction between self-efficacy and self-concept. They describe self-efficacy as being 'an individual's belief that they have the capability to succeed at a particular task in the future (Bandura, 1977, 2001). This involves determination of effort, persistence and goal setting (Lai, 2011). It is a way of measuring 'expectations about whether or not they can successfully perform a specific task at a later point in time' (Gutman and Schoon, 2013: 10). Self-efficacy is about how successful an individual is towards becoming skilled at a particular task (Gutman and Schoon, 2013).

Lai (2011) notes that those who have higher levels of self-efficacy tend to be more motivated and more successful on given tasks. In combination with this, cognitive strategies and our observations of our own self-efficacy, can 'predict achievement over and above actual ability' (Lai, 2011: 7).

However, the notion of self-concept is an interesting idea to explore. This is the ability to compare and assess how someone feels about their 'past performance in relation to others', and this is about 'affective appraisal of one's performance in an academic domain, relative to others' (Gutman and Schoon, 2013: 10).

As pupils evaluate their own cognition, they will inevitably become more aware of their emotions related to learning. Figure 6.1 represents how metacognition can act as a bridge or support when faced with challenging situations and as pupils become emotionally aware of strengths and weaknesses (Lai, 2011).

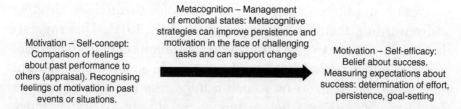

Motivation – Self-concept: Comparison of feelings about past performance to others (appraisal). Recognising feelings of motivation in past events or situations.

Metacognition – Management of emotional states: Metacognitive strategies can improve persistence and motivation in the face of challenging tasks and can support change

Motivation – Self-efficacy: Belief about success. Measuring expectations about success: determination of effort, persistence, goal-setting

Figure 6.1 The journey from self-concept to self-efficacy with metacognition acting as a support or bridge

Motivation is required for both academic and non-academic outcomes and one way that metacognition can support the development of motivation is by supporting accuracy of judgement (see Chapter 2 for more detail on this). Accurately judging yourself can be a challenge. For example, in maths pupils may truly believe that they do not know many strategies to use when faced with a problem but when they start using metacognition to start thinking and focusing on what they do know as opposed to what they do not know, they would realise that they do have some skills.

Figure 6.2 shows a model of how metacognition, motivation, self-concept, self-efficacy and self-belief may be interlinked.

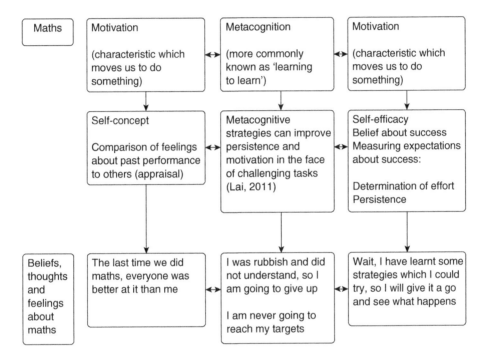

Figure 6.2 Beliefs, thoughts and feelings about maths in terms of self-concept, metacognition and self-efficacy are interlinked (self-talk can go backwards and forwards) (adapted from Lai, 2011)

What is the change that is required to motivate pupils? What strategies or interventions can be put into place to change the mindset from negative self-talk to recognising what they already know about the task in hand?

Feedback

All educators are aware of the impact feedback can have on pupil motivation, progress and attainment. It is one of the most powerful tools in a teacher's repertoire. In the book *Visible Learning: Feedback* by Hattie and Clarke (2019) describe it 'as relating to actions or information provided by an agent' (e.g. teacher, peer, book, parent, internet, experience).

Feedback is the information required to fill the gap between what is understood and what needs to be understood. Providing feedback and how pupils respond to it can lead to improved effort, motivation and engagement. It is a tool which builds self-concept and self-efficacy, improves behaviour, gives an indication of how well pupils are progressing and if they have reached their goals (Hattie and Clarke, 2019).

Hattie and Clarke (2019: 5) advise that the quality of feedback is crucial. Rather than giving feedback about trying harder next time, giving constructive feedback is far more effective.

Pupils find it more motivating when feedback is centred around three main elements:

- the quality of the work and not in comparison to others
- specific strategies/elements required to improve the piece of work
- feedback acted upon since the last piece of work and improvements made since.

Feedback should be linked to challenging goals. This will allow the feedback given to be more specific and beneficial to the student. The classroom environment should be built upon a mutual culture of trust. It should be one where pupils feel safe enough to make mistakes and not laughed at by their peers. Educators must be mindful of pupil self-esteem and self-efficacy when creating a climate of trust.

Although Hattie and Clarke (2019) state that 'feedback thrives on errors and misconceptions', they also state that both negative and positive feedback can be beneficial to pupils but this is dependent on the self-efficacy of the pupil in question. Feedback should be centred around the task and what the individual could have done. It can cause self-evaluation at a personal level and lead to change.

Feedback does not work alone. It should also be 'combined with effective teaching and learning strategies to have the greatest impact'. Hattie and Clarke (2019) also state that sometimes it is better to re-teach than to just provide feedback.

Educators are aware that identifying and planning for misconceptions where they can be explored and challenged are important. This is an opportunity where prior learning can be activated and links to new information can be made visible. It also gives teachers the opportunity to provide scaffolds (Hattie and Clarke, 2019).

Although pupils prefer immediate feedback, sometimes delayed feedback can also be very powerful because it gives pupils the opportunity to discover the errors themselves. Feedback can also improve motivation. Motivation depends on four key elements: mindset, rewards, the Goldilocks effect and praise. We will now explore the use of rewards and the Goldilocks effect in relation to motivation.

The use of rewards

The use of rewards has always been a controversial issue as a device to inspire learning. It is what is known as classical conditioning. Classical conditioning was thought to be the holy grail at explaining human behaviours, including communication, cooperation, controlling our emotions and learning (Levy, 2020). Learning can happen consciously and unconsciously, but classical conditioning happens below the level of unconscious and conscious pathways, and underpins both positive and negative learned behaviours (Levy, 2020).

Conditioning is a type of learning that is associated with behaviours towards the learning, takes place through rewards and punishments and helps with our understanding of why people act a certain way. It is also thought that the environment affects an individual's behaviour.

The behaviourism branch of psychology 'assumes that all behavior is determined by one's environment' (Levy, 2020).

Classical conditioning is a way of understanding and explaining behaviours in both animals and people and is defined as 'learning through association' (McLeod, 2018). It is thought that when two stimuli are paired together, new learning occurs. This involves 'associations being made between an environmental stimulus and a naturally occurring stimulus' (Levy, 2020). Classical conditioning eventually leads to involuntary or reflex responses.

A famous example of this is the experiment conducted by the Russian psychologist, Ivan Pavlov, in the 1890s and is more commonly known as Pavlovian conditioning (McLeod, 2018). Pavlov taught dogs to link the sound of bells to feeding. Initially, the dogs would only salivate when they were presented with meat powder (conditioned stimulus) and did not respond to the ringing bell at all, which was the neutral stimuli. Pavlov rang the bell (neutral or unconditioned stimulus) just before giving the dogs meat powder. He did this repetitively. The dogs learned that there was a link between the ringing bell and being fed. Eventually, the dogs began to salivate (behaviour in response to a stimulus), with anticipation, every time the bell was rung, even when there was no meat powder (Levy, 2020). According to Levy (2020), 'The conditioned stimulus (CS) and unconditioned stimulus always occur together, so with repeated pairings, an association is made'.

Other classical conditioning examples include:

- sights or smells of certain foods, which may remind you of your childhood and these may make you feel hungry or excited
- a familiar smell may remind you of someone
- listening to certain songs may bring back certain emotions you felt when you first heard the songs. (Levy, 2020)

Levy (2020) states that there are three stages of classical conditioning as follows:

- Stage 1 is the pre-learning stage of new behaviour. A natural response has not been learned yet, from an unconditional/neutral stimulus.
- Stage 2 is the process of an unconditioned/neutral stimulus becoming a conditioned stimulus. This is a repetitive process and takes time to develop.
- Stage 3 is when both the unconditioned/neutral and conditioned stimulus create a new conditioned response.

According to Levy (2020) 'research has demonstrated that classical conditioning alters human behavior'. The key focus of classical conditioning is to reinforce desired behaviours and to eliminate undesired behaviours, and it is often used to help drug users deal with cravings. Although there are many uses of it, it is usually used in cognitive behavioural therapies (Levy, 2020).

Using rewards, which is classical conditioning, can be a beneficial strategy for some, but not all, pupils, temporarily (Lai, 2011) (see Chapter 2). Usually for pupils who require this type of intervention, educators notice that after a while, the reward impact wears off and the type of reward received requires changing several times throughout the year.

The issue with using this form of classical conditioning in the class-room is that although the behaviour may change temporarily the ideas of self-concept and self-efficacy remain the same.

In his book *Drive*, Pink (2011) further unpicks the deeper internal factors that motivate us. Although he focuses on the business world, he states that understanding what motivates people in the world of business can also directly apply to the world of education. He goes a long way to dispel the commonly held belief that people are only motivated by extrinsic factors.

The 'carrot and stick' (Pink, 2011) does not work for a variety of reasons and the message conveyed by presenting a reward is that 'the task is undesirable'. Firstly, the reward has to be 'enticing enough': if it is too small there will not be compliance. Secondly, the reward has to continuously increase size to sustain the same level of achievement. For example, if you pay your children to clean their bedrooms, 'once the initial money buzz tapers off, you'll likely have to increase the payment to continue compliance,' (Pink, 2011: 54). Rewards eventually become addictive and counterintuitive.

Pink (2011: 59), lists 'the seven deadly flaws' of extrinsic rewards as follows:

1. They can extinguish intrinsic motivation.
2. They can diminish performance.
3. They can crush creativity.
4. They can crowd out good behaviour.
5. They can encourage cheating, shortcuts, and unethical behaviour.
6. They can become addictive.
7. They can foster short-term thinking. (Pink, 2011: 59).

The other aspect to consider is that this approach does not change a pupil's belief about themselves and does not help them manage their emotions when they are faced with challenges. It would be beneficial to delve further into motivation to really understand how a more positive and permanent behaviour change can be achieved, to improve better outcomes for our pupils.

Although educators are aware that it is far better to develop the intrinsic reward of learning, there are occasions where extrinsic rewards can be beneficial. Pink (2011) explores this further and suggests that on the whole people are not motivated by financial (extrinsic) rewards, there must be a 'baseline', and rewards must be adequate and fair.

It is difficult to motivate staff without a 'healthy baseline'. Once this is in place, there are occasions when extrinsic rewards can be used successfully. Pink (2011) uses the candle problem to illustrate an example of when using extrinsic motivation would be useful. In the 1930s, Karl Dunker used candles to better understand the science of behaviour. Sitting at a wooden table, people were given a candle, tacks and a book of matches. The task was to attach the candle to the wall, without the candle dripping onto the table. Dunker found that some people tried to attach the candle directly to the wall, whilst others tried to melt the wax and stick the candle to the wall. However, the tacks came in a box of their very own. The idea was for people to overcome something called 'functional fixedness', where you can only see one use for the box. This is not an 'algorithmic' solution for this challenge, where a set path is followed. This type of challenge requires an 'heuristic' approach (Pink, 2011).

In the 1960s, Glucksberg offered cash as an extrinsic reward for solving the candle problem. He found that it took longer to solve the challenge. This was due to the fact that the only thing people can concentrate on when offered a monetary prize is the prize itself.

As mentioned earlier, some pupils will not need rewards but for those who do, rewards stop working after a while. Even when rewards are changed several times in a year, nothing appears to work. It may be partly to do with the addictive nature of rewards but may also be a signal to say that the pupil no longer requires extrinsic rewards and they have moved on to intrinsic motivation (Pink, 2011).

Challenge and the Goldilocks effect: helping pupils reduce cognitive overload

What does an appropriate level of challenge look like? According to the EEF guidance on metacognition and self-regulation (2018: 19), this 'requires expert knowledge both of a given subject, and of pupils in the classroom', which also includes accurate assessment. John Sweller devised the 'cognitive load theory' in 1988, which is about how much information our working memories can hold at any one time. This helps with our understanding of the 'Goldilocks' effect, where challenge is 'not too hard, not too easy, but just right' (EEF, 2018: 19). Thinking about how the memory works may be beneficial as the working memory is crucial to learning and it is where all the initial processes of information take place, but its capacity is limited (see Chapter 11). However, the working memory can be used more efficiently through the explicit teaching of meta-cognitive strategies. For example, instead of pupils relying on their working memories to remember how to solve a calculation, this can be freed up by displaying worked examples of maths calculations. The focus then shifts onto practising the skill of the calculation rather than having to remember how to carry out the calculation. Another benefit of this type of modelling and displaying the calcula-tion in the classroom, is that lower attaining pupils can access the learning too. Modelling and providing worked examples are two ways of creating the 'Goldilocks' effect. Other strategies include pro-viding structured planning templates and breaking down activities into steps (EEF, 2018). See Chapter 11 for more on cognitive load theory.

Among the many reasons why motivation is important, the main reason is that motivation is required to accept learning challenges. The EEF guidance (2018) advises that an appropriate level of chal-lenge is required in order develop metacognitive strategies. Challenge enables pupils to have a better understanding about how they are progressing in 'their knowledge of tasks, strategies, and of themselves as learners' (EEF, 2018: 7). Not only does challenge need to be at an 'appropriate level' but 'pupils must have the moti-vation to accept the challenge' (EEF, 2018: 7). It is also suggested that activities should be designed so that cognition is not over-loaded, particularly when applying new metacognitive strategies. Without challenge, pupils cannot develop new metacognitive strat-egies, reflect deeply on what they are learning or understand themselves as learners. If tasks are designed with 'deliberate diffi-culties' and these difficulties make them 'struggle' (EEF, 2018: 18) then they are more likely to be able to recall the knowledge from their long-term memories (Bjork, 2011).

How can this information help teachers when lesson planning? See Figures 6.3 and 6.4 to help manage cognitive load during lesson planning.

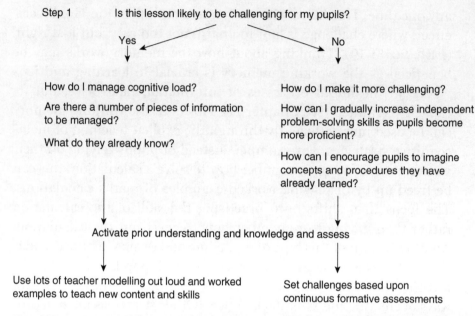

Figure 6.3   Step 1 of the lesson planning process

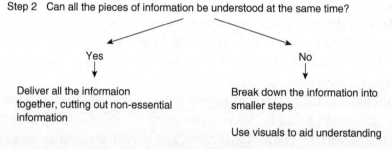

Figure 6.4   Step 2 of the lesson planning process

Bloom's taxonomy

Bloom's taxonomy was created by Benjamin Bloom in the 1950s to provide educators with a framework for developing critical thinking. The framework consists of six levels of hierarchy in the following order starting with remember, understand, apply, analyse, evaluate, with create being at the top of the pyramid. Remembering is at the bottom of the pyramid as it is about recalling basic concepts and facts. Next comes understanding, which is involved with explaining ideas or concepts. After that comes the stage of applying or demonstrating the new information in new situations. Drawing connections amongst the ideas comes next, then it moves onto evaluation, where decisions are justified, and finally it is the create stage, producing new work. This is a great starting point to develop understanding of the stages of the learning process (Bloom's Taxonomy, n.d.).

In his blog, Adam Boxer (2019) states that 'using command words from higher up the pyramid provokes deeper thought, higher order thinking and cognitive challenge'. He also states that the 'use of these command words or levels in Bloom's taxonomy predicts the level of challenge in a question, with higher order levels/command words predicting increased challenge'. So, how can questions based on Bloom's taxonomy be used to create challenge in lessons?

Boxer (2019) takes us on a journey through the use of command words and asks us to consider which command words makes tasks more challenging:

Task 1: 'Compare the typical features of an animal cell with the typical features of a plant cell'.

Task 2: 'Recall the typical features of an animal cell'.

He notes that 'compare' is level 4 on Bloom's taxonomy and 'recall' is only level 1 (Boxer, 2019). Using this example, Boxer (2019) illustrates that task 1 is more challenging due to the command word used. We are challenged further by being asked to think about whether task 1 is more challenging due to the fact that the word 'compare' was used or is it because it is asking for more to be done?

Keeping task 1 the same but changing task 2, Boxer (2019) asks us to consider the following comparison:

Task 1: 'Compare the typical features of an animal cell with the typical features of a plant cell'.

Task 2: 'Recall the typical features of an animal cell and the typical features of a plant cell'.

He notes that 'both animal and plant cells have mitochondria, cytoplasm, cell membrane, ribosomes and nucleuses. Only plant cells have vacuoles, cell walls and chloroplasts' (Boxer, 2019).

In this case, Boxer (2019) notes that responses to both tasks would be very similar. The command word has no relevance to the degree of challenge in either task. The challenge in both tasks is the same. Pupils may record the information in a list or in the form of an explanation. He concludes that writing a list does not prove that a pupil knows less than a pupil who writes an explanation; he argues that the 'command word doesn't necessarily *predict* or *determine* challenge' (Boxer, 2019).

Boxer (2019) suggests that command words can be 'superficial' and provides readers with another example to illustrate this through two more tasks:

Task 1: 'Describe the hormonal regulation of the menstrual cycle'.

Task 2: 'Describe the process of extracting solid copper sulphate from a copper sulphate solution'.

The command word has been kept the same, however, that is not the variable in this example. The unaccounted variable is the 'intrinsic difficulty of the content' (Boxer, 2019). Boxer argues that task 1 is more challenging due to the abstract nature of the task. This, he suggests, creates 'conflict with prior conceptions' and it is harder to understand. Another suggestion is that content demand is not given consideration in Bloom's taxonomy and it does not account for intrinsic difficulty.

Social and emotional learning

As mentioned earlier and according to the EEF guidance on metacognition and self-regulation (2018), motivation is a crucial factor in the development of self-regulation. Therefore, emotional support is of paramount importance when it comes to accepting challenge and continuing a task to fruition. It is at this point that failure can cause a person to give up. Motivation and failure are flipsides of the same coin.

This is where the EEF recommendation on social and emotional learning (SEL) can provide guidance. In this document, the CASEL (Collaborative for Academic, Social, and Emotional Learning) classification for social and emotional learning is mentioned. It has six core competencies for development which are: self-awareness, self-management, social awareness, relationship skills and responsible decision-making, with a list of skills associated with each core competency.

The EEF (2019) recommends six strands of social and emotional development: explicit teaching of SEL; modelling and implementing social and emotional skills within lessons; planning an SEL programme within the curriculum; using a SAFE curriculum, which is 'Sequential, Active, Focused and Explicit' (EEF, 2019: 9); reinforcing SEL skills through whole-school ethos and activities; and planning, supporting and monitoring SEL implementation.

The first recommendation is that social and emotional learning should be taught 'explicitly' (Durlak, Weissberg, Dymnicki, Taylor and Schellinger, 2011) and integrated into all subjects, taking its rightful place in the curriculum. It is not something that should be taught after 'crisis' has happened, but that schools should be proactive and include SEL in all areas of learning.

It is recommended that SEL should be both taught outside of academic lessons as well as within lessons, with pupils being given 'emotional vocabulary' in order for them to be able to articulate their thoughts and feelings and to develop self-awareness. 'Children's ability to recognise and express emotions can be supported with a class display,' and can be 'regularly referenced' (EEF, 2019: 11). The EEF (2019) suggests that the language of emotion is built on Jerome Bruner's principles of a spiral curriculum, where you revisit the same topics over time but build on them conceptually, activating or retrieving and consolidating prior knowledge to aid memory retention. The three principles are: cyclical, increasing depth, prior knowledge (Drew, 2020). The cyclical principle refers to the idea that throughout their schooling, pupils should return to the same topic on numerous occasions. When the topics are revisited, they should be taught 'at a deeper level' (Drew, 2020) and with increasing challenges. This links to the metacognition cycle. The principle of activating prior knowledge is also the metacognition part of the spiral curriculum, starting from what pupils already know (see Chapter 13 for more on curriculum).

Another recommendation is to develop 'self-calming strategies and positive self-talk to help deal with intense emotions' (EEF, 2019: 8), to improve self-regulation.

Social awareness should be developed through stories to develop pupil's 'emotions and perspectives' (EEF, 2019: 8). In addition to this, the EEF recommend that self-calming strategies are taught to develop self-regulation. Another suggestion is that self-awareness is taught explicitly through self-reflection to develop empathy for others. Teaching relationship skills are also important, which is 'our ability to interact positively with peers and adults, and to effectively navigate social situations' (EEF, 2019: 14).

There is an emphasis on developing communication and listening skills through role play and developing responsible decision-making by teaching and practising problem-solving strategies, all of which can be incorporated into daily lessons.

Other recommendations to improve social and emotional learning and to ensure progression of SEL in the curriculum through the years include: to balance direct instruction with group activities, to align school behaviour policies with SEL, to seek ideas from the whole school community, to ensure high-levels of parental engagement and reinforcement at home, and to monitor and evaluate impact (EEF, 2019: 9).

Progression of language is extremely important when it comes to social and emotional learning. RULER was developed in the US by Dr Marc Brackett at Yale University to develop emotional intelligence based on the following five skills: recognising, understanding, labelling, expressing and regulating emotions. According to Michael Eggleton (2020): 'RULER is underpinned by the vigorous and explicit teaching of emotional vocabulary used to identify and regulate emotions, supporting long-term wellbeing'. Eggleton discusses how he implemented a whole school project on emotional language development. This consisted of using an adapted 'language progression list', so that pupils could identify and articulate their feelings appropriately (see Chapter 14 for more on emotional intelligence).

Case study: Developing motivation for learning

Liam was a pupil who found it very difficult to stay focused in lessons due to a number of social and emotional barriers. Although he found it a challenge to focus on work in lessons, he was aware of where his weaknesses were, especially in maths, but could not articulate them due to a lack of language. Playtimes were particularly challenging, with ongoing feuds and fights most playtimes; and again he could not articulate his feelings due to the lack of language. His teacher realised that apart from the gaps in learning, his other barrier was a social and emotional one.

There were many children like Liam in the year group, who required explicit teaching of language of emotion. The curriculum for that year group was completely overhauled, to include emotive language in English with an emphasis on rapid progression of that language, developing sympathy and empathy for others through stories, and team-building activities which were taught both within lessons and separately. In addition to this, stress management strategies were taught when faced with challenging activities both within the lesson and outside of lessons. Recognition of stress factors and calming down strategies were also taught separately to lessons. Lots of work was done with parents to embed at home some of the strategies taught at school and also to ensure consistency. A range of strategies were taught to develop motivation and careful consideration was given to how to develop a feeling of success early on in the learning process; there was a focus on using positive praise. When mistakes were made, which contravened the behaviour policy, the appropriate sanctions were administered consistently and in line with the school behaviour policy.

After six months there was a real turn-around in Liam's behaviour. The number of playtime and lunchtime incidents reduced considerably, leading to more calming leisure time. Liam also began concentrating better in class and started to challenge himself. He was able to self-regulate during lesson time and was able to transfer the self-regulation strategies taught both inside class and out of class when faced with challenging situations in and out of school. Liam left the school not only ready for secondary school but also a confident learner, believing that he could achieve academically.

- What other ways are there to develop language?
- At which point did Liam turn his behaviour around?
- Which factors contributed to Liam's success?

Summary

- Motivation is an important factor for learning.
- Pupils who have higher levels of self-efficacy tend to be more motivated and more successful on given tasks.
- The use of external rewards must be considered carefully, be based on individual need and be temporary.
- Bloom's taxonomy is important and should be used carefully to support levels of challenge in the classroom.
- The amount of challenge and support should be considered carefully.
- There should be an emphasis on communication skills and in particular listening skills.

Think!

- How can warmth be created in the classroom environment?
- Why does listening need to be taught explicitly?
- How can pupil self-efficacy be developed?
- How can Bloom's taxonomy be utilised to scaffold learning?

Teacher metacognition

- What are your goals and ambitions?
- What motivates you to succeed in a task or activity?
- How do you stick to your goals?
- What prevents you from giving up on your goals, hopes, dreams?
- Why is creating a classroom atmosphere of challenge and support important?

Pupil metacognition

- How do you currently motivate pupils?
- Do the current strategies motivate all pupils?

- What other ways could pupils be motivated?
- Which pupils require extrinsic rewards in your class?
- Can they be weaned off extrinsic rewards?
- How can you link academic content to social and emotional learning?
- In your teaching practice, how can you facilitate social and emotional learning sensitively for vulnerable pupils?
- How can you measure the impact of social and emotional learning?

References

Bjork, R. (2011) On the symbiosis of learning, remembering, and forgetting. In A.S. Benjamin (ed.), *Successful Remembering and Successful Forgetting: A Festschrift in Honor of Robert A. Bjork*. New York: Psychology Press, pp. 1–22.

Bloom's Taxonomy (n.d.) *What is Bloom's taxonomy?* [online]. Available at: www.bloomstaxonomy.net/ (accessed 12 January 2020).

Boxer, A. (2019) *Challenge beyond Bloom's* [online]. Available at: https://achemicalorthodoxy.wordpress.com/2019/10/23/challenge-beyond-blooms/ (accessed 16 March 2021).

Deci, E.L., Koestner, R. and Ryan, R.M. (1999) A meta-analytic review of experiments examining the effects of extrinsic rewards on intrinsic motivation. *Psychological Bulletin*, 125 (6): 627–700. https://doi.org/10.1037/0033-2909.125.6.627

Drew, C. (2020) *Bruner's Spiral Curriculum – The 3 Key Principles* [online]. Available at: https://helpfulprofessor.com/spiral-curriculum/ (accessed 12 January 2020).

Durlak, J., Weissberg, R., Dymnicki, A., Taylor, R. and Schellinger, K. (2011) The impact of enhancing students' social and emotional learning: A meta-analysis of school-based universal interventions. *Child Development*, 82: 405–432. 10.1111/j.1467-8624.2010.01564.x

EEF (2018) *Metacognition and Self-regulated Learning: Guidance Report* [online]. Available at: https://educationendowmentfoundation.org.uk/public/files/Publications/Metacognition/EEF_Metacognition_and_self-regulated_learning.pdf (accessed 9 November 2020).

EEF (2019) *Improving Social and Emotional Learning in Primary Schools: Guidance Report* [online]. Available at: https://educationendowmentfoundation.org.uk/public/files/Publications/SEL/EEF_Social_and_Emotional_Learning.pdf (accessed 16 March 2021).

Eggleton, M. (2020) Emotions matter: Adapting RULER for UK schools to build emotional intelligence in children. *Impact: Journal of the Chartered College of Teaching* [online]. Available at: https://impact.chartered.

college/article/emotions-matter-adapting-ruler-uk-schools-emotional-intelligence-children/ (accessed 16 March 2021).

Gutman, L. and Schoon, I. (2013) The Impact of Noncognitive Skills on Outcomes for Young People: Literature Review. London: Education Endowment Foundation.

Hattie, J. and Clarke, S. (2019) *Visible Learning: Feedback*. Abingdon: Routledge.

Lai, E.R. (2011) *Motivation: A Literature Review*. Pearson Research Report [online]. Available at: https://images.pearsonassessments.com/images/tmrs/Motivation_Review_final.pdf (accessed 12 January 2020).

Levy, J. (2020) *Classical conditioning: How it works + potential benefits* [online]. Available at: https://draxe.com/health/classical-conditioning/ (accessed 12 January 2020).

McLeod, S. (2018) *Classical Conditioning* [online]. Available at: www.simplypsychology.org/classical-conditioning.html (accessed 12 January 2020). Cognitive load theory: Research that teachers really need to understand (nsw.gov.au).

Pink, D. (2011) Drive: The Surprising Truth About What Motivates Us. Canongate Books.

Sweller, J. (1988) Cognitive load during problem solving: Effects on learning. *Cognitive Science*, 12: 257–285.

Willingham, D. (2009) *Why don't students like school?* Pdf American Educator, Spring 2009, Why don't students like school, by Daniel T. Willingham (aft.org).

METACOGNITION, HOMEWORK AND REMOTE LEARNING

Contents

> ## In this chapter we will explore
>
> - Lockdown Spring 2020 and some of the challenges it brought
> - drawing upon research conducted into homework and its efficacy
> - the importance of parental engagement
> - fostering independent learning
> - the importance of social and emotional learning and maintaining relationships.

COVID-19 Lockdown Spring 2020

Due to the COVID-19 pandemic schools across the world faced unprecedented challenges. Severe disruption, with schools closing at short notice, not only sent shockwaves through communities but headteachers had very little time for training and were required to mobilise staff almost overnight to teach remotely.

Rightly so there was widespread concern about the impact this would have on pupil progress; the fear was that remote teaching 'would widen the gap' between pupils from poor backgrounds in comparison to those from more 'affluent backgrounds'. What became clear immediately was that 'children from the poorest families were the least likely to have access to the devices needed and internet access at home' (Bubb and Jones, 2020).

Being beyond the range of their existing role, school leaders nevertheless stepped up to the challenge, as they faced dealing with this huge crisis in their communities.

Due to navigating their ships through a pandemic with limited guidance, knowledge and information, headteachers have risen to the challenge, even though their roles became amplified to keeping their whole school communities safe from a deadly virus.

Throughout the pandemic, numerous challenges have been thrown up, creating barriers to existing processes for 'providing moral, social, personal and professional support and motivation' (Bubb and Jones, 2020).

The main concerns with remote teaching were that teachers were not familiar with how to deliver high quality teaching and learning remotely and they were unable to provide immediate verbal and non-verbal feedback, like they did in the classroom.

In order to find answers to some of the challenges of remote learning, let us consider research into homework and how the research around homework can help us to tailor our teaching for remote education at home.

What does the research say about homework?

Homework is given by teachers to pupils to complete outside of class and usually independently. Generally, at primary level, this consists of practising spellings, reading and practising maths strategies. Sometimes homework includes more inquiry type activities and other times more directed tasks such as test revision.

Even before COVID-19 appeared on our shores, many pupils struggled with independent study. However, the global pandemic has highlighted further these issues as well as identifying huge gaps in remote learning in our society.

There is no doubt that forming strong links with parents and home is beneficial to pupils, however, not all parents are able to find room to provide a quiet learning space. In addition to this, the curriculum, learning theories and learning strategies have changed and certainly the curriculum has changed beyond recognition.

How effective is homework?

The evidence points to homework not being particularly effective at primary level, whilst being very effective at secondary school level. Hattie's (2009) work shows that homework has a larger impact on older and higher-attaining pupils in secondary, rather than in primary. The main reason for this is that these pupils have better understanding of the activity and already have some resilience and self-efficacy and can persevere if the task becomes difficult. Instead of 'reinforcing negative attitudes or misconceptions when studying without teacher guidance', they are able to continue with it and be successful at completing the task.

At primary level, however, the evidence is limited; the findings have pointed to having 'low impact for very low cost' (EEF, 2018b). Classes where homework was given and not given were compared. It is clear that pupils who do carry out homework are more successful.

What is unclear is if it is the homework that contributes to this success.

The studies show that homework can improve pupil attainment, if it 'is used as a short and focused intervention' (EEF, 2018b). This, however, applies to primary school only and depends on the quality of the homework rather than the quantity. Although it has been found that schools which give more homework perform better, this increase is very small in primary schools. It is unclear 'whether this relationship is due to the homework itself, rather than other school factors' (EEF, 2018b).

There are a number of factors to consider. Firstly, in primary schools, homework 'does not appear to lead to large increases in learning' (EEF, 2018b). In addition to this, primary practitioners are aware that homework is related to increased parental engagement. Another aspect of homework, which primary practitioners are aware of, is that it is more beneficial to design homework tasks which are 'short' and 'focused' and 'which relate directly to what is being taught' (EEF, 2018b). These tasks are more effective when they are 'built upon in school' (EEF, 2018b). Finally, understanding the purpose of homework seems to have a more positive impact. At present what is unclear is whether this is true for remote learning during the pandemic.

At secondary level, although the reasons are unclear, homework can be a successful intervention to improve outcomes of pupils. The findings (EEF, 2018b) suggest that homework can impact on learning by an average of 'five months' additional progress'. When this has been investigated further, it appears there are a number of reasons contributing to the findings. This evidence suggests 'that how homework is set is likely to be very important'. It appears that when homework is used as a short, sharp, focused intervention, it can raise attainment by up to eight months, which is the maximum. Effect sizes are more likely to be 'up to three months' progress on average', particularly if it is set frequently (e.g. learning vocabulary or completing problem sheets in mathematics every day). This is similar to the findings for primary level. Another similar finding was that homework has greater impact when related to school learning 'rather than an add-on'. Another way to improve the impact of homework is to provide pupils with 'high quality feedback on their work' (see more on feedback in Chapter 5). The length of time homework is set for also has an impact on effectiveness. The recommended time is between one and two hours per school night, any longer and it becomes ineffective.

Usually at primary level, homework tends to consist of spelling practice and reading; may include answering comprehension questions and maths skills. Sometimes homework may consist of extended tasks or projects.

At primary level, however, the evidence is limited. The benefits of homework appear to be of very little value when set regularly, and what seems to be more important is the quality of the activity set not the quantity. The EEF *Remote Learning: Rapid Evidence Assessment* (2020d) has also found this to be the case.

Parental engagement

There is extensive evidence which indicates that parental engagement and support is crucial for all pupils. Recommendations include: involving parents in their child's learning journey, encouraging parents to support their children with homework tasks and helping to develop skills such as literacy or computing (EEF, 2020).

Maintaining positive relationships with parents is crucial for the academic success for all pupils. The EEF, in its *Working with Parents to Support Children's Learning Guidance Report* (2018c) states that there are a number of ways schools can engage parents, which can ultimately determine academic outcomes. Some recommendations are:

- providing regular feedback on children's progress
- offering advice on improving the home learning environment
- running more intensive programmes for children struggling with reading or behaviour.

The value of parental engagement cannot be underestimated. Much research has been conducted in this area of work, which shows that when parents are involved in their children's education, their attendance improves, engagement and regular completion of homework takes place and behaviour improves (Goodall, 2020).

However, Goodall (2020) argues that homework is not about doing more and more worksheets or checking the homework, but rather, 'Effective parental engagement with learning means the attitude towards and support for learning in the home' (Goodall and Montgomery, 2014).

Although it is clear that parental engagement contributes to and impacts on pupil success at school, what is less understood is how to improve attainment by engaging pupils from disadvantaged back-grounds. In particular, 'developing effective parental engagement to improve their children's attainment is challenging' (EEF, 2020c).

However, findings (EEF, 2020c) have indicated that supporting parents 'with their first child will have benefits for siblings'. It has also been indicated, whilst studying meta-analyses in the USA, that there was a positive impact of approximately two to three months in both primary and secondary schools.

An important point to note is that parents may not be as well-resourced as schools are in providing support for their children: 'We also need to realise that not all families will have everything we might like them to have, and not taking account of that could further disad-vantage some of our most vulnerable students' (Goodall, 2020).

Parents will understandably be worried about their children's learning and parents may lack self-confidence themselves, which could be a huge barrier. In addition to this, many families will not have enough devices for everyone to work on simultaneously. This creates additional barriers for families. As educators, we must reas-sure parents that it is acceptable not to know all the answers.

There is research available, particularly from early years and pri-mary, in reading and maths showing that the link between how well parents are involved in their child's education raises their child's actual academic progress. Clark (2007) states that 'involvement with reading activities at home has significant positive influences not only on reading achievement, language comprehension and expressive language skills (Gest, Freeman, Domitrovich and Welsh, 2004), but also on pupils' interest in reading, attitudes towards reading and attentiveness in the classroom (Rowe, 1991)'.

Jay, Rose and Simmons (2018) state that 'parents and the home environment are generally recognised as making a substantial contri-bution to children's mathematics learning'. The parent-teacher has become more significant during the pandemic.

Although it is too early to tell what the actual cause of this is, parental engagement seems to be a huge factor contributing towards this.

Remote learning

Before discussing remote learning in its online form, it is important to note that safeguarding is a crucial aspect to consider when planning online teaching for children. There are many safeguarding resources available from the NSPCC and National Safety Online.

COVID-19 has certainly created a plethora of challenges for teachers having to provide home learning as well as teach full timetables during the day. Nevertheless, educators stepped up to the mark and provided creative ways for home-learning to take place in either paper form or online, with either live and recorded lessons, or both, known as blended learning.

During the COVID-19 pandemic and the lockdown, there was the notion that remote learning would be easier and reduce workload for teachers. In reality, however, there were many challenges; not only were there technical issues, but ensuring pupil–teacher interaction without the teacher being physically present became a top priority. Replicating exactly what happens in the classroom online was a huge challenge.

In addition to this schools were tasked with the mammoth role of educating not only children but also parents in the pedagogy of home learning.

Preliminary results indicate that remote learning has proved to be beneficial, as educators have taken to social media platforms such as Twitter indicating that the lockdown has not had much of an impact on learning as previously thought. Bubb and Jones (2020) also found this to be the case.

What became clear in the UK was that there was indeed a huge digital divide, whether this was as a result of not having devices or being digitally illiterate. According to Bubb and Jones (2020) and their research in Norway, they concluded that:

> those who already utilised digital learning platforms had fewer barriers to remote education compared with schools that had formerly made little use of technology or where pupils did not have devices and the internet at home. Research in England (NFER, 2020) concluded that schools which had already established a virtual learning environment had higher student engagement levels than those without, especially for disadvantaged children.

In order to identify 'methods that schools could use to support remote learning during school closures caused by the 2020 coronavirus pandemic (COVID-19)', the EEF carried out a study (EEF, 2020d). Being aware that schools may use a range of approaches during the pandemic, the EEF worked through already 'existing meta-analyses and systematic reviews to find the best evidence for a wide range of approaches' (EEF, 2020d: 3).

The Education Endowment Foundation, in its rapid evidence assessment on remote learning (2020d), concluded that:

- Teaching quality is more important than how lessons are delivered.
- Ensuring access to technology is key, particularly for disadvantaged pupils.
- Peer interactions can provide motivation and improve learning outcomes.
- Supporting pupils to work independently can improve learning outcomes.
- Different approaches to remote learning suit different tasks and types of content. (EEF, 2020d: 4).

Bob and Jones (2020) note that these findings are 'largely based on other (non-pandemic) situations'. An important factor which needs to be taken into consideration is that in the EEF *Remote Learning: Rapid Evidence Assessment* (2020d) there have not been enough 'high-quality studies' which have focused on 'remote learning in school-aged education' with many studies focusing on 'reviews' which 'combine evidence from school-aged education, university education and adult learners' (EEF, 2020d: 3). Some of the approaches highlighted may be beneficial for older pupils. This means that careful consideration must be given to the best use of an approach given a pupil's age and cannot be directly transferred.

When it comes to remote learning, due to the fact that teachers are not present with their pupils, metacognition becomes even more important. The EEF has broken down the metacognitive learning sequence into five parts: activate, explain, practise, reflect and review.

The 'activate' part of the lesson is the retrieval of knowledge where pupils recall what they had learnt previously and how this will help their learning in the current lesson or unit of work. This is an important metacognitive skill.

The 'explain' part of the lesson is when teachers explicitly teach the metacognitive skills in context and explain the purpose of using them and when to use them.

The 'practise' stage is when pupils repeatedly practise the strategies and skills required, so that they become fluent in them. This is where scaffolds are used and gradually decreased over time. This will enable them to become independent learners.

The 'reflect' stage is where, after completing a piece of work, pupils reflect on it. This valuation will enable them to become self-regulated learners.

The 'review' stage usually happens some time after the learning, as it aids memory retention.

It is not expected that the sequence be taught in one lesson.

Fostering independent learning

One of the EEF recommendations is that supporting pupils to work independently can improve learning outcomes. This becomes much more important when there is no face-to-face teaching. Let us explore some ways forward in supporting pupils to become more independent.

According to Informed Teaching's blog entitled, 'Going 'live' – rising to the challenge of remote learning (2020), the Harvard Division of Science found that pupils 'benefit from taking an active role in lessons'. Therein lies the dilemma of whether to provide pre-recorded or live lessons online.

Naturally, many would argue that live lessons are better, other than the obvious downside being teachers and pupils staring at a computer screen for most of the day. Another factor to consider would be how to engage pupils who are not directly in front of the teacher. In addition to this, with pre-recorded lessons pupils who do not understand a particular concept or who need more practice can pause the video and rewind it, but with live lessons this is not possible.

In the classroom, getting pupils to answer questions, interact and discuss topics/issues/learning is easy but creating the same conditions for learning online is a huge challenge. Of course, no one can deny that face-to-face teaching is the best method, however, how does this translate online? Can it fully translate online?

This is where the purpose of education comes into play. Educators around the world would like to develop more independence in learners.

Becoming an independent learner takes times and for some requires explicit teaching and training – not everyone is naturally organised. However, this becomes a challenge when teaching pupils remotely. Another consideration is that some pupils have to not only manage their own time but 'teach' their younger siblings, as parents are working from home too.

One of the stands in the EEF guidance on *Metacognition and Self-regulated Learning* (2018a: 7) is: 'Explicitly teach pupils how to organise and effectively manage their learning independently'.

The three main recommendations for developing independent learning include:

- planning in guided practice, where support is taken away slowly, depending on pupil proficiency
- developing accuracy of judgement about 'how effectively they are learning' by giving 'timely, effective feedback'
- supporting 'pupils' motivation to undertake the learning tasks'. (EEF, 2018a: 7)

According to the EEF, there are a range of strategies pupils can use to help them learn more independently. These include: setting short-term goals, adopting powerful strategies for attaining these goals, monitoring performance for signs of progress, restructuring their physical and social context to make it compatible with their goals, self-evaluating their methods, and attributing causation to results and adapting future methods (EEF, 2018a: 23).

In her blog entitled: 'Getting metacognition into remote learning', MacNeill (2021) suggests practical ideas to develop this, including:

- Develop pupil organisational skills by providing students with timetables and daily guides with breaks built in.
- Model thinking processes so pupils can apply these independently. This could be in video format or in written format, which pupils could refer to when they get stuck. Providing planning scaffolds for learning can also develop organisational skills. This will also alleviate anxiety.
- Within the lesson, whether live or pre-recorded, give pupils prompts and reminders about what to do if they get stuck.
- Where there is a live element to the lesson, encourage discussion about starting strategies. One way to do this is to encourage

pupils to type their answers into the chat bar. If the lesson is pre-recorded, ask a question to get pupils thinking, and encourage pupils to pause the video and think about the answer.

- Learning can be scaffolded in a number of ways, including by activating prior knowledge – before introducing a new topic, start off by having revision lessons from a previous linked topic.
- Another way to scaffold is to ensure there are learning objectives and success criteria so pupils can keep track of their plan, monitor and evaluate cycle. This also helps to develop organisation skills. Checklists are less specific than success criteria and can give a quick overview instead.
- In addition to this, asking pupils to pause pre-recorded lesson and planning in breaks into live lessons, allows pupils the opportunity to pause and reflect on their learning. This time could be used to encourage pupils to re-read their work and identify misconceptions. Planning in time at this stage is important so that pupils can practise skills and strategies repeatedly. It will also foster effective habits for regular review.

MacNeill (2021) suggests keeping 'a log of their performance for their own purposes' and using that 'to inform the questions they would like to ask of the teacher or the areas they think they need to develop'.

Develop self-awareness by encouraging pupils to self-reflect via questioning about what they did and how they felt and what made them successful, when they encountered challenges.

Parents may not be aware of the 'struggles' their children encounter with remote learning and may feel completely overwhelmed and start correcting everything. For very young children, parents could be included in the self-reflection process. Encouraging parents to ask children whether anything needs changing not only develops parental awareness but pupil awareness also.

Motivation

In Chapter 6, we explored motivation and using reward systems effectively. Motivation to learn becomes even more important during remote learning.

What has become clear during the third COVID-19 lockdown in 2021 in the UK is that the main challenges associated with providing a like for like curriculum online is how to keep pupils motivated. Without the motivation to turn on their devices, pupils will not learn, despite the best lessons being planned and prepared.

How do schools motivate pupils when there is no teacher around? Live lessons may provide the ultimate platform for developing motivation but with computer screens in the way, forming a barrier, it is still not easy. With pre-recorded lessons, it becomes even more challenging to motivate pupils. However, some teachers have found creative ways to do this through the online platforms their schools have chosen, but it is much too early to see if this can be sustained for long periods of time.

Another important aspect is that although some pupils benefit from less classroom distractions whilst learning at home, there may be more distractions at home, which provide instant gratification, such as gaming (Bubb and Jones, 2020). Pupils need self-control, which is part of the 'metacognitive process' to be able to focus on learning (EEF, 2018a: 23).

What becomes clear is that the effectiveness of online learning is age dependent. Li and Lalani (2020) state that due to younger pupils being easily distracted, they require a more 'structured environment'. They advise that online learning needs to break the norms of teaching, and instead of replicating the classroom via videos, engagement and collaboration tools that foster inclusion, personalisation and intelligence need to be promoted, as suggested by Dowson Tong, Senior Executive Vice President of Tencent and President of its Cloud and Smart Industries Group.

Home-school contact and vulnerable pupils

As mentioned earlier in the chapter, parental engagement has a huge impact on pupil progress and this can be seen as a scaffold leading to independent learning. Bubb and Jones (2020) also reported that during COVID-19 home-schooling, the crucial role of parents/carers became more apparent and provided parents/carers with a 'deeper insight into their child's learning'.

The strengthening of the relationships between teachers and parent/carers had a positive contribution to the learning of pupils and many parents spoke very highly of teachers. This in itself is a huge 'driving force for school improvement' (Bubb and Jones, 2020), which is in line with EEF findings on parental engagement (EEF, 2020c).

Naturally there has been widespread concern about the remote learning of vulnerable pupils. In the research conducted by Bubb and Jones (2020) they found that schools had prioritised well for this group and had increased the level of contact.

It has also been reported that with less distractions in the classroom, many vulnerable pupils have performed better, with more contact between teachers and parents/carers and relevant services. Giving pupils the 'choices in their ways of working and ordering assignments' seems to have had a positive influence on their learning. The research also showed that 'there was consensus among the groups that pupils became more independent during remote learning: 74% of teachers, 64% of parents, 71% of Grade 1 to 4 pupils and 78% of Grade 5 to 10 pupils agreed' (Bubb and Jones, 2020).

Scaffolding learning and providing feedback

The EEF (2020d) identified from a number of reviews that scaffolding and feedback were increasingly important in remote learning, in particular metacognitive scaffolding providing greater impact. This could come from either teachers themselves or from prompts 'built into the technology that encourage learners to think about successful strategies for learning or when to request help' (EEF, 2020d: 14).

In his book, *Visible Learning for Teachers: Maximising Impact on Learning*, Hattie (2012) emphasises the importance of teachers providing immediate feedback to pupils as a tool to develop motivation and self-efficacy. Feedback also helps pupils develop accuracy of judgement (see more on feedback in Chapter 6).

It is clear with remote learning that when pupils are not face-to-face with teachers, particularly where verbal feedback is not always possible, the development of self-efficacy, motivation and accuracy of judgement, through providing pupils with written feedback, becomes even more crucial.

According to Bubb and Jones (2020), the impact of personalisation has been hugely beneficial in remote learning. There was a shift in accepting feedback, as it was 'seen as more useful during home-school than normal, which is an important but surprising finding given that one would assume there would be severe practical obstacles in setting up the necessary dialogue to constitute effective feedback' (Bubb and Jones, 2020).

Pupils commented positively about feedback received and two-thirds stated that the feedback helped more during remote teaching. From the pupils' perspective, they stated that digital technology allowed teachers to 'see how good all the pupils are, and not just those who always raise their hands in class' (Bubb and Jones, 2020).

Although parents/carers were not aware about how much feedback was usually given to pupils, teachers stated they 'probably commented on more assignments per student than normal' and also divided their attention more fairly (Bubb and Jones, 2020).

Despite some pupils being able to concentrate better at home, there are others who find school more motivating, with teachers reporting that parental support and monitoring had a greater impact on pupils' work.

Taking ownership of their own learning

Bubb and Jones' (2020) study found that a motivating factor of remote learning was that some children enjoyed taking ownership of their own learning, and being responsible for their own learning motivated some children. Being able to 'manage by figuring things out and fixing things', appeared to be hugely rewarding. Some pupils disagreed, stating that they had been independent from before the pandemic. Perhaps we need to develop our understanding of individual online motivational tools and techniques?

Li and Lalani (2020) state that for those who do have access to digital technology, 'learning online can be more effective in a number of ways'. There has been research to show that pupils can retain 25–60 per cent more when learning online as opposed to 8–10 per cent when in the classroom. One of the advantages is that learning happens much more quickly online: 'e-learning requires 40–60 per cent less time to learn than in a traditional classroom setting'. Another advantage is that 'students can learn at their own pace, going back and re-reading, skipping, or accelerating through concepts as they choose'. However, preliminary findings suggest that children who are usually less likely to seek adult and peer support, and who usually lack skills in developing relationships, are likely to require face-to-face teaching.

Case study: How a school implemented remote learning during the global COVID-19 pandemic

Lockdown 1

During the first lockdown in March 2020, the school had successfully installed Google Classroom for each class and teachers began setting work, marking and conversing with pupils. Teachers kept in touch, regularly, with families and pupils via the telephone.

Partial Lockdown 2

Google Classroom was used for homework setting only, and only in Year 6 as a trial. This threw up a number of challenges, some of which were that some pupils had devices, some had no internet or devices. A solution was to provide paper copies for the pupils who had no internet and/or device. However, some pupils began completing the online homework and the paper copies of the homework, even though it was the same homework.

In addition to this, the Remote Learning Leader attended online training sessions and cascaded their learning to staff through a training session on pre-recorded lessons, just in case a 'bubble' had to close. Not only was the purpose to highlight the importance of safeguarding but also to show how it was possible to deliver metacognition, how to build motivation and feedback into lessons remotely.

Lockdown 3

The school put into place a like for like curriculum online. Staff were mobilised on the first INSET (In-service training day) to start recording lessons, with support from SLT (Senior Leadership Team). Devices and internet connections were arranged for the most vulnerable pupils. E-safety leaflets were written and given to parents, as well as e-safety lessons for all pupils. Parents were advised to set up a clear learning space, and pupils who were struggling with completing tasks were taught how to manage their time effectively. Parents were also regularly updated via the newsletter about new online teaching websites and apps.

(Continued)

They toyed with the idea of conducting daily Google Meets for the class but this was not feasible, so teachers conducted a weekly Google Meet to talk to their classes. Parents commented positively on the weekly Google Meets.

Teachers used Screencast-O-Matic to record a video for themselves in the corner of the presentation, so pupils could see a familiar face. As well as teaching at school, providing online learning and photocopying home learning packs, teachers also became the first port of call for technical issues from families. Teachers found that their workload had increased phenomenally this time round.

Due to the limitations of time for marking discovered during the second lockdown and due to teacher workload increasing tremendously, teachers worked on a half-day rotation basis, with the other half-day spent either teaching keyworkers and vulnerable children or making phone calls to the parents of the pupils who did not submit online learning. Some families requested paper copies of the online learning instead of being glued to the computer screen all day. Parents were impressed with the quality of the teaching resources and the way the teachers were supporting pupils at home.

Preliminary findings were that most pupils were completing work to a good standard and some were excelling with online learning, particularly in English, maths, science, art and design and technology. The pupils who were finding it challenging to complete their work online and via the home learning packs received extra support in the form of increased telephone calls to guide parents and their children through the lessons and the learning process. Some of the ways they motivated pupils weekly included through online Star of the Week, singing lessons, art lessons and growth mindset assemblies.

After a few weeks, questionnaires were sent out to parents, pupils and staff about the effectiveness of the online provision. Due to the fact that it became unsustainable for teachers to work at the rate they were working and due to the fact that most parents, pupils and teachers wanted less screen time, the school decided that on Wednesday afternoons there would be no online learning. Instead parents were provided with a list of other learning activities to replace the online learning, where they could spend some time together and/or get out into the fresh air.

After about four weeks, the school noticed a decline in motivation in the remote learners, and they swiftly responded by writing parent guides on how to keep children motivated.

- How was staff efficacy increased during the pandemic?
- How did the school evaluate its provision?
- What did the school do to refine and improve its provision?

Summary

- The effectiveness of homework depends on the quality not quantity of tasks set.
- Homework is more effective for secondary than for primary pupils.
- Parental engagement is important, to help support pupils in their self-regulation and self-efficacy.

Remote and online learning:

- Prioritise safeguarding and e-safety due to pupils spending a longer amount of time online.
- Strengthen their already existing partnerships with parents and carers in order to keep motivation levels high and develop confidence.
- Motivation to study becomes even more important.
- Feedback becomes even more important in remote teaching to develop self-efficacy and accuracy of judgement.
- Balance online learning with other types of learning in the home environment.
- Constantly refine and evaluate practice of remote and online learning.
- More focus is required on developing the social and emotional aspects of teaching and learning.
- A support network becomes even more crucial.
- More focus is required on maintaining relationships building between pupil and teacher and between peers.

Think!

- Are there any types of learning which may be more suitable for remote learning?
- Which subject areas might be better suited for remote learning?

(Continued)

- What are the most important factors which need to be considered when setting homework, remote and/or online learning?
- What support could be provided for parents to be more involved in remote and online learning?
- How independent are learners in your school?
- What strategies do you use to develop independent learning?
- How well does homework task setting foster independence?
- Does independent learning require more instruction, structure and practice?
- How are social and emotional skills developed in the classroom and what are the implications for these during remote and online learning?

Teacher metacognition

- How do you usually plan lessons?
- How do you need to break down the lesson for online learning?
- What pedagogies would engage pupils effectively online?
- How could you ensure that pupils will understand the instructions given online?
- Where do you ask pupils to pause the video to practise skills?
- How can you get pupils to become more interactive online and how do you engage them?
- How can you get pupils to practise skills required for the lesson, within the online platform we are using?
- How could you give feedback efficiently and effectively?
- How do you ensure that you continuously build social and emotional skills and relationships?

Pupil metacognition

- Which pupils require more instructions to watch the videos?
- Which pupils need to understand the benefits and the reasons for pausing the videos and having a go at practising the skills?
- Which pupils need to be engaged more in remote learning?

- Which pupils need support in developing their social and emotional skills and how can this be done remotely?
- Which pupils need more motivating?
- Which pupils require more scaffolding?

References

Bubb, S. and Jones, M.-A. (2020) Learning from the COVID-19 home-schooling experience: Listening to pupils, parents/carers and teachers. *Improving Schools*, 23 (3): 209–222. doi: 10.1177/1365480220958797

Clark, C. (2007) Why it is important to involve parents in their children's literacy development [online]. Available at: https://eric.ed.gov/?id=ED496346 (accessed 29 January 2021).

EEF (2018a) *Metacognition and Self-regulated Learning: Guidance Report* [online]. Available at: https://educationendowmentfoundation.org.uk/public/files/Publications/Metacognition/EEF_Metacognition_and_self-regulated_learning.pdf (accessed 9 November 2020).

EEF (2018b) *Teaching and learning toolkit* [online]. Available at: https://educationendowmentfoundation.org.uk/public/files/Toolkit/complete/EEF-Teaching-Learning-Toolkit-October-2018.pdf (accessed 16 March 2021).

EEF (2018c) *Working with Parents to Support Children's Learning Guidance Report* [online]. Available at: https://educationendowmentfoundation.org.uk/public/files/Publications/ParentalEngagement/EEF_Parental_Engagement_Guidance_Report.pdf (accessed 16 March 2021).

EEF (2020a) Home learning approaches: Planning framework [online]. Available at: https://educationendowmentfoundation.org.uk/public/files/Publications/Covid-19_Resources/Resources_for_schools/Home_learning_approaches_-_Planning_framework.pdf (accessed 29 January 2021).

EEF (2020b) Home learning planning framework: This is the plan for a learning sequence, and won't take place within a single session [online]. Available at: https://educationendowmentfoundation.org.uk/public/files/Publications/Covid-19_Resources/Resources_for_schools/Home_learning_approaches_Planning_framework_%E2%80%93_worked_examples.pdf (accessed 29 January 2021).

EEF (2020c) Parental engagement [online]. Available at: https://educationendowmentfoundation.org.uk/pdf/generate/?u=https://educationendowmentfoundation.org.uk/pdf/toolkit/?id=139&t=Teaching%20and%20Learning%20Toolkit&e=139&s= (accessed 29 January 2020).

EEF (2020d) *Remote Learning: Rapid Evidence Assessment* [online]. Available at: https://educationendowmentfoundation.org.uk/public/files/Remote_Learning_Rapid_Evidence_Assessment.pdf (accessed 16 March 2021).

Goodall, J. (2020) Engaging parents during school closures. *Impact: Journal of the Chartered College of Teaching* [online]. Available at: https://impact.chartered.college/article/engaging-parents-during-school-closures/ (accessed 29 January 2021).

Goodall, J. and Montgomery, C. (2014) Parental involvement to parental engagement: A continuum. *Educational Review* 66 (4): 399–410.

Hattie, J. (2009) *Visible Learning: A Synthesis of Over 800 Meta-Analysis Relating to Achievement*. London: Routledge.

Hattie, J. (2012) *Visible Learning for Teachers: Maximising Impact on Learning*. London: Routledge.

Informed Teaching (2020) 'Going 'live' – rising to the challenge of remote learning [online]. Available at: www.informedteaching.com/post/a-shift-towards-independent-learning (accessed 16 March 2021).

Jay, T., Rose, J. and Simmons, B. (2018) Why is parental involvement in children's mathematics learning hard? Parental perspectives on their role supporting children's learning. *SAGE Open*. doi: 10.1177/2158244018775466

Li, C. and Lalani, F. (2020) The COVID-19 pandemic has changed education forever: This is how [online]. Available at: www.weforum.org/agenda/2020/04/coronavirus-education-global-covid19-online-digital-learning/ (accessed 4 February 2021).

MacNeill, S. (2021) Getting metacognition into remote learning. Herts for Learning blog [online]. Available at: www.hertsforlearning.co.uk/blog/getting-metacognition-remote-learning (accessed 4 February 2021).

8

METACOGNITIVE STRATEGIES IN ENGLISH

Contents

- Reading
- Metacognitive reading strategies
- Writing
- Metacognitive writing strategies
- References

> ## In this chapter we will explore
>
> - metacognitive reading and writing strategies
> - the Question–Answer Relationship strategies
> - different ways of activating prior knowledge for reading
> - ways in which the skills of tracking could be developed in both reading and writing.

Reading

Reading is one of the greatest gifts a child could be given.

> It has astonishing benefits for children: comfort and reassurance, confidence and security, relaxation, happiness and fun … It builds self-esteem, vocabulary, feeds imagination and even improves their sleeping patterns. (Literacy Trust, 2020)

When a parent and child read together, an emotional bond develops through the discussions which take place. Reading is a portal, opening up worlds and experiences that most of us can never experience in real life; it is a way of living a thousand lives. Not only are fluent reading skills required as we move through each stage of our lives but reading helps us to learn about empathy and gives us a framework for navigating our way around an increasingly challenging world. Unfortunately, not all children learn to read fluently enough and some children grow up to be illiterate, which impacts hugely on their life chances. Teachers recognise that reading is very much a personal experience and children enjoy learning new words and vocabulary. However, learning to read is a very complex process shrouded by mystery. This is partly due to reading being a largely hidden process.

Flavell, who in 1979 first coined the term metacognition, describes reading as being a marriage of three elements: 'interaction among the reader, the text, and the context in which reading takes place' (Teng, 2020). According to Teng (2020) metacognitive strategies can be very useful, not only for those of whom English is an additional language but for all pupils due to the process of learning to read being extremely complex.

There is no doubt that one of the most effective ways of improving reading comprehension is to give pupils a love of reading and promoting developing reading for pleasure, as there is a 'growing body of evidence to indicate that there are strong links between self-initiated reading and attainment' (Gamble, 2013: 19). Children who are intrinsically motivated read for pleasure. However, there appear to be negative associations with children who require extrinsic motivation. The depth of text comprehension is also affected by the type of motivation that leads to reading for pleasure. For reading to become a life-long process both inside and outside of the classroom, educators should talk about books and reading with passion. Reading for pleasure is critical in developing a love of reading. Pupils who are already good at reading also have a well-developed repertoire of metacognitive strategies to plan, monitor and evaluate their reading. However, disadvantaged pupils and those with poor reading skills need such skills to be taught explicitly.

Question–Answer Relationship strategy

A study of the impact of teaching metacognitive strategies to EAL (English as an additional language) pupils was published in the January 2020 edition of the UKLA journal, *Literacy*. Teng (2020) conducted a small-scale study consisting of two groups: a control group with no metacognitive teaching and a group where there was explicit teaching of metacognition strategies. This was centred around developing 'metacognitive prompts' from the Question–Answer Relationship (QAR) framework suggested by Raphael and Au (2005) with the questioning being designed around the proposals from Wilson and Smetana (2011).

The QAR strategy is an established method that involves applying questioning strategies to texts in order to improve reading comprehension. There are four types of questions:

1. Right There questions have only one answer that can be found at one place in the reading text.
2. Think and Search questions have answers that can also be found in the text, but because there may be more than one correct answer, students must put different parts of a story together in order to answer them.
3. Author and You questions are not answered directly in the text and require the reader to read between the lines, using prior knowledge and information from the text to make inferences.

4. On Your Own questions are related to students' experiences and feelings on a topic and can be answered without reading the text. (Raphael, 1982, 1984, 1986)

It is important to note that the answers to question types 1 and 2 can be found in the book, while answers to question types 3 and 4 are based on what the learner knows.

For young pupils the challenge is immense, especially when 'processing sufficient information to make sense of various types of reading material' (Teng, 2020: 1). Pressley (2002) states that although Grade 6 pupils (Year 7 in England) can deceive educators into thinking that they are fluent readers, when it comes to comprehension they often cannot articulate their understanding of the text or remember what they have just read. As well as 'word recognition and vocabulary, comprehension strategies need to begin in primary' (Pressley, 2002). Primary educators are well aware that comprehension activities can be taught long before pupils begin to decode words – literally from birth.

Other comprehension strategies

Amongst the many priorities at primary level, reading usually takes centre stage. Schools plan parent reading workshops to guide less experienced parents into what reading could look like at home. This usually begins with talking about picture books and reciting nursery rhymes. With the thinking processes in place, eventually the decoding catches up with the comprehension, with the scene set for pupils to get off to a flying start. Pressley (2002) states that 'It is now understood that long-term instruction of sophisticated comprehension strategies clearly improves student understanding and memory of texts that are read'. By long term, Pressley means to start reading from a very young age. The more experience we have as a reader, the better our comprehension will be. How do we start the reading comprehension process before the actual skills of decoding are learnt?

Both comprehension and meaning-making are the foundations for dialogue for picture books (Roche, 2015). Dialogue itself is a pedagogical approach to access deeper thinking skills. Dialogue enables both pupils and educators to access metacognitive thinking. When we read, we are experiencing lives created from the guidelines and procedures of stories. This can be challenging to understand.

Whilst reading, we employ three strategies to mitigate these difficulties (Roche, 2015): contrast, confrontation and metacognition, based on Bruner's ideas.

The first strategy is contrast, when the reader experiences different 'versions of the same event or sequence of events' (Roche, 2015), where learners seek similarities and differences to develop a deeper understanding of the text. An example would be comparing different versions of *The Little Red Riding Hood* story and comparing it to *The Wolf's Story* for example. As pupils listen to different versions with differing viewpoints, not only does their understanding develop but they are able to extend their growing knowledge of texts, and in this case their empathy with characters in books becomes enhanced.

The second strategy is confrontation, when learners scrutinise their own ideas about reality when faced with 'superior claims' (Roche, 2015) and they change their original perspective in light of this and create their own reality.

The third strategy is metacognition, where pupils 'reflect, not only on their own view of reality, with the intention of changing or deepening it, but also how they came to know it in the first place' (Roche, 2105: 148).

Even in younger readers, reading comprehension can be developed at a deeper level before decoding has taken place, through picture books and dialogue. Moir, Boyle and Woolfson (2020) state that the use of metacognition and self-regulated learning have been well documented and these strategies enable progression of academic skills.

According to Teng (2020) reading comprehension includes a range of aspects: 'background knowledge, vocabulary, fluency, active reading skills and critical thinking'. Due to reading being a primarily hidden process, this becomes particularly challenging for younger pupils.

Teng (2020) conducted a study with twenty-five Grade 5 EAL pupils and an equal number of pupils in a control group in a Hong Kong international school. Metacognition was taught explicitly to one group of twenty-five pupils over a period of ten reading lessons. After the study, two types of reading tests were administered, pupils' notes were examined, evaluations from reflections were studied as well as group deliberations, which were enabled by the teacher. The control group were not taught any metacognitive strategies. Teng (2020) found that the group receiving explicit teaching of metacognition had improved outcomes compared to the control group. This showed that teaching metacognition in reading to second language English learners could be of benefit.

It is therefore important to explicitly teach or highlight to pupils the 'mental and emotional processes' (Teng, 2020) that occur during reading. Although developing reading strategies is a particularly stressful process in young learners (Teng, 2020), for pupils for whom English is an additional language it becomes even more challenging, EAL pupils can benefit from explicit instruction on comprehension strategies (Block and Pressley, 2002). Good readers naturally set goals for themselves, know how they remember the information, monitor their comprehension and evaluate their level of success. These are metacognitive strategies. Cognitive strategies are having enough information to be able to make sense in different types of contextual reading, having background knowledge, understanding of vocabulary, having reading fluency, active reading skills and critical thinking skills.

It has been suggested that when pupils develop an awareness of the nature and demands of reading, this can have a positive impact on reading outcomes such as activating prior knowledge, making connections to the text, questioning the text, determining contextual importance and summarising. This leads to pupils being able to self-regulate their reading and choosing appropriate strategies to improve their understanding (Teng, 2020).

Metacognitive reading strategies

This section will focus on metacognitive reading strategies solely and should not be replaced with other crucial reading comprehension strategies but used in conjunction.

According to Teng (2020), there are a number of metacognitive strategies which need to be explicitly taught for reading comprehension, which are: activating prior knowledge, making connections to the text, questioning the text, determining contextual importance and summarising. These strategies in combination with reading aloud strategies, such as QAT, can be very powerful.

Activating prior knowledge

One of the EEF recommendations is that activating prior knowledge at the beginning of lessons or units of study is an effective way to strengthen the memory and build into higher thinking concepts. Drawing out pupil understanding and knowledge is called retrieval practice. There are many ways to do this and regular testing and quizzing has been found to be effective. However, there are other ways of retrieving knowledge and understanding, which we will look at below.

Activating prior knowledge through predicting

'"Retrieval practice" is a learning strategy where we focus on getting information out' (Agarwal, Roediger, McDaniel and McDermott, 2020: 2). It is a way of strengthening the memory where information is less likely to be forgotten. It does not require more time or money but can be a very 'powerful strategy for improving academic performance' (Agarwal et al., 2020: 2). There are, however, different types of retrieval practice. The two types we will explore here are isolated and embedded.

> In reading, isolated retrieval practice could include retrieval of the names of characters, places and events, or recalling the definitions of words. However, retrieving the meaning of words can also be embedded in other tasks. For example, depending on the stage of pupils' understanding of vocabulary and comprehension, activating prior knowledge through predictions when reading is often used where pupils are naturally required to draw upon facts in order to be able to make predictions. (Mughal, 2020)

There are many ways to activate prior knowledge. It is important to distinguish between the types of activating prior knowledge for different types of text. For fictional texts activating prior knowledge would be in the form of predicting (Tennent, Reedy, Hobsbaum and Gamble, 2016).

There is no doubt that activating prior knowledge, in this way, in reading is crucial to the development of comprehension and the deeper thinking skills required to aid understanding of text. However, there are different types of predicting. When pupils predict what is going to happen next in a story, they are required to activate their prior knowledge. Without this it is not possible to make a prediction, as pupils are required to draw upon the last event that happened or draw further back into the story.

For non-fictional texts, activating prior knowledge may be in the form of factual knowledge. However, we are all too aware that it is not possible to equip pupils with all the prior knowledge required to access the phenomenal amount of texts out there. Even through having a broad and balanced curriculum, it is impossible to expose pupils to every single life experience required to build up prior knowledge. In his book, *Understanding Reading Comprehension*, Wayne Tennent (2015) discusses the types of knowledge which need developing in reading comprehension and how carefully selecting texts with the right amount of prior knowledge can act as a lever to facilitate reading comprehension.

Activating prior knowledge through making connections to the text

Making sense of texts requires the ability to identify links between the text and other things. There are three different connections which could be made (Tennent et al., 2016), originally mentioned by Keene and Zimmerman (1997):

1. Connecting text to 'own life experiences'.
2. Connecting text to another text which the pupil has already read.
3. Connecting the text globally, through other media such as videos, films, music and trips.

For this strategy to be successful, educators will need to consider whether the chosen text or part of the text allows for pupils to be able to make the connections mentioned, ensuring the 'text potential' allows for this (Tennant et al., 2016).

Making connections to reading texts

Making connections to the text is very important for comprehension and may contribute to the development of metacognitive comprehension strategies. According to Wise (2020), 'an effective strategy for readers to understand text is to make connections to their personal experiences and background knowledge'. One way readers can monitor their own thinking is by making connections to the text. It enables them to stay 'actively engaged while reading and leads to an overall better understanding of the text'.

Below, you will find the three types of connections which can develop reading comprehension:

1. Text to self: The child makes links from what they read to an aspect in their own life.

Here are examples of questions which could be asked:

- Have you visited this type of setting before?
- Have you been to a similar setting?
- Are you similar to any of the characters in the text?
- Have you met similar characters before?
- How does this text make you feel?

This may need to be taught explicitly and the thinking process modelled to pupils, as well as providing examples. This may take a lot of practice before pupils can answer these questions independently.

2. Text to fictional text and/or picture books: The child links what they read to something they have read before.

Comprehension can be improved by linking fictional and non-fictional for each unit of study. This helps strengthen background knowledge, vocabulary and interestingly, motivation.

> Such units improve students' background knowledge when informational texts activate or build prior knowledge for fictional texts on the same topic, vocabulary when they provide opportunities to encounter the same word or group of conceptually related words in a variety of different texts, and motivation when they offer multiple entry points suited to individual preferences for fictional or informational texts. (Soalt, 2005)

In addition, reading two or more texts on the same topic provides pupils with 'multiple perspectives on a single subject' (Soalt, 2005). The multiple perspectives include affective and objective points of views.

When the texts are compared and contrasted by teachers, this helps to develop and expand pupil understanding, and is also a way of enriching the 'engagement experience', particularly in older pupils (Soalt, 2005).

Another benefit is that using non-fictional texts and picture books is a way of building up contextual knowledge by creating a scaffold for readers of differing abilities and for those for whom English is an additional language. They create scaffolds for readers at a variety of different levels and help build the contextual knowledge necessary for working with longer texts.

All the benefits stated above between fictional and non-fictional texts also apply to picture books. Roche (2015) states that she has witnessed 'interthinking' – development of thinking through collaborative speaking by Littleton and Mercer (2013) – in her own classroom, where there was a 'buzz of excitement' as pupils became engaged and 'animated' when discussing picture books and lots of 'light bulb' moments.

3. Text to world: The child links what they read to an aspect that they know about the world.
4. Thinking aloud strategies.
5. Metacognition in reading is when a reader thinks about the cognitive processes required to achieve comprehension, which involves monitoring, understanding and self-regulating mental processes. (Wilson and Smetana, 2011)
6. Recognition about lack or difficulty of understanding or when the reader requires more information.
7. Being aware that there are a number of known strategies to choose from.
8. Choosing a strategy or strategies to enable comprehension.
9. Teaching students to be metacognitive is a key element to developing effective readers (Pressley et al., 1998). Students using QAT become metacognitive by seeing the teacher model her metacognition with the Think Aloud, engaging in the analysis of strategies with questioning, and engaging in the sharing of metacognitive processes through the Think Aloud.

Questioning the text

Questioning the text is an important metacognitive process. In *Guiding Readers – Layers of Meaning*, Tennent et al. (2016) use a great example of choosing texts based on their potential to create cognitive conflict, which promotes the thinking skills to question texts. The example given in the book is from the Lord Fox story and the sentence is: 'Lord Fox pulled up in his red Ferrari and did a wheel spin on the gravel driveway'. The language used in the text of lords, ladies and suitors may well give the impression that it is written in the nineteenth century. This would create the cognitive conflict to question the text. Pupils would need to go back through the text and track their understanding of it, to see if they had misread something. Teaching explicit metacognitive strategies is crucial for developing effective readers. Pupils who use 'QAT become metacognitive by seeing the teacher model her metacognition with the Think Aloud, engaging in the analysis of strategies with questioning, and engaging in the sharing of metacognitive processes through the Think Aloud' (Pressley et al., 1998).

Echo reading

Usually used in small group reading, echo reading is used to read short sections of text. It can be used to develop both fluency and print knowledge. The strategy involves pointing to the words as they are read, in order to make the connection between the words printed in front of the reader and the audible words. The idea is that pupils get to hear what fluent readers should sound like and this in turn develops their reading fluency. This begins with the teacher modelling the reading for pupils and then the pupils read afterwards, prior to reading independently. The strategy acts as a scaffold and the finger pointing helps pupils to explicitly see every single word (https:// strategiesforspecialinterventions.weebly.com/echo-reading.html).

Reflection

Metacognition is also beneficial for assimilation of 'new ways of thinking' (Gamble, 2013: 63). Gamble suggests that the key to this is providing pupils with opportunities to reflect upon reading tasks. During the reflective process, educators can make pupils explicitly aware of the strategies they use in order to 'accommodate new ways of thinking'.

Writing

Writing is an area where disadvantaged pupils seem to get even further behind than their peers. There are many reasons for this and in this section we will focus on the metacognitive strategies of writing only.

Metacognition is described by Tarrant and Holt (2016) as thinking about how we learn and how we think. In the classroom, metacognitive knowledge is concerned with how well pupils know themselves as learners and their understanding about how they learn.

Explicit teaching of the hidden thinking processes behind meta-cognitive thinking strategies and regulation can be very powerful when it comes to writing.

Tarrant and Holt (2016) describe the first step in this process as being able to talk about metacognition and verbalise how we learn. Development of critical thinking is paramount. Pupils need to be able to articulate their thinking to engage in critical discussion. The basis of initiating metacognitive responses is the development of verbal language.

Voicing of thought language and learning directly through dialogue is something that needs to be taught explicitly. There are many benefits of metacognition to pupils and teachers alike. Developing an understanding of learning and applying that learning leads to breaking down of barriers and improved self-esteem.

Although pupils can make 'an average seven months' additional progress according to the' EEF Metacognition and self-regulation Toolkit (2018), due to its invisibility it becomes a challenge to implement.

> Anything based entirely within a classroom relies upon a teacher buying into the concept, using it correctly, and if necessary demonstrating the difference it makes to their students. This can inherently be a tough sell to teachers, especially those who for a number of reasons may be entrenched in their pedagogical belief. (Lockyer, 2015: 44)

An article entitled 'Metacognitive strategies' (2015) states that explicit teacher modelling is great for maths instruction. However, this is also beneficial for developing thinking skills required for writing. This article agrees with thinking aloud strategies being used for the development of metacognition. They state that thinking aloud strategies 'help students to consciously monitor and reflect upon what they are learning'. This is most effective when teachers periodically stop whilst teaching to verbalise their thoughts, especially when reading aloud. This enables pupils to sequence their own thinking processes and helps them to 'create their own strategies' as a basis to develop understanding in comprehension.

In this article 2015, checklists and success criteria are suggested as great resources for solving word problems. Success criteria can, however, be used for all lessons from processes to more creative subjects such as art and writing. Some may argue that teachers should give free reign to pupils when teaching such creative subjects. However, pupils need to be taught the basic skills and components before being able to fully utilise the freedom to experiment.

The closest analogy to writing is that it is like baking a cake. If we were not aware of the ingredients needed for a particular cake, it would probably go horribly wrong. However, if we know the basic ingredients required and the skills used to combine the ingredients together successfully, we can then start changing some of the ingredients and experimenting to create more delicious cakes.

Children's Cognitive Development and Learning by Usha Goswami (2015) is a comprehensive piece of research which takes us on a cognitive learning journey through children's development. The thorough research highlights the fact that speaking and spoken language is the basis for the development of metacognition. Dialogical learning is probably the only way we can construct meaning but this has to be carefully planned and engineered.

The thinking out loud process written above explicitly models the use of writing targets and success criteria, as pupils are shown clearly where and how to spot improvements made. This is a visual way of displaying the hidden processes of writing and creates the awareness required for metacognition to develop in writing. In addition to this, the use of dialogical learning in combination with metacognitive strategies can be a powerful combination to enable all pupils to make for rapid progress. Dialogical teaching and learning is defined by the University of Cambridge as being based on the following principles:

1. Knowledge isn't fixed – it means different things to different people in different times and places.
2. The dialogue between these different perspectives leads to new understandings and new knowledge.
3. Teachers and students can become more fully engaged in learning in an environment where these differences are respected and rigorously explored.
4. Such exploration, where meanings are constructed from the inside by learners in dialogue, rather than imposed from the outside, leads to powerful learning.
5. Learning through dialogue leads not only to content knowledge but improved thinking skills.

Opportunities for constructive dialogic learning must be created in the classroom. Stephen Lockyer backs up this argument in his book *Thinking About Thinking* where he says: 'Put simply, effective cognition can impact students by almost another nine months in one school year. More importantly, a lot of metacognitive strategies don't show up in end-of-year results, but their effect is instead seen in sustained results in the following years. This is the definition of intervention – giving a sustainable impact rather than a quick fix' (Lockyer, 2015). See more on dialogical teaching in Chapter 12.

Metacognitive writing strategies

Using writing targets and explicit success criteria

Using a combination of writing targets and explicit success criteria can have a positive impact on pupil progress in writing. The writing target and success criteria should be visible at all times whilst writing. Asking pupils to underline the writing target helps them keep track of it and they can revisit it when they require reminding. It enables pupils to see where they have used elements of the success criteria and this promotes a feeling of success, which further motivates them to challenge themselves and drives their learning forward. This is extremely powerful in combination with teacher modelling of writing, verbalising the thought-processes out loud.

For example, when writing a story with a setting description, we would have already read a selection of texts which start with setting descriptions and analysed the use of vocabulary, sentence structures, imagery, atmosphere and impact created by the authors. We would also be ready with our plans. It is beneficial for the teacher to read out loud the learning objectives and success criteria with the class and recap each skill and the purpose to prompt pupil thinking skills. Modelling checking pupil's individual targets and writing them into the success criteria means it is on display throughout the writing process. As the writing is modelled by the teacher, physically ticking off success criteria is a way of modelling the thinking process to keep track of writing.

Teacher modelling and thinking aloud

Teacher modelling and thinking aloud is a great strategy for any topic, in order to develop metacognitive thought processes. The case study below shows an example of developing metacognitive thinking and strategies through writing.

Case study: Transcript of modelling writing aloud

Background to the writing lesson

A sequence of lessons had been taught where the outcome of the writing had been explained. The children would be writing a report to demonstrate their understanding that adaptation may lead to evolution.

In previous science lessons children had learned key scientific terms such as adaptation, environment and evolution. In history lessons, in the previous term, they learnt about the Industrial Revolution. Knowledge about the Industrial Revolution was retrieved and further notes were added onto the flipchart from the previous term.

Children had also studied images of the peppered moth and dark coloured moths resting on light and dark trees, followed by teaching about lichen growing on trees and what happened to the lichen during the Industrial Revolution.

The class had studied a book called *Moth* by Isabel Thomas and how the Industrial Revolution may have caused adaptation in the peppered moth.

After studying the story, children then read non-fictional texts on moths, collecting keywords and phrases and made notes. They also studied moths outside and drew diagrams and labelled them.

After that they planned their writing and practised writing sentences with the keywords and phrases collected.

Modelling of writing lesson

After modelling and getting children to practise sentences, the teacher began to model writing the first paragraph, from a plan that had been written by one of the pupils. As well as containing bullet points about what the pupil wanted to write, the plan also contained keywords, phrases and sentence openers. This was displayed along with the learning objective and the success criteria.

The teacher starts modelling:

(Continued)

Where do I get the information from? I know, I will look at my plan. My first paragraph is about what happened during the 1880s, when it took place, what it was called and what happened but I need to keep it general at the moment and I can be more specific later on. I will start off by writing: 'A change happened in Britain'.

The teacher re-reads the sentence and says:

Actually I do not like that sentence. I am wondering how I can improve it ... I know, I will change the beginning of the sentence and include the modifier 'greatest' to make my writing more exciting and draw the reader in. Let me rewrite my sentence ...

The teacher rewrites the sentence and starts verbalising as she writes it:

'One of the greatest changes happened in Britain', I know, I will add in the the phrase 'during the 1800s'. I will read it out again to see if it makes sense: 'One of the greatest changes happened in Britain during the 1800s'. I like that sentence now that I have added a modifier.

My next sentence will be about what this greatest change was called, so I am going to write:

'It was called industrial revoltion'. Does it make sense?

The teacher re-reads the sentence and discovers that it does not make sense.

Oh dear, it does not make sense. I forgot to write the determiner in! Let's re-read it again.

She rewrites the sentence.

Let me read it again and see if it makes sense. 'It was called the industrial revoltion'. Yes, that makes perfect sense!

At this point, unable to contain himself, one of the children shouts out:

> Miss, miss you have made a spelling mistake! Oh dear! What mistake have I made?

She re-reads the sentence and pauses at the word 'industrial' and sounds out the syllables.

> In-dus-tri-al. That is correct.

She then pauses to read the next word.

> Re-vol-tion! Oh dear, that does not say revolution. Right let me say it out loudly again, re-vo-lu-tion. Got it right this time!

The teacher then proceeds to check on capital letters.

> The next thing to check is to see if I have capital letters in the correct places. What do we know about capital letters? We know that the names of places and proper nouns have capital letters. Is the Industrial Revolution a proper noun or a common noun? Common nouns are table, apple, chair etc. ... I know that the Industrial Revolution is a proper noun, so I will change the small letters to capital letters.

The teacher proceeds to change the letters. She moves on to model the next two sentences.

> I have written: 'One of the greatest changes in Britain happened during the 1800s. It was called the Industrial Revolution'.

The teacher pauses here for a moment to check to see if she has met part of the success criteria.

> Have I met the success criteria yet? Let's see. I can see that I can tick off 'I can use technical vocabulary' because I have used the word 'Britain' and the words 'Industrial Revolution'.

> Now I do not like the first sentence! How can I improve it? I know I will change the word 'happened' to the word 'occurred'. Let's see

(Continued)

how that sounds. 'One of the greatest changes in Britain occurred during the 1800s. It was called the Industrial Revolution'.

Oooh! I like that now! My next sentence is going to be about what happened overall during that time.

According to my plan, I can see that I have notes on it being 'a time of human growth and exciting discoveries', so I will now write this into a sentence.

The teacher starts writing and reading aloud.

'It was a time of human growth and exciting discoveries were made'. Hmmm, it doesn't sound right. What could I do to improve it? I know, I will extend it to add more detail.

She re-reads it again.

'It was a time of human growth and exciting discoveries were made'. I am going to cross out the full stop and extend the sentence.

The teacher reads it again, this time adding extra detail.

'It was a time of human growth and exciting discoveries were made, which have changed our lives forever'. Oooh, I really like that now. Let's read what we have written so far.

'One of the greatest changes in Britain occurred during the 1800s. It was called the Industrial Revolution. It was a time of human growth and exciting discoveries were made, which have changed our lives forever'.

- Which parts of the modelling incorporate explicit teaching of metacognition?
- How does modelling ticking off the success criteria help with meta-cognitive processes?
- Which metacognitive strategies are being developed through the writing process?

Summary

- Reading comprehension can be developed even before decoding is learned.
- When reading, prior knowledge of the text can be activated by predicting what is going to happen and by making connections to the text.
- Reading comprehension can be affected by background knowledge, vocabulary, fluency, active reading skills and critical thinking.
- Linking non-fiction, fiction and picture books can be very powerful at developing contextual knowledge and can provide the scaffold, particularly for disadvantaged pupils.
- Setting goals in both reading and writing can be beneficial for all, but particularly for less experienced readers and writers.
- Modelling the thinking processes of both reading and writing are important metacognitive strategies.

Think!

- In your class, who are the pupils who can naturally keep track of their reading?
- Which pupils find it challenging to track their reading?
- Which metacognitive strategies could pupils be taught to help them with this?
- Why is thinking aloud important in both reading and writing?
- Why is modelling and making mistakes in writing, as a teacher, an important part of a lesson?

Teacher metacognition

- When planning a unit of study, which metacognitive strategies do you need to include?

- Are there some metacognitive strategies which need developing first in order for the lesson or unit of study to be a success?
- Which metacognitive strategies need to be taught explicitly?
- How can you ensure that you include a range of strategies in a unit of study?

Pupil metacognition

- What will pupils find challenging about this unit of work or lesson?
- What gaps do they have in their subject knowledge?
- What gaps do they have in their metacognitive knowledge?
- Which scaffolds will they need to fill the thinking gaps?

References

Agarwal, P.K., Roediger, H.L., McDaniel, M.A. and McDermott, K.B. (2020) *How to Use Retrieval Practice to Improve Learning* [online]. Available at: http://pdf.retrievalpractice.org/RetrievalPracticeGuide.pdf (accessed 5 February 2021).

Block, C.C. and Pressley, M. (Eds.) (2002) Comprehension Instruction: Research-based Best Practices. New York: Guilford Press.

EEF (2017a) *Improving Literacy in Key Stage 1: Guidance Report* [online]. Available at: https://educationendowmentfoundation.org.uk/public/files/Publications/Literacy/KS1_Literacy_Guidance_2017.pdf (accessed 3 February 2021).

EEF (2017b) *Improving Literacy in Key Stage 2: Guidance Report* [online]. Available at: https://educationendowmentfoundation.org.uk/public/files/Publications/Literacy/KS2_Literacy_Guidance_2017.pdf (accessed 16 March 2021).

EEF Metacognition and Self-regulation Toolkit (2018) *Teaching and Learning Toolkit*. Available at: educationendowmentfoundation.org.uk

Flavell, J. (1979) Metacognition and cognitive monitoring: A new area of cognitive-developmental inquiry. *American Psychologist, 34*: 906–911.

Gamble, N. (2013) *Exploring Children's Literature* (3rd edn). London: Sage.

Goswami, U. (2015) *Children's Cognitive Development and Learning*. York: Cambridge Primary Review Trust.

Littleton, K. and Mercer, N. (2013) *Interthinking: Putting Talk to Work*. London: Routledge.

Lockyer, S. (2015) *Thinking About Thinking*. CreateSpace Independent Publishing Platform.

Metacognitive strategies Inclusiveschools.org (2015). *Metacognitive Strategies* [online]. Available at: https://inclusiveschools.org/metacognitive-strategies (accessed 30 May 2020).

Moir, T., Boyle, J. and Woolfson, L.M. (2020) Developing higher-order reading skills in mainstream primary schools: A metacognitive and self-regulatory approach. *British Educational Research Journal, 46* (2): 399–420. https://doi.org/10.1002/berj.3584

Mughal, A. (2020) What is the best way to plan retrieval practice in primary schools given the range of different subjects and developmental ability? [online]. Available at: www.positiveproof.co.uk/articles.php?page=4 (accessed 3 February 2021).

National Literacy Trust (2020) Reading to children is so powerful, so simple and yet so misunderstood [online]. Available at: https://literacytrust.org.uk/blog/reading-children-so-powerful-so-simple-and-yet-so-misunderstood/ (accessed 16 March 2021).

Pressley, M. (2002) Metacognition and self-regulated comprehension. In A.E. Farstrup and S.J. Samuel (eds), *What Research Has to Say About Reading Instruction* (3rd edn). Newark: International Reading Association, pp. 291–309.

Raphael, T. (1982) Improving question-answering performance through instruction. Reading Education Report No. 32. University of Illinois at Urbana-Champaign: Center for the Study of Reading.

Raphael, T. (1984) Teaching learners about sources of information for answering comprehension questions. *Journal of Reading, 27* (4): 303–311.

Raphael, T. (1986) Teaching question answer relationships, revisited. *The Reading Teacher, 39* (6): 516–522.

Raphael, T. and Au, K. (2005) QAR: Enhancing comprehension and test taking across grades and content areas. *The Reading Teacher, 59* (3): 206–221. https://doi.org/10.1598/RT.59.3.1

Roche, M. (2015) Developing Children's Critical Thinking through Picturebooks: A Guide for Primary and Early Years Students and Teachers. Abingdon: Routledge.

Soalt, J. (2005) Bringing together fictional and informational texts to improve comprehension. *The Reading Teacher, 58*: 680–683. https://doi.org/10.1598/RT.58.7.8

Tarrant, P. and Holt, D. (2016) Metacognition in the Primary Classroom: A Practical Guide to Helping Children Understand How They Learn Best. Abingdon: Routledge.

Teng, M.F. (2020) The benefits of metacognitive reading strategy awareness instruction for young learners of English as a second language. *Literacy, 54*: 29–39. https://doi.org/10.1111/lit.12181

Tennent, W. (2015) Understanding Reading Comprehension Processes and Practices. London: SAGE.

Tennent, W., Reedy, D., Hobsbaum, A. and Gamble, N. (2016) *Guided Reading – Layers of Meaning*. London: UCL IOE Press.

Wilson, N.S. and Smetana, L. (2011) Questioning as thinking: A metacognitive framework to improve comprehension of expository text. *Literacy, 45*: 84–90. https://doi.org/10.1111/j.1741-4369.2011.00584.x

METACOGNITIVE STRATEGIES IN MATHS

Contents

In this chapter we will explore

- the problem with maths
- barriers to mathematical learning
- how children learn maths
- alleviating anxieties and building confidence in maths
- metacognitive strategies in maths.

The problem with maths

Maths is like marmite; you either love it or hate it. However, when it comes to emotions there is no binary but a complex mass of feelings which can sometimes overwhelm people particularly when it comes to learning maths. This phenomenon of mathematical fear can become overwhelming and destructive to mathematical learning.

There seems to be more of a correlation between emotional status and learning in maths learning compared to reading. In reading, for example, pupils who lack confidence may not be engaged in reading whereas if pupils lack confidence in maths, this appears to have a deeper emotional response than simply not engaging.

There is evidence to suggest that maths is very closely related to confidence and belief. Classroom practitioners encounter lack of confidence in their classrooms every day.

According to a research by National Numeracy (n.d.), one of the issues with maths is having a 'negative attitude' as opposed to lacking in ability.

The barriers about beliefs in maths tend to be more challenging to break through than in other subjects. There tends to be the belief that achieving a poor grade in maths equates to being 'bad at maths', and it is a belief that seems to be 'easily accepted' (Boaler, 2016). According to Bell (2018), learning maths seems to be reserved for the educationally elite, that is to say that it is for the intellectually gifted and not for the whole of society. Boaler (2016) agrees with this. Alarmingly, in the UK not being able to 'do maths' is often worn as a badge of honour. National Numeracy (www.nationalnumeracy.org) expand on this to say that although we do not refer to any other life skills in this way, it is perfectly satisfactory to have a fixed mindset towards maths. Being a geek is usually associated with maths, with negative connotations. Negative mindset can lead to the further development of anxieties. However, good maths skills are required in all walks of life and not just in school. It may even be the best protection against unemployment, low wages and poor health (Schleicher, n.d.).

Bell (2018) suggests that 'maths anxiety' is something which needs to be included in initial teacher training programmes and that there needs to be a nationwide emphasis on developing confidence in maths. The EEF also recognise the notion of maths anxiety. They describe it as being 'a type of anxiety that specifically interferes with mathematics, and is not the same as general anxiety' (EEF, 2017: 23).

Maths anxiety can have a huge negative impact 'on pupils' learning by overloading their working memory or causing them to avoid mathematics' (EEF, 2017: 23). Although maths anxiety usually increases the older you get, the first signs tend to appear in children in Key Stage 1.

Pupils will avoid circumstances where they have to use mathematical knowledge and skills (National Numeracy, n.d.). Many adults feel bewildered and do not know where to turn to for support as well as believing that it is probably too late to learn. In addition to this, there is far more importance attached to developing literacy skills and these are favoured compared to numeracy skills. The truth of the matter is both literacy and maths are important life skills and should be given equal weighting, although building confidence in maths may require more effort and time.

The EEF math guidance for Key Stage 2 and Key Stage 3 (2017) recommends that firstly practitioners should be aware of maths anxiety and realise that is a huge barrier for some children. Maths anxiety may manifest itself as 'freezing, sweating and fidgeting', and pupils should be supported to overcome their anxieties using teacher professional judgement.

One of the recommendations that both Bell (2018) and National Numeracy (n.d.) make is that a shift in culture is required in order to raise levels of numeracy.

In her paper called *Mindsets and Maths/Science Achievement* first published in 2008, Carol Dweck emphasises the link between mindsets and maths. There is some evidence to suggest that one of the factors impacting progress and achievement in maths and science could be dependent on pupils' mindsets. Pupils, and indeed practitioners, who believe that intellectual learning of maths and science is fixed, appear to perform badly in comparison to those 'who believe that their abilities can be developed (a growth mindset)' (Dweck, 2008: 2).

There is some research which shows that a fixed or negative mindset could be responsible for the 'underachievement of women and minorities in math and science' (Dweck, 2008: 4).

Dweck explains the reported findings of an experiment conducted by Dar-Nimrod and Heine (2006). This was an experiment to ascertain whether mindsets did impact on academic achievement of women. Before being given challenging maths activities, different explanations were given to each of two groups of female college students. In order to manipulate a fixed mindset one group was told that 'the gender difference was genetically based', whereas in order to manipulate a growth mindset the other group was told that 'the gender difference originated in the different experiences that males and females have had' (Dweck, 2008: 5). Dar-Nimrod and Heine (2006) found that the group who were given the explanation based on the different experiences of male and females (growth mindset) outperformed the other group.

Good, Aronson and Inzlicht (2007) found that mindset towards maths, particularly for female students, was an important influence on their sense of belonging in maths, their longing to continue with maths courses in the future, and how well they achieved in maths.

Although there is much negativity regarding women studying maths, women who had growth mindsets were not affected by negative stereotypical views. Regardless of such views, this did not prevent females from having a sense of belonging in maths. They also had the intention to continue with mathematical learning in the future and continued to achieve highly. Negative stereotypical views, however, did affect the women who had fixed mindset about maths and this affected their longevity in mathematical studying with a reduced goal to take up maths and ultimately resulted in a decrease in the final scores (Good, Aronson and Inzlicht, 2007).

National numeracy (n.d.) say that a combination of bad experiences and not understanding the 'everyday relevance' of maths contribute to the further decline in confidence and that 'this continues to influence how they feel about maths throughout their adult lives'. Although the causes of a negative mindset around maths are complex and varied, the 'bad memories' resurfacing and emotions linked to the memories are likely to compound the issue.

Alleviating anxieties and building confidence in maths

In *Mindsets and Maths/Science Achievement*, Dweck (2008) details some issues associated with fixed mindsets and how a growth mindset can be facilitated:

a. mindsets can predict math/science achievement over time;
b. mindsets can contribute to math/science achievement discrepancies for women and minorities;
c. interventions that change mindsets can boost achievement and reduce achievement discrepancies; and
d. educators play a key role in shaping students' mindsets. (Dweck, 2008: 2)

The EEF guidance Improving Maths in the Early Years and KS1 (2020), explores what the foundations for learning maths are and how best to support these. It makes five recommendations:

1. Develop teachers' subject knowledge of maths and how children learn maths.
2. Commit time for children to learn mathematics and assimilate mathematics into the curriculum throughout the day.
3. Develop understanding of links between manipulatives and maths.
4. Use assessment and questioning to start teaching from what pupils already know.
5. 'Use high quality targeted support to help all children learn mathematics'. (EEF, 2020)

However, the EEF guidance on Improving Maths in Key stages Two and Three (2017) has eight recommendations as follows:

1. Use assessment to build on pupils' existing knowledge and understanding.
2. Use manipulatives and representations.
3. Teach pupils strategies for solving problems.
4. Enable pupils to develop a rich network of mathematical knowledge.
5. Develop pupils' independence and motivation.
6. Use tasks and resources to challenge and support pupils' mathematics.
7. Use structured interventions to provide additional support.
8. Support pupils to make a successful transition between primary and secondary school.

Not only are positive attitudes required for all types of learning but having a positive mindset can help in the 'development of self-regulation and metacognition'. The longevity of motivation is dependent on 'deliberate and sustained effort'. The EEF also suggests that due to the complexity of motivation and due to the fact that it may be affected by personal beliefs and whether or not it is liked and whether or not it has any purpose. 'Many pupils hold negative attitudes about mathematics, and pupils' attitudes tend to worsen as they get older' (EEF, 2017: 22).

In schools, historically, there has always been more of a focus on developing literacy skills and often more time is devoted to it within the curriculum. This can often leave very little time allocated to maths learning.

Just as there is no binary when it comes to growth and fixed mindset, your mindset appears to impact on mathematical learning. Although the EEF (2017) suggests that emotions may be linked to our learning of maths, more research needs to be carried out in this area.

The studies around how mindsets affect learning, continuing with maths learning and earning potential are fascinating, however, it is not possible to one day have a fixed mindset and the next to suddenly have a growth mindset towards maths.

Metacognitive maths strategies

It would appear that the priority for mathematical learning is to develop a more positive culture around maths and ensure that everyone understands the benefit of mathematical learning. There needs to be a significant mind shift from viewing maths as being reserved for the elite few to recognising that it should be for everyone.

There are recommendations on how to achieve this and these will be explained here.

The benefits of teaching about neuroplasticity for mathematical achievement

Dweck (2008) suggests that teaching pupils about neuroplasticity can help them overcome some of the barriers towards learning maths.

There is a commonly held perception that the brain is in a stationary position and does not change. Being gifted and talented are also seen as being personal attributes which do not change over time. When pupils are 'taught that the brain is like a muscle that gets stronger and works better the more it is exercised', they are able to imagine this actually happening and this can be 'extremely motivating' (Dweck, 2008: 9). They also realise that each time they challenge themselves and put effort into their learning, new neural connections are made and they become more intelligent. This new thinking seems to indicate that if pupils do not stretch themselves, they will not form new neural pathways, which is something they do not want to miss out on.

Although Dweck (2008) suggests using computer programmes to teach about neuroplasticity, this is not necessary. As long as practitioners include images about how neurons connect and how the brain grows, they will convey the important part of teaching this complex topic. There are many resources available to do this:

> Children's T.V. programs, educational spots, children's books, and children's computer programs and computer games can all be used to send these messages: that the brain grows new connections every time we face challenges and learn, and that great mathematicians and scientists are people who have engaged in this process more than other people. (Dweck, 2008: 12)

Dweck (2008) found that teaching growth mindset can change how pupils speak in a classroom environment, and also found that in fixed mindset schools, there tends to be perception that the focus is on testing and passing tests, however, in growth mindset schools the focus appears to be on growing your brain.

Motivation

The EEF (2017: 7) suggests that motivation in maths is crucial in developing self-confidence and self-efficacy. Pupils should be encouraged 'to take responsibility for, and play an active role in, their own learning'.

Reflection is a process which enables the development of metacognition and an understanding of the plan, monitor and evaluate cycle. Motivation goes hand in hand with this process and it is a way to help pupils become more independent.

Some points to consider would be:

- Are pupils able to recognise which strategies they already have and choose the most effective one to solve a maths problem?
- Are pupils able to monitor whether the selected strategy has been fruitful?
- Can pupils consciously change their strategy in light of recognising that it is not working?

This is quite a complex process, which initially would need to be taught explicitly and support would need to be provided. This is where modelling would be an effective strategy to use to develop pupils' thinking. Another way could be to ask pupils questions as they work through an activity (Lai, 2011).

Wittwer and Renkl (2010) suggest that worked examples could be used to teach pupils how to think clearly. As pupils become more independent and as they gain mathematical fluency, these strategies could be slowly removed.

Self-explanation is another strategy which could be used to develop metacognition and self-regulation in maths. Talking through the process of planning, monitoring and evaluating to each other and to teachers can be beneficial in developing the metacognitive process (Kramarski and Mavarech, 2003).

Adult mindsets

What pupils think about their own maths ability can be affected by the adults' maths mindsets and how they provide feedback to their pupils.

'Fewer assumptions are made about inherent ability (vs effort) as the basis of success' (Dweck, 2008: 8) in cultures where large numbers of maths and science graduates (including females) are produced, which are mainly in the Eastern and South Asian countries. Researchers found that Japanese teachers and parents placed more emphasis on effort, as cause of success, rather than ability, as is usually the case in the US. UNESCO, OECD and EUROSTAT collected data for 2004, which showed that Japan had the highest percentage of female graduates in maths and computer science out of the 30 countries studied.

Giving praise and feedback

Maths is a subject where there are right and wrong answers, and often pupils are praised for achieving the correct answers. This should not be the sole focus. The emphasis should be on the thought processes pupils employ to obtain their answers, whether or not their answers are correct.

The emphasis should be on 'process praise/feedback [which] includes feedback about strategies, effort, perseverance, challenge-seeking, improvement' (Dweck, 2008: 13), rather than on intelligence, aptitude or outcomes.

When teachers have a fixed mindset towards maths, research has indicated that only high achieving pupils make progress. In comparison to this, when teachers have a growth mindset towards maths, a larger range of pupils do well in maths. Dweck recommends that training should include growth mindset training, particularly those curricula which have guided by fixed mindsets (2008: 14). There are five other recommendations which Dweck has suggested, which should be included in teacher training sessions, as follows:

1. The most recent findings on brain plasticity and implications on pupils' ability to learn. Pupils should also be taught about neuroplasticity.
2. How pupils' long-term success can be achieved through dedication and self-improvement.
3. The fact that praising intelligence and/or outcomes do not promote pupil confidence. It is more important to shift the focus onto process praise and how it builds lasting confidence and motivation.
4. The importance for pupils at all levels to be challenged appropriately.
5. The above four suggestions could be woven into the curriculum. Teachers should be shown how to introduce new units and how to give feedback to promote the growth mindset. (Dweck, 2008: 14)

Shifting past underacheivement due to environment rather than genetics

Informing female and ethnic minority pupils that prior underachievement in maths is more to do with the environment than genetic factors seems to have an impact on mathematical achievement. Many pupils are deterred from taking up maths and sciences in higher education either because they have a fixed mindset or believe that they do not have the ability to learn and are less capable than others. More research needs to be conducted in this area, as most of the research so far has been small-scale studies (Dweck, 2008: 15).

Incorporating growth mindset into lessons prior to high stakes testing

Dweck suggests that an important message to get through to pupils is 'test assess current skills and not long-term potential to learn' (Dweck, 2008: 15). This is crucial because many pupils interpret disappointing test scores as a measure of the fixed mindset and become discouraged about future learning, potential and success. At the same time, those pupils who do well in the tests must not be given the opportunity to become complacent and assume that test scores indicate long-term achievement, success and potential.

Dweck (2008) also states that it is important for both teachers and parents to know what is being tested and to be able to convey that to pupils. Rather than drilling for tests, pupils would be better off learning about the growth mindset as a tool for motivation that leads to effective learning.

Teaching a range of maths strategies

There are two maths guidance reports created by the EEF; Improving Mathematics in Key Stages Two and Three Guidance Report 2017 and Improving Mathematics in the Early Years and Key Stage 1 Guidance Report 2020.

One of the recommendations made by the EEF (2017) suggests equipping pupils with a range of maths strategies. This will give pupils confidence, knowing that they are armed with a repertoire of strategies to draw upon even when faced with the most complex of tasks.

> If pupils lack a well-rehearsed and readily available method to solve a problem, they need to draw on problem-solving strategies to make sense of the unfamiliar situation. (EEF 2017: 6)

Other recommendations include 'demonstrating and developing the understanding of the relevance of maths in everyday life' (EEF Improving Mathematics in the Early Years and Key Stage 1 Guidance Report 2020). Giving purpose to learning helps pupils understand that mathematical skills are required throughout life.

'De-emphasising the "speed" of calculation' (EEF, 2020) is another recommended strategy. This allows pupils time to learn the strategy accurately and speed can be built upon at a later stage. It is also a way of building mathematical confidence.

Mistake-making and correcting can also be a powerful strategy to improve accuracy; it helps pupils accept 'that making mistakes is part of learning' (EEF, 2020) but this must be used with caution. Pupils who are more confident in their mathematical learning may benefit from recognising their mistakes and learning from them. However, those who are less confident will have difficulty recognising where they went wrong and how to correct their errors. They are, therefore, likely to lose confidence in their mathematical ability.

As well as 'freeing-up short-term (working) memory, encouraging a "growth mind-set" and taking responsibility in recognising one's own mind-set' (EEF, 2020) are also deemed important strategies when learning maths. One way of freeing-up working memory could be by displaying the modelling process in the classroom, where pupils are not relying on remembering how to carry out a calculation. Another way could be to give pupils a set of procedural success criteria to follow if they get stuck. When used in conjunction, these two approaches free up even more working memory and enable the development of the growth mindset.

Requiring 'pupils to monitor, reflect on, and communicate their reasoning and choice of strategy' (EEF, 2017: 15) is another recommended strategy. The EEF (2017) gives examples of encouraging pupils to question their thinking process. See Chapter 2 for examples.

The NRICH team (2011) also recommend 'Low Threshold High Ceiling' activities, as a way of developing confidence in all pupils as well as allowing all pupils to be able to access mathematical learning at their level. Low Threshold High Ceiling activities also allow 'everyone to get started and everyone to get stuck'. Using Low Threshold

High Ceiling activities is a type of pedagogy but also it is an 'approach which is grounded in a growth mindset philosophy (Dweck, 2007): everyone can do well in mathematics, regardless of their prior attainment, and making mistakes, struggling and persevering are all important' (NRICH, 2011).

Boaler (n.d.) also states that maths is 'an open, growing subject (as opposed to a closed, fixed subject); and that communicating, reasoning about, and justifying ideas are central acts in the work of mathematics'.

Giving pupils the opportunity to choose problem-solving strategies (EEF, 2017) takes the pressure off pupils and enables the building up of confidence. It also takes away the competitive element, particularly in mixed ability settings, as some pupils may not be able to use the same strategy as everyone else. Being able to use long division and short division requires pupils to know their times tables and multiples. Not all pupils know their times tables and some find it very difficult to learn them, recall and recite them out loudly. Such pupils are usually aware of their limitations and will avoid attempting any associated maths activities. The following case study illustrates how pupils can develop confidence in this area of learning, even when they are aware that they do not know their times tables.

Case study: Giving pupils the flexibility of choosing maths strategies

Laura had no confidence in maths. At the start of the academic year, as soon as maths lessons had started, Laura would make excuses to avoid learning maths. She had low self-esteem about her learning overall but her teacher realised that this was particularly so in maths. Laura was not the only pupil who felt such anxiety about maths; there were others. Division is a particularly cognitively challenging topic in maths. If pupils do not understand the concept of sharing, then moving on to the more abstract concept of dividing by numbers becomes very difficult. The first thing her teacher did was set up a Low Threshold High Ceiling activity. It was based on planning a birthday party and working out how many packets of sweets and chocolates would be required when planning a party for thirty people. This activity was designed to develop the concept of sharing, an understanding of what division meant and development of reasoning. This evened out the playing field for all learners and pupils realised that despite their differing levels of prior knowledge, they could all succeed.

The class thoroughly enjoyed the activity and as well as low attainers learning about the concept of division, the higher attainers were able to develop a deeper understanding of reasoning and were set challenges in which this could be developed. All pupils were given the opportunity to move on to the challenges at their own pace. In one lesson some pupils had secured the concept of sharing and had moved on to problem solving and reasoning.

After the initial lesson on sharing and dividing, over three weeks the teacher taught the class a range of division strategies such as: chunking, using factors, long division and short division, and ensured that pupils knew that they could choose the strategy that they felt most comfortable with.

Prior to the teaching on division a practice arithmetic paper was given to all pupils. Laura only managed to score 10 marks on this paper. However, after the teaching of division Laura scored 25 marks out of 40. Her confidence had grown and this was evident in the way she presented herself in class.

- How was prior knowledge activated in this lesson?
- Why was the sequence of lessons important to pupil's success of mathematical learning?
- How did the teacher make her pupils feel successful at mathematical learning?

Activating prior knowledge through embedded retrieval practice

The main purpose of retrieval practice is to consolidate learning by the process of recalling previously learnt knowledge. In classrooms there are two main types of retrieval practice in use: isolated and embedded. Isolated retrieval practice is where specific knowledge and/or skills are retrieved through tests, quizzes and questioning. Embedded retrieval practice is where knowledge and/or skills are retrieved through a different activity such as reading or problem solving. Recalling knowledge and/or skills from one subject domain to another, thereby forming links, is also a type of embedded retrieval (Mughal, 2020).

Coe (2020) states that, although retrieval practice is extremely useful, it is something that needs to be planned carefully, in order for it to be highly effective. Tests and quizzes no doubt help learners to 'actively search their mind or look up the answer' (Mughal, 2020). We are aware that re-reading notes or making notes are less effective at developing memory than retrieval practice. However, Coe (2020) throws caution to the wind. He brings up questions about which types of learning are best supported by retrieval (Coe, 2020). There seems to be a heavy reliance on using retrieval practice to elicit simple facts and endless lists of vocabulary (Dunlosky, Rawson, Marsh, Nathan and Willingham, 2013). Van Gog and Sweller (2015) argue that as learning becomes more complex, retrieval practice becomes less effective.

Although Rohrer et al. (2019) suggest that retrieval practice has no other benefit in maths than to elicit facts, retrieval practice could be used to embed such facts into long-term memory and develop critical thinking. Activating prior knowledge through problem solving may be worthwhile, it is still a way to practise isolated retrieval. 'Retrieval practice remains an effective way to improve meaningful learning of complex materials' (Karpicke and Aue, 2015).

One way of activating prior knowledge in order to embed knowledge would be through reasoning in maths. This would not only be a way to improve memory but also to develop higher order thinking skills where 'pupils were to use their knowledge in new situations, thereby improving their understanding of the learning material' (Mughal, 2020).

Summary

- Breaking down barriers to mathematical learning is crucial to improving outcomes.
- Giving pupils a range of maths strategies is important.
- There are different types of retrieval practice, which can be used to improve outcomes.
- The use of retrieval practice in the curriculum must be considered carefully and can depend on what it is that requires retrieving.

- Teaching both teachers and pupils about neuroplasticity is important.
- Praise to develop motivation and confidence.
- Developing a growth mindset in maths is crucial.
- Appropriate challenge for pupils at all levels is crucial.
- Females and minorities should be taught that the environment plays a huge part in mathematical underachievement.
- Convey to teachers, parents and pupils that tests assess current skills and not the potential to learn.
- Developing confidence in maths helps improve outcomes.

Think!

- How can the teaching of neuroplasticity contribute to mathematical learning?
- How can mistake-making be used in the classroom?
- How would you create an environment where making mistakes is recognised as part of learning?
- How can a growth mindset be developed in maths?
- How can confidence be developed in maths?
- How can both confidence and challenge be balanced in mathematical learning?

Teacher metacognition

- Were you good at maths at school?
- If not, how did you overcome any feelings of anxiety?
- How do you feel when teaching maths?
- Who are the pupils who struggle with maths in your class?
- What are their main barriers?
- How do the barriers manifest themselves?
- What could you do to help and support the pupils who lack confidence in maths?
- How could you show the pupils who struggle with maths that most people struggle with maths and that this is part of learning?
- How could you build confidence in mathematical learning?

Pupil metacognition

- How do your pupils feel about learning maths?
- How do they feel when you make mistakes?
- How could they overcome barriers to learning maths?
- How could their confidence be built up in mathematical learning?

References

Bell, D. (2018) Maths Anxiety Summit. Summit Report and Key Messages. *Maths Anxiety Trust*. Senate House UCL University of London, Learnus UK.

Boaler, J. (2016) Mathematical Mindsets: Unleashing Students' Potential through Creative Math, Inspiring Messages and Innovative Teaching. San Francisco, CA: Jossey-Bass.

Boaler, J. (n.d.) Our teaching approach [online]. Available at: www.youcubed.org/evidence/our-teaching-approach/ (accessed 4 February 2021).

Coe, R. (2020) Does research on retrieval practice translate into classroom practice? *Impact: Journal of the Chartered College of Teaching* [online]. Available at: https://impact.chartered.college/article/does-research-retrieval-practice-translate-classroom-practice/ (accessed 16 March 2021).

DfE (Department for Education) (2016) Trends in Maths and Science Study (TIMSS): National Report for England. https://dera.ioe.ac.uk/28040/1/TIMSS_2015_England_Report_FINAL_for_govuk_-_reformatted.pdf

Dunlosky, J., Rawson, K.A., Marsh, E.J., Nathan, M.J. and Willingham, D.T. (2013) Improving students' learning with effective learning techniques: Promising directions from cognitive and educational psychology. *Psychological Science in the Public Interest*, 14 (1): 4–58.

Dweck, C. (2007) Boosting achievement with messages that motivate. *Education Canada*, 47 (2): 6–10.

Dweck, C. (2008) *Mindsets and Math/Science Achievement*. Available at: www.growthmindsetmaths.com/uploads/2/3/7/7/23776169/mindset_and_math_science_achievement_-_nov_2013.pdf (accessed 16 March 2021).

EEF (2017) *Improving Mathematics in Key Stages Two and Three: Guidance Report* [online]. Available at: https://educationendowment-foundation.org.uk/tools/guidance-reports/maths-ks-2-3/ (accessed 4 February 2021).

EEF (2020) *Improving Mathematics in the Early Years and Key Stage 1: Guidance Report* [online]. Available at: https://educationendowment foundation.org.uk/public/files/Publications/Maths/EEF_Maths_EY_KS1_Guidance_Report.pdf

Good, C., Aronson, J. and Inzlicht, M. (2003) Improving adolescents' standardized test performance: An intervention to reduce the effects of stereotype threat. *Journal of Applied Developmental Psychology*, 24: 645–662.

Karpicke, J.D. and Aue, W.R. (2015) The testing effect is alive and well with complex materials. *Educational Psychology Review*, 27 (2): 317–326. www.jstor.org/stable/43548477

Kramarski, B. and Mevarech, Z.R. (2003) Enhancing Mathematical Reasoning in the Classroom: The Effects of Cooperative Learning and Metacognitive Training Bar-Ilan University. *American Educational Research Journal*, 40 (1): 281–310.

Lai, E.R. (2011) *Metacognition: A Literature Review*. Pearson Research Report [online]. Available at: https://images.pearsonassessments.com/images/tmrs/Metacognition_Literature_Review_Final.pdf (accessed 16 March 2021).

Mughal, A. (2020) What is the best way to plan retrieval practice in primary schools given the range of different subjects and developmental ability? [online]. Available at: www.positiveproof.co.uk/articles.php?page=4 (accessed 4 February 2021).

National Numeracy (n.d.) *Attitudes Towards Maths: Research & Approach Overview* [online]. Available at: www.nationalnumeracy.org.uk/sites/default/files/documents/attitudes_towards_maths/attitudes_towards_maths_-_updated_branding.pdf (accessed 16 March 2021).

NRICH (2011) Creating a low threshold high ceiling classroom [online]. Available at: https://nrich.maths.org/7701 (accessed 4 February 2021).

Rohrer, D., Dedrick, R.F., Hartwig, M.K. and Cheung, C. (2019) A Randomized Controlled Trial of Interleaved Mathematics Online First Publication. *Journal of Educational Psychology*. http://dx.doi.org/10.1037/edu0000367

Schleicher, A. (n.d.) Why is numeracy important? [online]. Available at: www.nationalnumeracy.org.uk/about/what-numeracy/why-numeracy-important (accessed 16 March 2021).

Van Gog, T. and Sweller, J. (2015) Not new, but nearly forgotten: The testing effect decreases or even disappears as the complexity of learning materials increases. *Educational Psychology Review*, 27 (2): 247–264.

Wittwer, J. and Renkl, A. (2010) How effective are instructional explanations in example-based learning? A meta-analytic review. *Educational Psychology Review*, 22 (4): 393–409.

10

METACOGNITIVE STRATEGIES ACROSS THE CURRICULUM

Contents

> ## In this chapter we will explore
>
> - what makes science, art, design and technology, drama, PE, technology subjects more prone to being naturally metacognitive in nature
> - the difficulties associated with transferring metacognitive skills into English and mathematics
> - what metacognition looks like in science, art, design and technology, drama, PE, technology.

Metacognition in non-academic subjects

Educators are all too aware that metacognition is most effective when taught within subjects and not as a bolt on. Another equally important aspect of metacognition is the fact that some subjects lend themselves well to being metacognitive in their very nature than others. One of the reasons why metacognitive strategies may be easier to teach in subjects such as science, design and technology (DT), drama, art and PE is that they are very creative subjects.

According to Xiaoyu, Weijan and Liren (2019), 'Metacognition refers to the knowledge and regulation of one's own cognitive processes, which has been regarded as a critical component of creative thinking'. However, there is controversy around the role of metacognition in developing critical thinking:

> the current literature on the association between metacognition and creative thinking remains controversial, and the underlying role of metacognition in the creative process appears to be insufficiently explored and explained. (Xiaoyu, Weijan and Liren, 2019)

When metacognitive knowledge is used to 'correct cognitive strategies' (Xiaoyu, Weijan and Liren, 2019), these appear to be important for creative thinking. Some studies have shown that domain-specific creativity can be attributed to metacognitive knowledge (Lizarraga and Baquedano, 2013). According to Lizarraga and Baquedano (2013) there was some 'correlation between metacognitive knowledge and visual-spatial creativity (e.g. drawing and titling four drawings from provided lines)' (cited in Xiaoyu, Weijan and Liren, 2019). Similarly, Erbas and Bas (2015) reported that mathematical creativity was developed through metacognitive knowledge. This would suggest that fluency in mathematical skills could play a crucial role in developing reasoning.

Another important finding was from Fayenatawil, Kozbelt and Sitaras (2011), who studied artists and non-artists whilst they drew 'original drawings' and discovered that the 'artists who possess much more metacognitive knowledge of plans, goals, and descriptions performed better than non-artists in an artistic creation task'.

Some studies have discovered that when metacognitive knowledge is taught, it does lead to 'creative problem solving' (Xiaoyu, Weijan and Liren, 2019). Abdivarmazan, Taghizade, Mahmoudfakhe and Tosan (2014) conducted an experiment to test this with a control group and an experimental group. The experimental group received explicit teaching of metacognitive strategies consisting of a total of eight sessions comprising of fifty minutes, whereas the control group did not receive any teaching of metacognitive strategies. They found that explicit teaching of metacognitive strategies 'can significantly improve creative problem solving'. Prior to these findings, Hargrove (2013) also discovered similar findings.

However, according to Xiaoyu, Weijan and Liren (2019), Preiss, Cosmelli, Grau and Ortiz (2016) did not find a correlation between teaching metacognitive strategies and the development of creativity.

Although there is contradictory evidence on whether the explicit teaching of metacognition leads to creative thinking, according to Xiaoyu, Weijan and Liren (2019) this may depend on fluency of cognitive skills. It appears that a variety of cognitive tasks are influenced by how fluent one may be in the subject (Koriat, Bjork, Sheffer and Bar, 2004), including reading comprehension (Alter, Oppenheimer, Epley and Eyre, 2007; Miele and Molden, 2010). There are other cognitive factors which could contribute to the development of creative thinking (Gilhooly, Fioratou, Anthony and Wynn, 2007). These include: goal setting (Storbeck and Clore, 2007), effort put into the task (Miele and Molden, 2010), and having a choice of strategies to choose from (Lucas and Nordgren, 2015).

Does the metacognitive experience reflected by processing fluency promote or prevent creative thinking? According to Xiaoyu, Weijan and Liren (2019), this is controversial due to a number of reasons.

Firstly, there are 'different types of creative thinking, such as divergent and convergent thinking'. How these types of thinking relate to the development of fluency is relatively unknown.

According to Xiaoyu, Weijan and Liren (2019), Benedek, Bergner, Könen, Fink and Neubauer (2011) found that 'different types of creative thinking have significant differences in processing mechanisms'.

One type of creative thinking is divergent thinking skills. Some divergent thinking activities rely on analytical thinking processes (Unsworth, Spillers, Brewer and Mcmillan, 2011). However, too much analytical thinking can halter creative thinking, as 'convergent thinking tasks', which are required for problem solving 'and the search for remote connections to memory' (Metcalfe and Wiebe, 1987), could be prevented.

Xiaoya, Weijan and Liren (2019) suggest that consideration, therefore, must be given to the different 'roles of processing fluency', in both 'divergent and convergent thinking'.

Whether or not metacognition leads to creative thinking, with the spotlight on developing metacognition in more academic subjects, such as English and maths, in recent years, it may be useful to draw upon strategies used in more creative areas of the curriculum to enable our understanding about what it could look like across the curriculum.

Metacognition in science

According to Sanium and Buaraphan (2019) metacognition is difficult to understand due to it being a wholly 'abstract process ... in one's mind'. For this reason, a number of studies have been carried out in Thailand to understand the benefits of metacognition in the context of science. The researchers found that twenty-two studies had been carried out in primary and secondary schools and the areas of study included: 'impact of metacognition on other research variables; teaching strategies to enhance metacognition; developing measurement tool for metacognition; impact of metacognition and teaching strategies enhancing metacognition and the impact of students' developed metacognition on problem-solving skill'.

The findings in each area were very interesting. In category 1, which was the impact of metacognition on other research variables, the study focused on the 'relationship between metacognition and critical thinking' (Sanium and Buaraphan, 2019: 3). This was carried out by conducting a critical thinking test and a questionnaire on metacognition. Overall, there was a significant and positive correlation between some subcategories of metacognition and critical thinking skills. However, some subcategories of metacognition had a negative effect but according to the report the reasons for these negative findings are unclear.

The category for 'effect of a metacognition training with attribution training to effort on problem-solving skills' was split into three groups (Sanium and Buaraphan, 2019: 4). There were two experimental groups, with the first group receiving explicit teaching of metacognition and a focus on effort, the second group receiving only explicit teaching of metacognition, while the third group was the control group. The results were as predicted with both experimental groups showing significant scores compared to the control group, who 'received lower problem-solving skill scores' (Sanium and Buaraphan, 2019: 4). It is unclear whether or not the group who had received training on attribution to effort scored the highest.

The research on 'students' scientific problem-solving ability, metacognition development and scholastic achievement in work and energy topic by using metacognitive strategies' (Sanium and Buaraphan, 2019: 4) was also interesting. The results showed that teaching metacognitive strategies had a positive impact on pupil achievement as it enabled pupils to improve their scientific problem-solving ability. There were also significant positive findings in the areas of decision-making, and cooperative learning combined with metacognitive thinking.

Although there were only three studies at primary school level, with the other nineteen studies on secondary school pupils, some of the findings could be beneficial to primary school pupils.

Sanium and Buaraphan (2019) state that of Piaget's 'four stages of cognitive development' – sensorimotor, pre-operational, concrete and formal – in Thailand, pupils at primary are at Piaget's concrete operational stage of development. One of the reasons could be due to limited cognitive development in pupils aged between seven and twelve, in this particular study. This is explained as a reason why most of the metacognition research was conducted at secondary level. In the UK, however, due to a more formal curriculum, the formal stage is reached at primary school level. In addition to this, the EEF guidance

(2018) signposts research which shows that metacognitive thinking can be developed in very young children.

Overall, research in the area of impact of metacognition on other research variables shows that when metacognition is developed in pupils, this can have a positive impact not only on achievement but also on problem solving, critical thinking skills, decision-making and awareness.

What are some of the metacognitive strategies that could be applied to primary school pupils?

Strategies in science

According to InnerDrive (n.d.), a number of metacognitive strategies could be taught within science. These include: the plan, monitor and evaluate cycle, building up diagrams gradually, modelling answers and discussion, concept mapping, creating metacognitive conflict, retrieval practice and making predictions.

Plan, monitor, evaluate

First of all, time must be scheduled in plan, monitor and evaluate. When planning a fair test to assess a question or query in science, pupils are required to use the plan, monitor and evaluate cycle. Dye and Stanton (2017) found that when presented with a self-regulation structure to use, pupils performed better in their learning, using questions such as: 'what is the outcome?' and 'have I carried a similar task before?' Usually, in primary schools, pupils are given structures which enable them to plan their investigations. Such structures or scaffolds also have predictions and evaluations built into them. These scaffolds really prompt pupils to think about improvements they would make if they were to carry out a similar experiment. This strategy could be applied to other domains of scientific teaching.

This would suggest that pupils need training in how to provide feedback. In addition to this, time needs to be dedicated for evaluating, when lesson planning, and consideration should be given to redoing projects or redrafting pieces of work.

Building up diagrams gradually

In *Making Every Science Lesson Count*, Allison (2017) suggests building up scientific diagrams in stages and not revealing the whole diagram at the same time. Developing diagrams gradually not only improves 'conceptual understanding', through teacher modelling and explaining the 'different layers and functions' as they draw, but also deepens pupils' understanding of complex scientific vocabulary (InnerDrive, n.d.).

Badger, Horroks, Turton and Lewis (2019), in their article entitled 'Using technology to promote metacognition', also state that whilst using PowerPoints showing worked examples to reduce cognitive overload (Sweller, 2006), particularly in maths and science, has been a success, it can be more valuable to gradually work through problems on the board, making mistakes and talking through the thought processes.

Modelling answers and discussing

Modelling scientific answers and discussing is another metacognitive strategy which could be used. Sanium and Buaraphan (2019: 6) found when there was an 'instructional model' provided 'with metacognitive reflection strategies', this resulted in a higher achievement score across all groups of pupils. Through evaluating what a good scientific answer would be as opposed to a less favourable answer, pupils' evaluating skills can be developed. Just as in writing, teacher thinking out aloud and modelling their thinking whilst writing a model answer will enable pupils to develop their thinking processes, when answering such questions.

Concept mapping

Not only does concept mapping allow pupils to process knowledge about a particular scientific topic but it can be used to break down knowledge into smaller, more specific areas. It can also help retrieve information about what pupils already know about a particular topic and enable them to make links between topics and other areas of learning (see Chapter 13).

Metacognitive conflict

By eliciting what pupils' scientific ideas are and then challenging them, this creates metacognitive conflict. This conflict is necessary for creativity and innovation.

Retrieval practice

Although there are a number of different types of retrieval practice, there are two main types to focus on for science. There is usually more of a focus on 'isolated retrieval practice of science terminology' (Mughal, 2020). However, embedded retrieval practice can also be used.

An example, is sorting and classifying materials. This is where pupils are recalling and using vocabulary specific to the task, deepening their understanding of the vocabulary and making links to other subject domains. (Mughal, 2020)

Making predictions

Activating prior knowledge of scientific vocabulary and concepts is usually conducted through predictions, particularly when carrying out an investigation, 'where pupils are naturally required to draw upon facts in order to be able to predict. This is embedded retrieval practice' (Mughal, 2020).

Metacognition in art and design and technology

Although metacognition in art and design and technology and how metacognition could be developed in these subjects are not well understood, some of the strategies above could be useful in developing metacognition in both subjects. Kavouski et al. (2019: 1) found:

> that metacognitive thinking plays an essential role in design idea generation and development and that it is an important part of the creative process in design. Moreover, the resulting model illustrates how components of metacognition interact and can provide insights to educators seeking to enhance the design process and its outcomes for learners.

When pupils are planning to make something, part of the decision-making process involves a degree of metacognition. Similarly, in both art and design and technology, pupils are required to constantly make decisions about their creations. This enables pupils to reflect deeply about what they are doing and why and also helps develop metacognitive thinking.

The idea behind Kavouski, Miller and Alexander's (2019: 1) study was to identify a 'rich qualitative data to construct and validate a detailed conceptual model of metacognitive processes in architectural students' design-thinking and design-making'. They describe architecture as being 'a multidimensional process'. It is a subject which requires students to analyse, reason, use their intuition and express their ideas creatively (Powers, 2017). According to Kavouski, Miller and Alexander

(2019), researchers have found that metacognition can impact on pupil performance and that there is a direct correlation between metacognition and creative thinking. Creative thinking can be improved by 'focusing on metacognition'. They also suggest that metacognitive strategies can provide an insight into the 'creative thought process and allow them to control this process'. Due to the fact that design in its nature is usually open-ended, pupil 'motivation and willingness to engage' can diminish as learning can become 'confusing and frustrating'. This is something which needs to be given careful consideration when planning such subjects. They further suggest that the research of Dunlosky and Metcalfe (2009) indicates that metacognition can help pupils conquer such issues and improve their learning potential.

Metacognition in drama and physical education

Highly creative subjects such and drama and physical education are great for developing metacognition. This may be due to their creative nature or it may be because they are subjects which require natural and constant evaluation as you work through tasks.

Drama

The use of drama can improve metacognition. Drama lends itself very well to the planning, monitoring and evaluating process. For example, when acting out a scene from a text, pupils have decisions to make from the outset, where not only is prior knowledge from the text required but also prior knowledge of each other's strengths. Where consideration is lacking in strengths, pupils need to be able to support each other in order to deliver an effective performance and in effect become the scaffold for each other. Decisions need to be made on: who the characters will be; how the words and actions will be expressed; what impact they are trying to have on the audience; where the most effective place is to deliver the performance; how they will move around the place; how they will need to work in a team to deliver their best performance. Support and scaffolding can be provided by the educator here by ensuring feedback is given in a timely manner. All these thought processes require a certain degree of reflection. During the drama session – the monitoring stage – pupils are required to constantly draw on prior knowledge, evaluate and make changes to the elements. After the drama performance, whole class reflection of performance, expression of voice, teamwork, use of physical space, and facing the audience could provide further reflective processes to take place and targets could be given for next time (Burt's Drama, 2020).

Physical education

Physical education just like drama is a subject where pupils have awareness of their progress and learning. However, in some areas, accuracy of judgement can be affected due to the fact that sometimes there is success despite having poor skills. One way of alleviating this is to give pupils the opportunity to plan physical education activities, where they can 'self-monitor their learning' (Maclean, 2013). According to Maclean (2013), an example is 'BEEF' in basketball, where B = Balance, E = Elbow, E = Eyes, F = Follow Through. In addition to this, pupils can monitor their skills by carrying out paired or groupwork. The peer support provides the monitoring required to improve skills required. Just as in drama, evaluation can be planned in whilst practising skills and afterwards can provide much needed reflection.

Metacognition in technology

Badger et al. (2019) list strategies which they have used to develop metacognition in technology. They state that with the increase in 'tablet technology' it is easier than most people think to use the 'think aloud' strategy. It is a strategy which has been successful in their classrooms.

Due to the issue of teacher commentary being lost after the lesson, as pupils try to keep up with note-taking, Badger et al. (2019) suggest using a technology called *Explain Everything* (explaineverything. com). This online whiteboard app, which is interactive, allows for the making of screencasts. These can be saved and be used before the lesson, during and afterwards for consolidation or for revision purposes.

Another strategy that has been shown to be highly effective, compared to re-reading and high-lighting, is screen casting by pupils (Dunlosky, 2013). This strategy, according to Badger et al. (2019), is used 'when students are correcting their work'. After practice exams pupils pick a maximum of three questions where errors have been made. Pupils are required to explain what the error was in their thinking.

This is similar to the Dot and Circle technique described by Still (2020), which is when a dot in the margin denotes an error on the line but pupils are not told what the error is and have to work out what the mistake is. This can be done in isolation or by talking to a peer, depending on the direction of the educator and level of need. Once found and corrected, pupils circle the dot, indicating that the correction has been done.

When explaining their errors and what they did to correct these errors, their misconceptions can be elicited. As a result, assessment can become more accurate and feedback can be tailored more effectively. As previously stated by Sanium and Buaraphan (2019), researchers in Thailand suggested that primary school pupils lacked metacognitive development due to not reaching the formal stage of cognitive development; this view seems to be echoed by Shamir, Mevarech and Gida (2009). However, one of the reasons given is that the research tools used may not be appropriate, so it is not about not reaching the required cognitive development, but rather because young pupils lack the language they require to explain their thinking. In other cases, it may be that due to the 'adult–child dynamics', some children may be more reticent about explaining their thought processes (Badger et al., 2019). The tools used by Badger et al. were developed so as not to solely rely on language but included video prompts, as a scaffold in order to develop the dialogue.

This suggests that time must be set aside for exercise such as these, and providing pupils with scaffolds to develop the language of metacognition or reflection, in order to explain their thinking, becomes important.

Case study: Developing the metacognitive strategy of looking for errors and correcting

Charlie began Year 6 with very low self-esteem and confidence in all areas of learning. He constantly called out in class and took very little care of his work. As soon as lessons started, he would make excuses to go to the toilet and walk around the classroom drinking water.

Charlie did not respond well to feedback and refused to act upon it. His teacher decided to carry out pupil conferencing combined with actively looking for errors and correcting. She would read the feedback aloud to Charlie and ask him to correct the error straight away. As a result of creating an environment where mistake-making was seen as a learning opportunity, Charlie became more focused and engaged in learning, he began to take pride in his work and the calling out stopped.

- Why did Charlie walk around the classroom as soon as lessons started?
- Why did Charlie avoid learning?
- How did the pupil conferencing help Charlie become more focused and engaged?
- How did actively seeking out and correcting errors help Charlie take on feedback more readily?

Summary

- Metacognition can be developed through all subjects. e.g. science, art, design and technology, drama and physical education.
- Support and scaffolding can be provided by the educator by ensuring feedback is given in a timely manner.
- Reflection and evaluation are key components of these subjects.
- Innovation often takes place after the assimilation of cognitive and creative skills.
- Metacognitive strategies learned in the creative subjects can be transferred to English and maths.
- There is a link between creativity and metacognition.
- Further research is required to identify the aspects of metacognitive which may influence creative thinking.

Think!

- Which of the strategies do you already use in the classroom?
- Which of the strategies would you like to try out?
- In which areas of planning would you allocate more time to develop metacognitive strategies?
- How would you scaffold pupils' use of metacognitive language, to enable pupils to be able to explain their thinking?

Teacher metacognition

- As a learner, which strategies do you already use yourself?
- How can these strategies be used in a range of subjects?
- What would these strategies look like in different subjects?

Pupil metacognition

- Which strategies do your pupils find easier to use?
- Which strategies do pupils find challenging to use?
- How can you enable a range of metacognitive strategies in your classroom?

References

Abdivarmazan, M., Taghizade, M.E., Mahmoudfakhe, H. and Tosan, M.A. (2014) A study of the efficacy of meta cognitive strategies on creativity and self confidence and approaching problem solving among the third grade junior school students of the city of Rey. *European Journal of Experimental Biology*, 4: 155–158.

Allison, S. (2017) Making Every Science Lesson Count: Six Principles to Support Great Science Teaching. Carmarthen: Crown House Publishing.

Alter, A.L., Oppenheimer, D.M., Epley, N. and Eyre, R.N. (2007) Overcoming intuition: Metacognitive difficulty activates analytic reasoning. *Journal of Experimental Psychology: General*, 136: 569–576. doi: 10.1037/0096-3445.136.4.569

Badger, C., Horroks, S., Turton, C. and Lewis, H. (2019) Using technology to promote metacognition. *Impact: Journal of the Chartered College of Teaching* [online]. Available at: https://impact.chartered.college/article/using-technology-promote-metacognition/ (accessed 16 March 2021).

Benedek, M., Bergner, S., Könen, T., Fink, A. and Neubauer, A.C. (2011) EEG alpha synchronization is related to top-down processing in convergent and divergent thinking. *Neuropsychologia*, 49: 3505–3511. doi: 10.1016/j.neuropsychologia.2011.09.004

BERA (2011) *Ethical Guidelines for Educational Research*. London: BERA.

Drama Games and Metacognition – BURT'S DRAMA https://burtsdrama.com/2020/02/19/drama-games-and-metacognition/

Dunlosky, J. (2013) Strengthening the student toolbox: Study strategies to boost learning. *American Educator*, 37: 12–21.

Dunlosky, J. and Metcalfe, J. (2009) Metacognition. SAGE Publication.

Dye, K.M. and Stanton, J.D. (2017) Metacognition in Upper-Division *Biology Students: Awareness Does Not Always Lead to Control*. Department of Celullar Biology, University of Georgia, Athens.

Erbas, A.K. and Bas, S. (2015) The contribution of personality traits, motivation, academic risk-taking and metacognition to the creative ability in mathematics. *Creativity Research Journal*, 27: 299–307. doi: 10.1080/10400419.2015.1087235

Fayenatawil, F., Kozbelt, A. and Sitaras, L. (2011) Think global, act local: A protocol analysis comparison of artists' and nonartists' cognitions, metacognitions, and evaluations while drawing. *Psychology of Aesthetics, Creativity and the Arts*, 5 (2): 135–145. doi: 10.1037/a0021019

Gilhooly, K., Fioratou, E., Anthony, S.H. and Wynn, V. (2007) Divergent thinking: Strategies and executive involvement in generating novel uses for familiar objects. *British Journal of Psychology*, 98 (4): 611–625. doi: 10.1111/j.2044-8295.2007.tb00467.x

Hargrove, R.A. (2013) Assessing the long-term impact of a metacognitive approach to creative skill development. *International Journal of Technology and Design Education*, 23: 489–517. doi: 10.1007/s10798-011-9200-6

InnerDrive (n.d.) Developing metacognition in science class [online]. Available at: https://blog.innerdrive.co.uk/developing-metacognition-in-science-class (accessed 16 March 2021).

Kavousi, S., Miller, P. and Alexander, P. (2019) Modeling metacognition in design thinking and design making. *International Journal of Technology and Design Education*, 30. doi: 10.1007/s10798-019-09521-9

Koriat, A., Bjork, R.A., Sheffer, L. and Bar, S.K. (2004) Predicting one's own forgetting: The role of experience-based and theory-based processes. *Journal of Experimental Psychology: General*, 133: 643–656. doi: 10.1037/0096-3445.133.4.643

Lizarraga, M.L.S.D.A. and Baquedano, M.T.S.D.A. (2013) How creative potential is related to metacognition. *European Journal of Education and Psychology*, 6: 69–81. doi: 10.30552/ejep.v6i2.95

Lucas, B.J. and Nordgren, L.F. (2015) People underestimate the value of persistence for creative performance. *Journal of Personality and Social Psychology*, 109 (2): 232–243. doi: 10.1037/pspa0000030

Maclean, D. (2013) PE and metacognition [online]. Available at: https://prezi.com/y6llzldck185/pe-and-metacognition/ (accessed 16 March 2021).

Metcalfe, J. and Wiebe, D. (1987) Intuition in insight and noninsight problem solving. *Memory and Cognition*, 15: 238–246. doi: 10.3758/BF03197722

Miele, D.B. and Molden, D.C. (2010) Naive theories of intelligence and the role of processing fluency in perceived comprehension. *Journal of Experimental Psychology: General*, 139: 535–557. doi: 10.1037/a0019745

Mughal, A. (2020) What is the best way to plan retrieval practice in primary schools given the range of different subjects and developmental ability? [online]. Available at: www.positiveproof.co.uk/articles.php?page=4 (accessed 4 February 2021).

Oppenheimer, D.M. (2008) The secret life of fluency. *Trends in Cognitive Science*, 12: 237–241. doi: 10.1016/j.tics.2008.02.014

Powers, M.N. (2017) Self-regulated design learning: A foundation and framework for teaching and learning design. London: Routledge.

Preiss, D.D., Cosmelli, D., Grau, V. and Ortiz, D. (2016) Examining the influence of mind wandering and metacognition on creativity in university and vocational students. *Learning and Individual Differences*, 51: 417–426. doi: 10.1016/j.lindif.2016.07.010

Sanium, S. and Buaraphan, K. (2019) Research about metacognition in science education: A case of basic education in Thailand. *Journal of Physics: Conference Series*, 1340. DOI: 10.1088/1742-6596/1340/1/012014

Shamir, A., Mevarech, Z. and Gida, C. (2009) The assessment of metacognition in different contexts: Individualized vs. peer assisted learning. *Metacognition Learning*, 4: 47–61.

Still, K. (2020). Available at: www.remembermore.app

Storbeck, J. and Clore, G.L. (2007) On the interdependence of cognition and emotion. *Cognition and Emotion*, 21 (6): 1212–1237. doi: 10.1080/02699930701438020

Sweller, J. (2006) The worked example effect and human cognition. *Learning and Instruction*, 16: 165–169.

Unsworth, N., Spillers, G.J., Brewer, G.A. and Mcmillan, B.D. (2011) Attention control and the antisaccade task: A response time distribution analysis. *Acta Psychologica*, 137 (1): 90–100. doi: 10.1016/j.actpsy.2011.03.004

Xiaoyu, J., Weijan, L. and Liren, C. (2019) The role of metacognitive components in creative thinking. *Frontiers in Psychology*, 10. https://doi.org/10.3389/fpsyg.2019.02404

11

METACOGNITION AND TEST PERFORMANCE

Contents

In this chapter we will discuss

- Cognitive Load Theory
- how memory works
- how long-term memory can be improved through activities such as exam preparation
- metacognitive strategies used to improve test performance, such as traces and exam wrappers
- how metacognition can increase performance through reflection in a structured way
- how to incorporate metacognition into exam practice.

Cognitive load theory: Research that teachers really need to understand (2017: 2) Centre for Education Statistics and Evaluation, states that 'significant implications for teaching practice is cognitive load theory.' In this document Daniel Wiliam has been cited as stating 'the single most important thing for teachers to know' (Shibli and West, 2018). Cognitive load theory is steeped in evidence base and gives teachers 'theoretical and empirical support for explicit models of instruction.' It is based on two elements: that the human brain has limits to the amount of information it can process and at the same time that the human brain has no limits to 'how much stored information can be processed at one time' (Centre for Education Statistics and Evaluation, 2017: 2).

The theory aims to facilitate the working memory, maximising learning, through explicit instruction, due to the fact that it is an efficient way that human brains learn.

Explicit instruction involves teachers clearly showing students what to do and how to do it, rather than having students discover or construct information for themselves (Centre for Education Statistics and Evaluation, 2017: 2).

The Centre for Education Statistics and Evaluation, 2017: 2 state that according to Hattie, during explicit instruction, it is the teacher who decided on the learning objectives and success criteria, sharing them with pupils, models how to use them, checks for understanding and evaluates them. Asking pupils to repeat back the instructions is also part of explicit instructional direction. Another word for all of these supporting tools would be scaffolds, which are required to move from novice to expert learner, without overloading the memory.

The working memory can become overwhelmed by the simplest of cognitive activities. Although relatively little is known about cognitive load theory, there are 'widely accepted theories about how the brain stores and processes information' (The Centre for Education Statistics and Evaluation, 2017: 2). It has been assumed that 'human memory can be divided into working memory and long-term memory; that information is stored in the long-term memory in the form of schemas; and that processing new information results in 'cognitive load' on working memory which can affect learning outcomes' (The Centre for Education Statistics and Evaluation, 2017: 2).

The working memory

There are various models that can help to visualise current understanding of the working memory. Memory could be seen as goods in a shopping bag. Shopping bags are used to temporarily hold shopping so that it can be transported and transferred to more appropriate storage such as the cupboard, fridge or freezer. Our working memories can be seen as shopping bags, where the knowledge is transferred to long-term memory.

Successful thinking relies on four aspects: mental model of the world, what you know, change in long-term memory, how much effort is required.

Working memory can become full but the same does not happen to long-term memory. There is strong evidence to show links between working memory and academic achievement. In a podcast interview by Jamie Scott (EEF, 2019), Dr Tracy Alloway, an award-winning cognitive psychologist, explains why understanding working memory is so important. She describes working memory as being an 'active memory', one that is used to 'actively engage with information'. The working memory absorbs new information and 'matches' it with the long-term memory. Alloway uses the analogy of Post-it notes to describe how much information the working memory can hold due to having 'limited space' and being a temporary form of storage. A Post-it note keeps information active for a limited period of time. If we never engage with this information again, it is quickly lost.

Alloway and her team conducted a 'government funded' study across England in primary schools, with children aged five to six years of age, with the aim of finding out what it is that makes learners successful at this age. They spoke to parents and carers and teachers and sat in lessons.

One working memory test they used was 'the backward digit test'. This was where children were asked to memorise a series of three digits backwards such as: 567. They found that the average five-to-six-year-old could memorise two of these digits backwards, whereas adults could remember a string of four or five digits backwards. This usually depends on how 'actively engaged' their working memory is with the information.

Although IQ can be a 'key predictor to learning', Alloway and her team discovered that working memory was more important than IQ. Measuring working memory at age five, gave accurate predictions of success in national testing, six years later. The degree of working memory at age five could be used as an accurate prediction at how well pupils would do in reading, writing and maths.

The results of the study were surprising. EEF (2019) mentions in her podcast that her team found that working memory is not dependant on any other factor. It did not depend on the level of education of the mother, who is usually the 'primary caregiver'. It did not depend on whether children had someone reading stories to them at home or whether children were given rich outdoor experiences. This suggests that children's 'learning potential of success in the classroom' can be measured by using a simple working memory test. Due to the 'symbiotic relationship' between the working and the long-term memories, children with poor working memory can still access information from the long-term memory. Those with poor working memory can still draw from their long-term memory but it 'might take longer to build up a store' through investing in 'time, effort and engagement' (EEF, 2019).

Poor working memory can manifest itself through non-desirable behaviours and it can be mis-identified in the classroom as being lazy and showing a lack of attention. Pupils usually appear to be very quiet and disengaged and can be invisible.

Alex Quigley (EEF, 2019) states that our working memory can be affected when we have too many things to think about all at once. For example, when we are writing, we need to remember which vocabulary to choose, sentence structures to create particular effects, correct usage of grammar, genre types and neat handwriting to name but a few elements. At the same time we are thinking about new knowledge.

One way to not overload the working memory is to 'chunk' information into 'smaller steps' (EEF, 2019). Teachers always recognise when pupils begin to struggle with working memory and are adept at breaking learning into smaller chunks.

A trial was carried out across 127 primary schools with Year 3 children, aged between seven and eight years, where teaching assistants were trained to deliver an intervention. This consisted of explicitly teaching arithmetic strategies such as verbalising counting aloud strategies and using fingers to help children count. It is usually assumed that children do this naturally but often they do not. They found that these strategies quickly became internalised. Although some metacognitive skills are subject specific, some are not. The thinking aloud strategy can be used across the curriculum, in all subjects. Chunking can be used in reading, writing, maths and science to break down large numbers or concepts. Without knowledge you cannot be strategic. The question to consider is: how much knowledge is required to become a strategic learner? The other question to consider is how domain specific the strategies are.

We must be mindful that our working memory can be affected when we are tired or emotional. This is important for classroom practitioners to bear in mind when working with those with poor working memory.

An example of working memory

Let us now look at an example of using working memory:

> How would you multiply 43 and 28 together without using a calculator?

Firstly, the two numbers would have to be held in your working memory. Secondly, you would need to draw upon multiplication rules and strategies. Thirdly, you would need to choose the appropriate strategy to carry out the calculation mentally. Your chosen strategy would be the one that you think is cognitively least challenging for you. Then you would need to carry out the calculation of the separate parts, simultaneously calculating and holding the products of each calculation in your head, whilst you work out another calculation. Then you would need to add together both products to reach the final answer.

It certainly is challenging holding information in your working memory whilst working on another part of a calculation.

Other examples of when we rely on our working memories include memorising recipes, telephone numbers, PIN numbers, registration numbers of vehicles, calculating food shopping bills (Gathercole and Alloway, 2007).

Although it is important for pupils to be taught a broad and balanced curriculum, emotional preparation for tests cannot be underestimated. More able pupils already have self-regulation skills in place, to set goals, monitor their feelings and emotions and reflect on how well they perform on test papers. Lower attaining pupils, who do not have well-developed self-regulation, will need support to develop good study skills and to be able to self-regulate.

Like with anything of this nature, pupils must be given every opportunity to build their confidence by practising test papers and getting used to answering test style questions. The metacognition strategies taught during lessons will go a long way to help prepare them for the tests. However, there are test specific metacognitive strategies that cannot be left to chance and must be taught explicitly, to give pupils optimum chance of succeeding in such challenging testing.

All educators want their pupils to be successful and achieve their potential, particularly during exams. Even though we are many years on since Flavell's (1979) ideas about there being either very little or too much focus on solely the cognitive, this is still relevant today, if not more so than when first introduced in 1979:

> Lack of hard evidence notwithstanding, I am absolutely convinced that there is, overall, far too little rather than enough or too much cognitive monitoring in this world. I believe this is true for adults as well as for children, but it is especially true for children. (Flavell, 1979)

There is far too much emphasis and importance attached to assessment of cognition without metacognition and motivation. These two crucial elements of self-regulation go relatively unnoticed as they are not a priority for cognitive testing. However, educators are all too aware that without the foundations of metacognition and motivation, a pupil will not reach their true cognitive potential.

Recently, there has been much focus on intelligence being defined as 'memory is the residue of thought' (Willingham, 2008: 20), whereby memory is formed by thinking about something over and over again. Thinking about something over and over again may help you to remember it and the amount remembered may increase. However, without practise the benefits of using metacognition to deepen understanding and thereby improving memory will be long forgotten.

Although retrieval practice is being used in classrooms across England, the way retrieve practice is implemented in the classroom has been questioned by Coe (2019). In as much as retrieval practice is used for low stakes knowledge retrieval, the benefits of using retrieval to monitor cognitive progress has gone relatively unnoticed. With an increasingly complex curriculum, there needs to be greater importance placed on how to use different types of retrieval practice to improve outcomes for all (Mughal, 2020).

Being taught metacognitive strategies can stimulate cognitive and metacognitive knowledge. For example, when preparing for a test, your metacognitive knowledge may tell you that you do not know an area of learning very well, so you set yourself a goal to learn more about a particular topic. Flavell (1979) suggested one way to improve subject knowledge might be to read through notes. However, Willingham (2008) found that even when pupils revised by reading their notes over and over again they were not able to recall facts required for exams. He also found that pupils knew very little about memory, how to commit something to memory to be recalled at a later time.

If knowledge gained is not practised regularly, it is soon forgotten. The task of recalling knowledge is very challenging for both children and adults because the brain is required to 'actively search memory and recall the relevant information' (Pintrich, 2002).

One way to alleviate the cognitive challenge of pure recall and retrieval is to teach metacognition alongside cognition (see Chapter 2).

Although the Cognitive Load Theory is relatively unknown to the psychology community, teachers may find it useful as a means to understanding how to balance support and challenge for learners, with the emphasis being that the 'human brain can only process a small amount of new information at once', however, it 'can process large amounts of stored information at once' (CESE, 2018: 2).

In 1974, Baddeley and Hitch presented a theory of the working memory. The working memory is where we hold and utilise minute pieces of new information for a limited time. It has been described as the ability to hold something in your memory whilst carrying out another task. It is like having a messy desk, where the workspace is limited and things start falling off the edge (Jacobson: What is Working Memory?).

This model includes speech and vision as separate components which is controlled by the central executive system, responsible for attention (Smith and Firth, 2018).

Baddeley (2000) suggests that working memory is made up of four elements, which hold information for limited amounts of time: phonological loop, visuospatial sketchpad, the episodic buffer and the central executive, each one with its own specialised function, working together to create the working memory, with the central executive controlling the three 'slave systems' (Smith and Firth, 2018).

A model of working memory

The simplest model used to describe how working memory works is from the study conducted by Baddeley (2000). In this model there are three pathways (phonological loop, visuospatial sketchpad and episodic buffer), from the central executive, which combine language, visual semantics and short-term episodic memory. Language is taken up by the phonological loop, visual semantics is taken up by the visuospatial sketchpad and the short-term episodic memory is taken up by the episodic buffer, all of which are stored in the central executive.

The phonological loop is concerned with sounds and converting sounds into speech in the brain. It is responsible for taking in and holding information as 'we are using them' (Smith and Firth, 2018). This also includes 'written language'. It has limited scope and can hold verbal information for less than two seconds (Smith and Firth, 2018).

The visuospatial sketchpad is the part that holds visual and spatial information. This area of the brain is concerned with completing 'simple visual tasks such as following a maze with your eyes' (Smith and Firth, 2018).

The episodic buffer combines information from the phonological loop, the visuospatial sketchpad, forming long-term knowledge and current experience into a coherent whole (Henry, 2012). Figure 11.1 is a visual representation of how the episodic buffer could combine information from those four key areas.

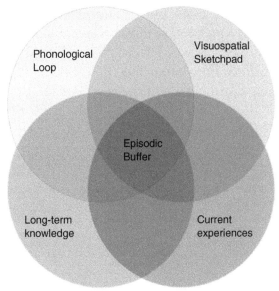

Figure 11.1 Image of episodic buffer combining information in the working memory

Once the information has been combined it is then transferred to the long-term memory (Henry, 2012). However, for some pupils, 'the visuospatial sketchpad and phonological loop are not directly connected but connect via the central executive', and this could cause difficulties associated with dyslexia (Thinkpix, 2020). Although 'there is much less known about the visuospatial sketchpad ... this can be measured separately using abstract visual information. In dyslexia, this is typically a strength and can be used to support auditory information' (Thinkpix, 2020).

Thinkpix (2020) also suggests that the auditory working memory is what links 'language, learning and behaviours', and describes the 'auditory working memory as a shelf', with those with poor working memory having items regularly falling off it.

Thinkpix (2020) lists a number of ways that poor working memory can manifest itself in the classroom, which include: inability to follow 'verbal instructions and follow sequences in PE', inability to be organised, calling out answers due to not being able to hold the answers in their minds, inability to remember messages, 'difficulty filtering out background noise, difficulty with remembering' and recalling times tables. This is where understanding of cognitive load can be beneficial.

There are three types of cognitive load: intrinsic load, which is to do with the complexity of the task; extraneous load, which refers to how well someone can block out irrelevant information or stimuli; and germane load, which refers to the relevant skills and knowledge and how the complex learning information is linked.

Table 11.1 outlines how balancing the different types of episodic memory can help optimisation of the cognitive load.

Table 11.1 Optimising cognitive load in the classroom

Intrinsic Load	Extraneous Load	Germane Load
Managing difficulty of subject knowledge (task)	Minimise extras e.g. design well thought out instructions	Maximise transference of knowledge
Control and enable	Minimise distractions and noise	Explicitly teach links between subjects, topics, domains, life experience
Correct level of challenge	Be mindful of overloading slides	
	Have routines to help what pupils already know	

There are many extraneous factors that need to be minimised to allow for effective teaching such as: decrease teacher talk, increase pupil talk, minimise outside noise and noise from neighbouring classes as this will fill working memory. Also reduce displays, acoustics, the number of visitors to the class, use a combination of text and symbols, simplify the structure of worksheets (Henry, 2012).

Long-term memory: procedural and declarative memory

Procedural memory is a long-term memory, which is unconscious. It helps with the performance and to achieve tasks without consciously thinking about it. The procedural memory is 'skill-based' (Weinstein, Sumeracki and Caviglioli, 2019: 6), an example being playing the piano.

However, declarative memory is another type of long-term memory, where you are required to report your memory or describe it. It is where you consciously remember certain events and facts.

Procedural memory usually develops by repeatedly practising something over and over again. It is demonstrated through your actions and 'does not involve directly reporting the contents of one's memory,' (Weinstein, Sumeracki and Caviglioli, 2019: 73). Some examples are walking and things you can do without being able to explain how you did them, for example finding your way home without being able to state the directions from a particular location (Weinstein, Sumeracki and Caviglioli, 2019: 73).

Procedural memory is slightly different from declarative memory in that retrieval through the procedural system can happen without realising it or subconsciously (Cohen and Squire, 1980). Learning how to drive is a good example of this, where new motor skills are practiced repeatedly and explicitly thought about at first and with repeated practice explicit thinking is no longer required and the skill becomes automatic.

Case study: Supporting pupils with poor working memory

Rob, like many pupils, found the classroom a challenge. He frequently called out in class and found it extremely difficult to follow instructions. Rob had limited spelling strategies and found reading and writing laborious but was quite good at mathematics and would often work very quickly, particularly in maths, so as to retain information. This meant that silly mistakes were made during classwork.

Behaviour management systems were put into place and applied consistently. Instructions were written out and copies given to all pupils to keep on their desks. Success criteria for each lesson were typed out and were also given to all pupils. Rob followed these diligently. Mistakes were picked up on and instant feedback was given for immediate correction. Within one term, Rob had stopped calling out in class and made rapid progress in all areas of learning. There was significant improvement in reading, writing and spellings.

- How did the support help with Rob's obvious challenges with poor working memory?
- What was the purpose of instant feedback?
- How did the instant feedback help with poor working memory?

Accuracy of judgement

When pupils start to learn more independently, their accuracy of judgement is usually quite poor. They are unable to tell which strategy works and which does not due to having unrealistic views of how 'well they have learned something' (EEF, 2018). Children, like adults, usually 'underestimate how much time and resource will be required to plan successfully' (EEF, 2018). This is called the 'planning fallacy' (cited in EEF, 2018 by Logan, Castel, Haber and Viehman (2012)). Explicit teaching about how to accurately judge how effective a particular strategy is will improve pupils' judgements of their own learning.

Spacing or distributed practice is a technique which can be used both when planning a curriculum (see Chapter 13) and when revising for exams to aid with the memorisation of material on the proviso that material is better retrieved when there is a larger gap as opposed to a smaller gap between being taught it. For example, if a particular topic is studied repeatedly over a weekend it will be forgotten easily rather than having a larger gap between revision periods (Smith and Firth, 2018). This is backed up by Cepeda, Vul, Rohrer, Wixted and Pashler (2008).

Although self-regulation involves making decisions around what to study, how long to study for and when to terminate studying, not all primary children have enough expertise or experience to be able to carry out this complex process (Kornell and Bjork, 2007). Due to being inexperienced learners, in primary schools particularly, pupils require guidance.

Explicit metacognitive strategies for exams

Let us now look at explicit metacognitive strategies for exams.

Retrieval practice

Argawal (2019) discusses whether pupil's 'factual knowledge' should be built up before moving into 'higher order learning'.

According to Daniel Willingham 'factual knowledge must precede skill' (2009). This view has been backed up by Diane Ravitch (2009) who states that it is not possible to think critically without having acquired a 'great deal of knowledge'. You need a lot of knowledge before you can compare, contrast and synthesise, skills which form part of critical thinking. It is a widely held belief that a lot of time needs to be spent on teaching factual knowledge. However, this can lead to misconceptions about how much knowledge is required for critical thinking to develop. How much knowledge is a 'great deal of knowledge'? And how long do you teach knowledge for before moving onto critical thinking? Can critical thinking be developed with some knowledge?

Even though Karpicke and Aue (2015) found that retrieval practice is crucial for using and applying knowledge for long-term memory, it is necessary to be mindful about what that looks like in the classroom. According to Coe (2019), careful consideration should be given to the type of quizzes designed for the classroom, as they may not lead to better outcomes.

There are two reasons why Coe (2019) is questioning the use of retrieval practice: a) although retrieval practice can improve memory of factual knowledge, there is no evidence about how it can improve the memorisation of complex information, and b) there has been no evidence of retrieval practice improving memory in maths other than factual knowledge. A good example would be the memorisation of times tables through rote learning, which does not work for all pupils.

The pitfalls of retrieval practice may be:

- educators might generate retrieval questions that focus solely on factual recall (these questions are easier to generate) rather than requiring any higher-order thinking
- questions might be too easy and boost confidence without providing real challenge, which is likely to be a key ingredient for generating the kind of learning hoped for
- there may be too much allocation of time to the quizzes, effectively losing the time they need to cover new material.

Spaced practice and flashcards

In her blog entitled, 'How to remember anything, forever', Daisy Christodoulou (2020) discusses the fact that memory decay is part and parcel of everyday life and shares strategies to overcome this. In order to remember something, you must have encountered it a number of times before. Christodoulou uses an example to illustrate this, about a book she read ten years before. Not only had she forgotten that she had read it, she couldn't remember the details contained within it, despite having highlighted sections and having folded a page. Christodoulou, 2020, states that this is called cryptomnesia.

> This is a concept in psychology, where you think you've come up with a brand-new idea of your own, when in fact it can be shown that you encountered the idea before. (Christodoulou, 2020)

Her blog also advises against cramming in revision just before an exam:

> Spending hours revising just before an exam doesn't help you remember for the long-term: you need to space the practice out. This is one of the oldest findings in psychological research, based on Hermann Ebbinghaus's experiments in the 1890s. (Christodoulou, 2020)

Some of the challenges of spaced practice are that there is no clear evidence to suggest how often spaced practice should be conducted and this very much depends on how confident you are with the subject matter. One solution is the use of algorithms in technology and Christodoulou suggests a flashcard app called Anki, to plug this gap.

The Remember More app and classroom programme also relies on this technology to improve memory. Developed by Kristian Still (2020, see www.kristianstill.co.uk) it is designed for busy educators and spaced retrieval practice is described as 'successive relearning'. Although memory decay and the 'conditions which produce forgetting' are not generally viewed positively, they do 'actually create opportunities to enhance our level of learning' (Bjork and Bjork, 2011).

Each time information is retrieved, it is altered and built upon. This creates 'additional retrieval routes'. These changes allow successful retrieval in the future, making testing a potent mechanism for enhancing long-term retention (Howard-Jones, 2014).

Many educational apps use 'spaced-repetition' to alleviate this problem and 'promote memory, and they also promote one of the most under-appreciated by-products of memory: the ability to make connections between different ideas' (Christodoulou, 2020).

Exam wrappers

One way of improving accuracy of judgements is by using a tool called exam wrappers. Exam wrappers are strategies whereby pupils sit an exam, and the mistakes are identified, analysed and corrected. It is a self-evaluation tool which helps to unpick errors and guides revision practice for exams.

Soicher and Gurung (2017) found that there is a surge in metacognition when taught on different courses. Lovett (2013) indicates similar findings. Soicher and Gurung suggest a possible reason for this could be that pupils did not notice the benefits of metacognition and therefore did not transfer metacognitive strategies across subjects automatically. This suggests that metacognitive strategies need to be taught explicitly (Brown and Palinscar, 1982) across subjects and in more than one subject, to have a greater impact.

It is possible to teach the same strategies across subjects, as often there is the same teacher preparing pupils for all the SATs subjects of reading, spelling, grammar and punctuation, and maths. It also becomes easier to spot whether or not some strategies are domain specific.

The exam wrapper technique was created by Marsha Lovett at Carnegie Mellon University. It was developed in response to students starting college with ineffective learning habits for higher order thinking. The wrappers were designed to give students the opportunity to evaluate their learning habits and make adjustments to how they studied and what they focused their time on when studying (Lovett, 2013).

Exam wrappers should be given out after pupils sit practice tests so that they can evaluate their performance. These should be designed to focus on particular skills or metacognitive strategies, should not be graded and should be kept quite short.

Pupil belief in the teacher's knowledge about them as learners and belief in their potential must be strong for the evaluation to have the desired impact. There are a number of things that teachers can do to create such a climate. One way is to start off with success first. In order to give pupils a sense of success, the teacher must engineer this carefully. That first taste of success will motivate the pupil to want to do well in future tests. When pupils begin to master these skills, further challenges could be provided.

Traces

Traces can be seen where pupils have internalised some metacognitive strategies and are beginning to know themselves as learners.

These are techniques to help the learner keep track and continuously evaluate where they are in their learning journey.

These techniques involve underlining keywords and phrases and making notes, so that pupils do not lose their place in their work. As learners become more independent, this technique also helps with accuracy of judgement and increased self-regulation.

One of the reasons why pupils do not perform as well as they should in exams is because they do not read and understand the questions correctly. Even pupils with well-developed metacognitive skills can make mistakes when reading test questions, especially under pressure. Underlining keywords and phrases can help with accuracy of understanding by enabling pupils to hone in on relevant information and then apply their skills and knowledge to answer the questions to the best of their ability.

Summary

- There are a number of memory systems which interplay and overlap with each other.
- Things can go wrong with any one of these memory systems and can affect our memories and how we learn.
- Memory can be developed in a variety of ways.
- Developing procedural and declarative memory could be beneficial for those with low working memory.
- There are a number of ways metacognition can help pupils improve memory.

Think!

- What is the correlation between accuracy of judgement and poor working memory?
- Who are the pupils in your class with poor working memory?
- How does this manifest itself in the classroom?
- For which classroom tasks do you already use procedural and declarative knowledge?

- In which subjects or topics could procedural memory be utilised to improve memory?
- How could retrieval practice, other than low stakes quizzes, be used in the classroom to aid memory retention?
- Do some subjects lend themselves to a particular type of memory being developed first, i.e. procedural memory?
- How could all types of memories be developed simultaneously?

Teacher metacognition

- What is your own working memory like?
- How do you feel when you are cognitively overloaded with information?
- If you have a good working memory, what do you do to understand the challenges associated for those with poor working memory?
- Which strategies do you use when learning something new, to aid memory retention?

Pupil metacognition

- Which behaviours are associated with poor working memory?
- How do these manifest themselves in the classroom?
- How do pupils behave when they feel cognitively overloaded?
- Who are the pupils who experience learning challenging due to a poor working memory?
- Which strategies do you use to reduce cognitive load, to enable all your pupils to succeed in learning despite the differences with working memory in your class?
- How could pupils with poor working memory become more independent in their learning?

References

Agarwal, Pooja, K. (2019) Retrieval Practice & Bloom's Taxonomy: Do Students Need Fact Knowledge Before Higher Order Learning? Washington University, in St. Louis. Available at: http://pdf.poojaagarwal.com/Agarwal_2018_JEdPsych.pdf

Baddeley, A.D. (2000) The episodic buffer: a new component of working memory. *Trends in Cognitive Sciences*, 4: 417–423.

Bjork, E.L. and Bjork, R.A. (2011) Making things hard on yourself, but in a good way: Creating desirable difficulties to enhance learning, in M.A. Gernsbacher, R.W. Pew, L.M. Hough and J.R. Pomerantz (Eds.), Psychology and the real world: Essays illustrating fundamental contributions to society (2nd edition). (pp. 59–68). New York: Worth.

Brown, A. and Palinscar, A. (1982) Inducing strategic learning from texts by means of informed, self-control training.

Cepeda, N.J., Vul, E., Rohrer, D., Wixted, J.T. and Pashler, H. (2008) Spacing effects in learning: A temporal ridgeline of optimal retention. *Psychological Science*, *19* (11): 1095–1102. doi: 10.1111/j.1467-9280.2008.02209.x

CESE (Centre for Education Statistics and Evaluation) (2018) *Cognitive Load Theory in Practice*. Sydney: NSW Government. Available at: www.cese.nsw.gov.au//images/stories/PDF/Cognitive_load_theory_practice_guide_AA.pdf (accessed 16 March 2021).

Christodoulou, D. (2020) How to remember anything, forever [online]. Available at: https://daisychristodoulou.com/2020/03/how-to-remember-anything-forever/ (accessed 4 February 2021).

Coe, R. (2019) *EEF Blog: Does research on 'retrieval practice' translate into classroom practice?* [online]. Available at: https://educationendowment foundation.org.uk/news/does-research-on-retrieval-practice-translate-into-classroom-practice/ (accessed 4 February 2021).

Cohen, N.J. and Squire, L.R. (1980) Preserved learning and retention of pattern analyzing skill in amnesia: Dissociation of knowing how and knowing that. *Science, 210*: 207–209.

EEF (2019) Working memory. *Trialled and Tested* [podcast]. 18 July. Available at https://educationendowmentfoundation.org.uk/news/trialled-and-tested-podcast-working-memory/ (accessed 26 December 2020).

Flavell, J. (1979) Metacognition and cognitive monitoring: A new area of cognitive-developmental inquiry. *American Psychologist, 34*: 906–911.

Gathercole, S.E. and Alloway, T.P. (2007) *Understanding Working Memory: A Classroom Guide* [online]. Available at: www.mrc-cbu.cam.ac.uk/wp-content/uploads/2013/01/WM-classroom-guide.pdf (accessed 4 February 2021).

Henry, L. (2012) The Development of Working Memory in Children. London: Sage.

Howard-Jones, P.A. (2014) Neuroscience and education: myths and messages. *Nature Reviews Neuroscience*. AOP; doi: 10.1038/nrn3817

Jacobson, R. (n.d.) What is Working Memory? [online]. Available at: https://childmind.org/article/what-is-working-memory/ (accessed 16 March 2021).

Karpicke, J.D. and Aue, W.R. (2015) The testing effect is alive and well with complex materials. *Educational Psychology Review, 27* (2): 317–326.

Kornell, N. and Bjork, R.A. (2007) The promise and perils of self-regulated study. *Psychonomic Bulletin & Review, 14* (2): 219–224. Available at: https://web.williams.edu/Psychology/Faculty/Kornell/Publications/Kornell.Bjork.2007.pdf (accessed 16 March 2021).

Logan, J.M., Castel, A.D., Haber, S. and Viehman, E.J. (2012) Metacognition and the spacing effect: The role of repetition, feedback, and instruction on judgments of learning for massed and spaced rehearsal, *Metacognition and Learning, 7* (3): pp. 175–195.

Lovett, M.C. (2013) Make exams worth more than the grade: Using exam wrappers to promote metacognition. In Kaplan, M., LaVaque-Manty, D., Meizlish, D. and Silver, N. (eds), *Reflection and Metacognition in College Teaching.* New York: Stylus Publishing.

Mughal, A. (2020) What is the best way to plan retrieval practice in primary schools given the range of different subjects and developmental ability? [online]. Available at: www.positiveproof.co.uk/articles.php?page=4 (accessed 4 February 2021).

Pintrich, P.R. (2002) The Role of Metacognitive Knowledge in Learning, Teaching and Assessing. Volume 41, Number 4. The College of Education, The Ohio State University.

Ravitch, D. (2009) Critical thinking? You need knowledge. The Boston Globe. Available at: https://duanechun.files.wordpress.com/2010/04/you-need-knowledge-the-boston-globe.pdf

Shibli, D. and West, R,. (2018) 'Cognitive Load Theory and its application in the classroom', *Impact Journal*, Chartered College of Teaching.

Soicher, R.N. and Gurung, R.A.R. (2017) Do exam wrappers increase meta-cognition and performance? A single course intervention. *Psychology Learning & Teaching, 16* (1): 64–73. doi: 10.1177/1475725716661872

Smith, M. and Firth, J. (2018) Psychology in the Classroom. A Teacher's Guide to What Works. Oxon: Routledge.

Thinkpix (2020) *Testing, testing: Memory working?* [online]. Available at: https://thinkpix.blog/2020/03/15/testing-testing-memory-working/ (accessed 4 February 2021).

Weinstein, Y., Sumeracki, M. and Caviglioli, O. (2019) Understanding How We Learn. Oxon: Routledge.

Willingham, D.T. (2008) Ask the cognitive scientist: What will improve a student's memory? *American Educator, Winter 2008–2009* [online]. Available at: www.aft.org/sites/default/files/periodicals/willingham_0.pdf (accessed 4 February 2021).

12

METACOGNITION, DIALOGUE AND LISTENING

Contents

In this chapter we will explore

- dialogue and why it should be taught explicitly
- what Socratic talking and dialogic teaching is
- what dialogical teaching could look like in the classroom
- why listening is important
- what self-regulated listening is and how to develop it in the classroom.

Dialogue

Dialogue and the ability to think are unique to human beings; they are what makes us human. From utterances as babies to fully formed and complex sentences, humans have the ability not only to communicate their basic needs but to reason and argue. Through language, humans are able to develop relationships and participate globally. In this increasingly challenging world, children should be given the language required to navigate their way through it. One of the first psychologists, Vygotsky (1962), suggested that speaking is initially a social construct, with it becoming a more individual act later in life. Through talking activities, pupils can construct their own knowledge and understanding of the world, however, this needs guiding by adults. Through social interactions children develop speech and sentences as well as meaning of words 'and the social relationships in which they are embedded' (Mercer and Hodgkinson, 2008). At school, teachers share their perspective with pupils, which allows them to construct meaning to their understanding of the world. Existing schemas are challenged with each new encounter in the classroom and through the process of reflection, misconceptions are altered. Through pupil–teacher interaction, each pupil creates slightly different variations of the meanings to hand (Mercer and Hodkingson, 2008). It is thought that in order to develop critical thinking skills, after shared construction, reinterpreting the information is essential. Some of the learning which happens in the classroom is implicit but teachers can direct the teaching to the main features of the activity. Focusing on these features enables pupils to be able to partake in the activity, whether that is with or without support.

Reflecting and thus making the learning explicit helps pupils critically view their understanding and provides them with an option to stick to their understating or change it. Talking about their learning in a different context appears to further facilitate critical thought (Mercer and Hodgkinson, 2008). Mannion and Mercer (2020) highlight the importance of listening as a 'gateway to understanding'. Teachers are more than aware that listening is crucial to learning but the misconception is that it is something that does not need to be taught; it is regarded as a 'passive skill'. The reality, however, is that there needs to be more of a focus on developing listening skills at the same time as speaking skills. Mannion and Mercer (2020) claim that 'if we explicitly taught listening skills to every child, we would likely see benefits in terms of their ability to acquire knowledge and skills in a range of contexts'. Although the importance of listening is recognised by practitioners, it appears to be one the least understood aspects of learning. This is due to its complex nature. However, it has become clearer more recently that not only can listening skills be taught explicitly but 'when done well, students learn more effectively'. Jiang, Kalyuga and Sweller (2017) highlighted the difference of novice learners and more experienced learners: 'novices learn best from instruction that combines reading and listening, while more knowledgeable learners benefit from a reading-only approach' (cited in Mannion and Mercer, 2020).

This is where developing the metacognition of listening can be beneficial, in particular how they learn from listening. Mannion and Mercer (2020) suggest five metacognitive strategies to develop listening. These are: 'enhancing awareness', with discussion of why it is hard to listen; 'self-monitoring', which consist of listening activities with timed pauses and recall; 'summarising', either through video or audio; 'selective attention', where pre-teaching of skills takes place; and 'cognitive connections'.

When it comes to dialogue, there is a common misconception that speaking does not have to be taught but that it is something that children should just pick up (Gaunt and Stott, 2019). However, educators realise that not all children 'just pick it up', and that speaking actually requires explicit teaching. Due to the nature of being exposed to language to varying degrees in the home environment, classroom dialogue becomes even more important. Teaching experience in this area is varied, so providing teachers with a framework would be beneficial and it would enable pupils to be able to 'engage in meaningful talk' (Gaunt and Stott, 2019: 2). Learning about effective use of dialogue in different situations for different listeners would have a huge influence on learning. There are many methods of teaching dialogue and we will explore two of them in this chapter: Socratic talking and dialogic teaching.

What is an Socratic talking and how can it be used in the classroom?

As in P4C, Socratic dialogue facilitates deep thinking skills, helps develop good listening skills, enables effective discussions to take place, building on and challenging others' ideas. It is not only used in P4C but can also be used in other subjects such as English, maths, history, geography, science and PHSE. It is a method which can be used at the beginning of a lesson or as 'part of the main activity' (Bibi, 2020).

Socratic dialogue or 'The Socratic Method' is thought to have originated from the philosopher Socrates, who lived around 470BC, although there is 'no written record of this' (Hymer and Sutcliffe, 2012). Our understanding of his methods are purely based on secondary sources of information, mainly from Plato, who was his student. Although elements of P4C can be embedded into other subjects such as English and history, it is crucial for the ten-step process of P4C to be completed to fruition (Gorard et al., 2015). The key difference with the Socratic method is that it is embedded into subjects based on similar principles.

In addition to this, Delić and Bećirović (2016) explain that there are a number of 'key points' which need to be taken into consideration when the Socratic method is used in learning.

The first part of the process is the 'inquiry' stage, where pupils' original ideas are partially altered but not totally opposed (Delić and Bećirović, 2016). One way could be by denying all knowledge and wisdom and whether or not they have the answer they should not offer any answers to the discussion. This would mean that the ownership of thinking and understanding would be transferred to the pupils (Hymer and Sutcliffe, 2012).

The second part of the process is the dialogue between the teacher and the pupils. When the teacher asks the questions the pupils combine 'their past experiences and their knowledge' (Delić and Bećirović, 2016) to form a coherent response. This depends on the age of the pupil and how much experience they have had when articulating answers.

The third part is involved in continuously reasoning incorrectly and then 'uses the counter example to clarify the problem' (Delić and Bećirović, 2016).

One way that this could look in the classroom could be via a 'compare and contrast framework' (Hymer and Sutcliffe, 2012) based on searching for the truth, facilitating what is already there and 'teasing' out information. Searching for the truth develops verbal and conceptual understanding. The Socratic method also hinges on feedback and developing intrinsic motivation but limiting the amount of praise used. Too much praise could hinder the thinking process, with pupils being misled into thinking that they have found all the answers. It is more effective to develop the intrinsic motivation by being 'driven by such things as intellectual curiosity, a creative restlessness and a passion truly to master a skill, puzzle or a knowledge domain' (Hymer and Sutcliffe, 2012). This process of learning is rewarding in itself because there is no need to influence anyone (see Chapter 6).

In her blog, Bibi (2020) states that Socratic seminars are an effective way of 'teaching to the top'. With scaffolds and differentiation all pupils can access higher order thinking. She shares two types of Socratic seminars which she conducts in her lessons: whole class and small group seminars (Bibi, 2020).

A whole class Socratic seminar may involve setting up an 'inner circle', which consists of the discussion group, and an 'outer circle', which forms the observers. Prior to the activity taking place the teacher would have decided the pupils for each circle. An observer from the outer circle is paired up with a speaker from the inner circle. The task of the observer is to make observations based on a variety of speaking and listening skills. Stimuli can be used at the beginning of the activity, although they are not required. Bibi (2020) suggests that pupils in the inner circle should be allocated roles depending on their strengths and what they need to improve on. During the discussion the role of the teacher is to facilitate and use questions to keep the flow of the discussion, to delve further or expand thinking. This activity should be planned for around fifteen to twenty minutes of the lesson. After the activity, the outer circle appraises and provides feedback for their partners in the inner circle. The ideas discussed within the inner circle are used to create a written response.

A small group session is exactly the same but set up for six to eight pupils and feedback is shared within groups not the whole class. For both, scaffolds and prompts may be given.

What is dialogical teaching?

Dialogic teaching is the exchanging of talk between teachers and pupils, which can have many benefits. It can be used to understand pupils' thinking and help engage them by developing their ideas and also identify misconceptions and overcome them. Through dialogic teaching pupils' spoken and written language can be extended in different contexts, allowing pupils to discover and demolish barriers to their understanding. They are able to explore and play with language in new and innovative ways and use it to build knowledge. Like P4C, it is based on Socratic questioning, however, it is not taught discreetly but through lessons.

In the EEF *Dialogic Teaching: Evaluation Report* by Jay et al. (2017), the intervention was carried out on Year 5 pupils across thirty-eight schools. A teacher-mentor was assigned in each school, who received the training and resources and implemented the intervention over two terms; the autumn and spring terms for twenty weeks during the academic year 2015/2016. 'The intervention was developed and delivered by a team from the Cambridge Primary Review Trust (CPRT) and the University of York' (Jay et al., 2017). The purpose of the intervention was to improve attainment in English, maths and science through the use of high-quality 'teacher and pupil talk in the classroom' (Jay et al., 2017: 4) after which pupils were tested. Teachers, mentors and headteachers were also interviewed as part of the study and case studies were carried out in three schools.

They were moderately confident that the intervention was solely responsible for the outcomes and nothing else. 'The Dialogic Teaching approach was highly valued by participating schools. Teachers reported positive effects on pupil engagement and confidence' (Jay et al., 2017: 4).

The main findings were: on average 'pupils made two additional months progress in English and science and one additional months' progress in maths, compared to children in "control schools"'

(Jay et al., 2017: 4). Another finding was that pupils on free school meals (FSM) made two additional months' progress in English, science and maths, although there were fewer pupils in this group in comparison to the non-FSM group.

Most teachers believed that in order to become fully embedded, it would take longer than two terms to implement. They also thought that measuring the impact for longer than two terms would be of benefit.

Due to the fact that this intervention is an alteration 'to classroom talk across the curriculum through training, handbooks, video and regular review meetings with mentors', there was the view that the effects of these could be differentiated (Jay et al., 2017).

What is clear is that Socratic questioning and dialogic teaching can be used for both philosophical debate, as in P4C, or for competitive discussions or to extend skills and knowledge as in dialogic teaching. However, there are key differences in their outcomes:

- Philosophical debate: used to seek the truth, discusses philosophical issues with no wrong or right answers – promotes diverse thinking and acceptance of it and enables the reaching of a 'tentative' conclusion. It is focused on learning and it is acceptable to change your mind (Hymer and Sutcliffe, 2012).
- Competitive discussions: used for victory seeking, could be used to debate two sides, building on reasoning to come to a proper conclusion. It is focused on performance and changing your mind indicates defeat (Hymer and Sutcliffe, 2012).
- Extending skills and knowledge: used to seek skills and knowledge, to develop exploratory talk, where pupils practise oral skills and build up ideas to develop a more coherent thinking process, to build knowledge, to alleviate misconceptions and reach the correct answer (Mercer and Hodgkinson, 2008). Changing your mind indicates success and a resilience to learning (growth mindset).

Although the outcomes of the different type of talk appear to be different, Robin Alexander (2018) emphasises that there should be an equal balance of teacher and pupil talk during discussions and that there is no 'right way to maximise talk's quality and power (for example, through small group discussion, or "interactive whole class teaching")'. This leaves it pretty much up to teachers to decide which strategies to choose based on the context of their classes.

Alexander (2019) sums up the purpose of dialogue as being a process to help children learn in collaboration with their teacher. This increases their 'sense of responsibility for what and how they learn'. Through dialogue pupils learn that knowledge is something which is 'negotiated and re-created' not only 'between self and others' but also 'between past and present'.

Listening

Mannion and Mercer (2020) cite that listening is the 'most fundamental', from Oxford (1993: 205). We spend most that is '45 per cent' of our time listening (Mannion and Mercer (2020). Due to its very nature, listening is usually given less attention. It cannot be recorded, assessed or measured in meaningful ways. 'Listening is invisible - it leaves no paper trail and cannot be detected or recorded in the way that speaking can', Mannion and Mercer (2020).

Although, the importance of listening is recognised by practitioners, it appears to be one of the least understood aspects of learning. This is due to the complex nature of it. However, of the 'four language skills: reading, writing, speaking and listening', listening is the most important.

Research (Buck, 2011) has shown that spoken language is different to written language. Three elements of speech, which are important for listening comprehension are:

1. 'Speech is encoded in the form of sound.
2. It is linear and takes place in real time, with no chance of review.
3. It is linguistically different from written language'. Mannion and Mercer (2020)

This suggests that the teaching of speaking and listening skills require different approaches than that of written forms of language.

Mannion and Mercer (2020) highlight the importance of listening as a 'gateway to understanding.' Educators are aware that listening is crucial to learning but the misconception is that it is something that does not need to be taught; it is regarded as a 'passive skill' (Mannion and Mercer, 2020).

Listening comprehension has been deemed to be a very complex problem-solving activity and since at least the 1950s researchers have understood the importance of it. It consists of 'a set of distinct sub-skills', Mannion and Mercer (2020).

The reality, however, is that there needs to be more of a focus on developing listening skills at the same time as speaking skills. There is a misconception that listening skills are generic and can be applied to all situations. To some extent this is true. However, the work of Jiang et al. (2017) highlighted the difference of novice learners and more experienced learners: 'novices learn best from instruction that combines reading and listening, while more knowledgeable learners benefit from a reading-only approach', Mannion and Mercer (2020).

Mannion and Mercer (2020) claim that 'if we explicitly taught listening skills to every child, we would likely see benefits in terms of their ability to acquire knowledge and skills in a range of contexts.' It has become clearer more recently that not only can listening skills be taught explicitly but 'when done well, students learn more effectively' (Mannion and Mercer, 2020). Mannion and Mercer (2020) state that a recent study by Ferrari-Briggers, Stroumbakis and Drini (2017), found that there is a positive association between critical-analytical skills and improved learning in maths and science. However, due to its complexity, listening is largely overlooked.

Mannion and Mercer (2020) draw upon a research review by Berne (1998) on second language learning to highlight key findings on listening comprehension: lower achiever listeners take cues from both sounds and meaning, whilst for the higher achievers there is a sole focus on just meaning; listening comprehension can be improved through the use of 'pre-listening activities, particularly those that provide short synopses of the listening passage or allow listeners to preview the comprehension questions', Mannion and Mercer (2020); using a scaffold such as video enables listening comprehension far better than audio; real listening passages in contrast to invented passages improves listening comprehension greatly; listening strategies should be taught as they improve comprehension; a variety of situations, different types of listening passages and different medium, where listening is required, should be used.

The metacognitive aspect of how pupils learn from listening can be beneficial, Wilson (2003). An interesting study conducted by Vandergrift et al. (2006) found that using Metacognitive Awareness Listening Questionnaire (MALQ) before and after teaching, was a way of capturing listening over time. It could also be used to enable metacognitive reflection and evaluation.

Developing the metacognition of listening can be beneficial in particular 'how they learn from listening', Mannion and Mercer (2020) and self-regulated listening.

They suggest five metacognitive strategies to develop listening. These are: 'enhancing awareness', where discussion is set up to explore reasons why it is sometimes hard to listen and to recognise what makes a good listener; 'self-monitoring' which consists of listening activities with timed pauses and recall; 'summarising' either through video or audio, where pupils write down three main ideas; 'selective attention' where pre-teaching of skills takes place; and 'cognitive connections' where pupils listen to new information and write how it 'relates to their pre-existing knowledge', Mannion and Mercer (2020).

Case study: Developing listening skills

Fatima had only been in the country for a year before starting Year 6. She was very shy and hardly spoke, in fact her teacher thought she was a selective mute. Her teacher set up lessons which involved teaching listening skills more explicitly. These consisted of lessons on why listening is important, how the whole class could contribute to an environment which positively promoted listening skills and how pupils could become better listeners. The teacher also arranged tasks which involved timed pauses to check for accuracy of listening. After watching videos pupils would jot down the main points, relevant to what they were learning about that day. Pupils were pre-taught knowledge and skills and made notes and they were able to relate the new knowledge to pre-existing knowledge. As a result of these actions Fatima made huge progress in her learning.

- Why did the teacher plan lessons on the teaching of listening skills?
- How did the teacher break down the teaching of listening skills?
- How did these lessons help, not only Fatima, but all the other pupils in the classroom?

Summary

- Talk is not automatically picked up but needs to be taught explicitly.
- All types of classroom talk requires giving pupils time to think and reflect.
- The type of talk chosen for particular activities depends on the desired outcome of the lesson or lessons.
- Listening carefully precedes speaking and needs to be taught explicitly.
- Listening skills needs to be taught separately to talking and should be taught explicitly.

Think!

- How can both speaking and listening be taught at the same time?
- Why is it important to teach listening skills explicitly?
- Why is it important to teach speaking skills explicitly?
- Which speaking and listening strategies are the most effective and why?
- How do speaking and listening skills contribute to the development of critical-thinking skills?

Teacher metacognition

- Which types of dialogue do you already use in the classroom?
- Which types of dialogue could you include in the classroom?
- In which activities could you use each type of dialogue?
- Which pupils do not usually speak during sessions?
- How could you encourage them to speak?
- What strategies could you use to develop speaking in the classroom?
- What are the main challenges in using dialogue?
- What are the main barriers to learning listening skills?
- Which listening strategies could be incorporated into lessons?
- How could challenges be overcome?
- How could you overcome these challenges?

Pupil metacognition

- How does the pupil feel when others are speaking?
- Do pupils find it easy to speak?
- If not, why not?
- How could pupils overcome the challenges and get their voices heard?
- Which pupils are good at listening?
- Which pupils need to be taught listening skills explicitly?

References

Alexander, R. (2018) Developing dialogic teaching: Genesis, process, trial. *Research Papers in Education*, 33 (5): 561–598, DOI: 10.1080/02671522.2018.1481140

Alexander, R. (2019) *Dialogic Teaching* [online]. Available at: www.robinalexander.org.uk/dialogic-teaching/ (accessed 16 March 2021).

Berne, J.E. (1998) Examining the relationship between L2 listening research, pedagogical theory, and practice. *Foreign Language Annals,* 31 (2): 169–190.

Bibi, Y. (2020) *Creating Independent Thinkers And Writers Through Socratic Seminars*. @msybibiblogs [online]. Available at: https://msybeebs.wordpress.com/2020/02/02/creating-independent-thinkers-and-writers-through-socratic-seminars/ (accessed 16 March 2021).

Delić, Haris and Bećirović, Senad (2016) Socratic Method as an Approach to Teaching.

EEF (2017) *Dialogic Teaching: Evaluation Report and Executive Summary* [online]. Available at: https://educationendowmentfoundation.org.uk/public/files/Projects/Evaluation_Reports/Dialogic_Teaching_Evaluation_Report.pdf (accessed 4 February 2021).

Ferrari-Bridgers, F., Stroumbakis, K., Drini, M. et al. (2017) Assessing critical-analytical listening skills in math and engineering students: An exploratory inquiry of how analytical listening skills can positively impact learning. *International Journal of Listening,* 31 (3): 121–141.

Gaunt, A. and Stott, A. (2019) *Transform Teaching and Learning through Talk: The Oracy Imperative*. Lanham, MD: Rowman & Littlefield.

Jay, T., Willis, B., Thomas, P., Taylor, R., Moore, N., Burnett, C., Merchant, G. and Stevens, A. (2017) *Dialogic Teaching: Evaluation Report and Executive Summary*. Project Report. London: Education Endowment Foundation.

Jiang, D., Kalyuga, S. and Sweller, J. (2017) The curious case of improving foreign language listening skills by reading rather than listening: An expertise reversal effect. *Educational Psychology Review*, 30 (1): 1–27.

Mannion, J. and Mercer, N. (2020) Teaching listening: The gateway to understanding. *Impact: Journal of the Chartered College of Teaching* [online]. Available at: https://impact.chartered.college/article/teaching-listening-gateway-understanding/ (accessed 16 March 2021).

Mercer, N. and Hodgkinson, S. (eds) (2008) *Exploring Talk in School*. London: Sage.

Oxford, R. (1993) Research update on teaching L2 listening. *System, 21* (2): 205–211.

Soodak, L.C. and Podell, D.M. (1996) Teacher efficacy: Toward the understanding of a multi-faceted construct. *Teaching and Teacher Education*, 12 (4): 401–411. https://doi.org/10.1016/0742-051X(95)00047-N

Vandergrift, L., Goh, C., Mareschal, C. et al. (2006) The Metacognitive Awareness Listening Questionnaire: Development and validation. *Language Learning*, 53 (3): 431–462.

Vygotsky, L.S. (1962) Thought and Language. Cambridge, MA: MIT Press. (Original work published in 1934).

Wilson, N.S. and Smetana, L. (2011) Questioning as thinking: a metacognitive framework to improve comprehension of expository text. *Literacy*, 45 (2): 84–90. https://doi.org/10.1111/j.1741-4369.2011.00584.x

13

METACOGNITION, SCHEMAS AND MEMORY DEVELOPMENT IN THE CURRICULUM

Contents

In this chapter we will explore

- the challenges involved in major assimilation
- our understanding of schemas and how the internal architecture can be built
- the reasons why sequencing of the curriculum is important to processing language and how this helps with memory development
- ways of incorporating memory development into the curriculum
- how theories of spacing and retrieval can be incorporated into the curriculum.

Assimilation of knowledge

In 1969, Paiget and Inhelder suggested that if new ideas do not fit our existing schemas, our schemas need to be changed; however, the closer the 'new knowledge and experience is to our existing schema, the better the integration of both new and old ideas' (Mercer and Hodgkinson, 2008). Similarly, in *Psychology in the Classroom*, Smith and Firth (2018) explain that essential information in our brains is grouped into schemas and not gathered in separately apportioned sections like in a 'computer hard drive. New information is best remembered if it can be linked to an existing structure'. It is completely natural to resist changing our view of the world, as often new ideas, experiences or information require deep-seated modification.

Let us look at some of the challenges involved in major assimilation. When a Year 5 teacher was teaching earth and space and discussing whether people always believed that the earth was round, due to their life experiences, pupils had only ever heard or believed that the earth was round. There was an element of shock when they discovered that some people had thought the earth was flat centuries ago. Even when presented with evidence of the earth being round such as seeing ships and boats disappear from view, pupils found the concept quite difficult to understand and 'this required a major accommodation of their ideas' (Mercer and Hodgkinson, 2008). They call this a 'radical revision of our pictures of the physical or social world and how it works'.

Due to the fact that 'we learn by connecting new ideas and ways of thinking to our existing view of the world, all new learning must depend on what a learner already knows'. The difficulty in the example above highlights the challenges involved when learning new things outside our existing schema, as 'we can only make sense of it in terms of our existing schemas' (Mercer and Hodgkinson, 2008). Learning does not usually happen abruptly. Learning is not a case of moving from not understanding something one minute to full understanding the next.

Figure 13.1 is an illustrative example of the assimilation of learning. The rectangle, in the centre of the figure, can represent years of learning.

Another example is comparing an adult's understanding of electricity to that of a child's. A pupil may use the word electricity to correctly identify what it is but may not have the ability or knowledge to explain the purpose, make links or explain how it works. The ideas may be too abstract to develop full understanding of it. The differences will be more apparent, especially to those who have studied physics. Our cognitive architecture (concepts, models, schemas) is continuously changing and developing in our minds and changes throughout our lives.

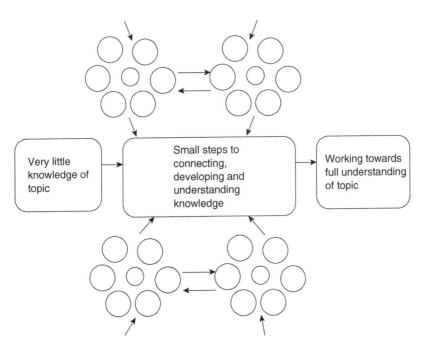

Figure 13.1 A model of assimilation of knowledge

Although Mercer and Hodgkinson (2008: 4) acknowledge the constructivist view of learning as requiring teachers to encourage 'pupils to relate new ideas and ways of thinking with existing understandings and expectations in order to modify them' (by setting up situations and challenges, they shift the focus to developing understanding instead: 'Working on understanding is, in essence, the reshaping of old knowledge in the light of new ways of seeing things' p. 4. 'Seeing things' is a metaphor for making learning explicit. Developing understanding can be one of the most challenging things to do.

Firstly, it is the pupil who can work on understanding, not the teacher. Teachers 'can encourage and support but cannot do it for them' (Mercer and Hodgkinson, 2008: 4). The process of reshaping takes into consideration 'old knowledge' as well as new experiences and this is where the teacher's expertise comes into play, to challenge a pupil's understanding.

Challenge necessitates the change in accommodation, as we change old ways of understanding to new ways. It is this challenge that can be uncomfortable for both adults and children because it is easier to hang on to misconceptions rather than to change (see Chapter 5 for more on this). Listening is one way to develop understanding (Mannion and Mercer, 2020) (see Chapter 12 for further information).

What is a schema?

A schema can be described as a cognitive framework upon which knowledge is built. When children are babies, they use their senses to learn about things which they come across in a safe and stimulating environment. You may notice some toddlers collecting all the toy cars, sometimes one at a time, and putting them into a long line. This pattern of behaviour of walking to and from becomes the 'foundation of learning' displayed between the ages of two and five (Nutbrown, 2011).

Sometimes, however, these cognitive frameworks can lead to eliminating important information and to confirming our already established beliefs and ideas. The downside to schemas is that they can confirm stereotypes and make it challenging to keep new information, which does not back-up our pre-existing ideas about the world (Cherry, 2019).

In 1932, Frederic Bartlett introduced the basis of understanding of the world as being in the form of mental structures. Although Jean Piaget coined the term schema, which was an idea he promoted, this learning theory was first used by Bartlett to explain what schemas might be (Cherry, 2019). Cherry (2019) explains that according to Piaget's 'theory of cognitive development, children go through a series of stages of intellectual growth'.

Piaget's theory of schema was one whereby 'both the category of knowledge as well as the process of acquiring that knowledge' is described. Piaget's explanation of schema development is that humans are continually acclimatising to their environments and as they absorb new material, new schemas are born as old schemas are adapted (Cherry, 2019).

Examples of schema

For example, a child may develop a schema for a horse first. The child knows that a horse is quite large. The child is also aware that it is hairy and has four legs and a tail. When the child comes across a cow, they may call it a horse initially. This would fit in with their understanding of a description of a horse. After all a cow has hair, four legs and a tail. When the child is informed that the animal is not a horse but a cow, their existing schema will become adapted and a new schema for a cow will be created (Cherry, 2019).

What would happen if the child came across a miniature horse, for example? They may incorrectly identify it as a dog due to their existing understanding of a dog being small and because their schema has already identified horses as being large. If the child is corrected at this point, the existing schema is adapted to include the understanding that whilst some horses are large, others can be small. Through this new experience, the existing schema becomes 'modified and new information is learned' (Cherry, 2019).

Piaget mainly studied childhood development, but everyone possesses schemas, which are continuously adapting and changing throughout our lives, as we assimilate new information. There are many types of schemas in operation at any one time. Some examples of schemas are: object schemas, for example a car; person schemas, about individuals, which can include information about their behaviour, personality and appearance; self-schemas, which are concerned with knowledge about yourself; and event schemas, which are about how you should behave and act in certain situations (Cherry, 2019).

Do schemas change?

There are two ways schemas can be changed: through assimilation and accommodation. The main differences are that assimilation is when new knowledge is combined with pre-existing schemas, however, in accommodation, existing schemas may be changed as the person learns new knowledge or skills (Cherry, 2019).

Schemas are usually easier to adapt when younger, and as people become older, they tend to become inflexible and more challenging to change.

As explained in Chapter 5, beliefs play a major role in the development of neuromyths and variance in teacher experience can also create misunderstandings in education. In a similar way, even 'when people are presented with evidence that contradicts their beliefs', they are still resistant to change their schemas (Cherry, 2019).

However, eventually people can modify their schemas to incorporate new information but this usually happens when people are presented with evidence on a continuous basis, which includes reasons why it needs to be modified.

Do schemas affect the learning process?

Schemas appear to play a very important role in the learning process. According to Cherry (2019), they can influence learning in many ways, for example: schemas affect what we give attention to as people are more likely to give consideration to things which are in line with their current schemas. Schemas can also affect how quickly learning occurs as people learn knowledge more easily when it is in line with their existing schemas. Schemas can also help us make sense of the world and, according to Cherry (2019), help us to 'simplify' it:

- Schemas help simplify the world. Schemas can often make it easier for people to learn about the world around them. New information could be classified and categorised by comparing new experiences to existing schemas.

- Schemas allow us to think quickly. Even under conditions when things are rapidly changing our new information is coming in quickly, people do not usually have to spend a great deal of time interpreting it. Because of the existing schemas, people are able to assimilate this new information quickly and automatically.
- Schemas can also change how we interpret incoming information. When learning new information that does not fit with existing schemas, people sometimes distort or alter the new information to make it fit with what they already know.
- Schemas can also be remarkably difficult to change. People often cling to their existing schemas even in the face of contradictory information. (Cherry, 2019)

The problem with schemas

Although using schemas to learn can occur without much effort and 'automatically', existing schemas can sometimes prevent 'the learning of new information' (Cherry, 2019). Prejudice is one example.

Sometimes our schemas can be affected by the beliefs we hold about a group of people and this can cause us to 'interpret situations incorrectly'. Sometimes when people's existing schemas or beliefs are challenged by a particular event, people may come up with 'alternative explanations that uphold and support their existing schema instead of adapting or changing their beliefs' (Cherry, 2019).

An example is our beliefs about what is masculine and what is feminine in society and the roles of men and women. We all have schemas for expectations on how each should behave. These beliefs can lead to, for example, stereotypes and gender expectations.

Cherry (2019) illustrates the problem with schemas by discussing a research study which was conducted where a group of children were shown images in line with gender stereotypes, for example, of a woman doing the dishes and a man fixing a car. Whereas another group were shown pictures which did not fit with some gender stereo-types, where instead a woman was fixing a car and the man was doing the dishes.

After some time, the children were asked to remember what they had seen. Researchers discovered that those who held gender stereo-typical views 'were more likely to change the gender of the people they saw in the gender-inconsistent images'. If they had seen an 'image of a man washing dishes, they were more likely to remember it as an image of a woman washing dishes' (Cherry, 2019).

This implies that schemas are notoriously difficult to challenge and change.

Schema development and memory in the curriculum

Developing a schema requires retrieval from long-term memory, making connections to other classroom and outdoor expereinces, linking knowledge to life experiences, activating prior knowledge of topic/subject studies, all of which require pupils to rely on drawing on their memories. All this recall rests on the foundation of language and as new information is assimilated, vocabulary becomes more sophisticated (see Figure 13.2).

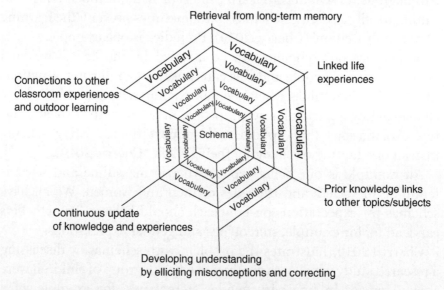

Figure 13.2 A model of developing a schema on the foundation of vocabulary instruction

In her book *The Curriculum: Gallimaufry to Coherence*, Mary Myatt (2018) explains that ultimately 'we are pattern-seeking species' and that we are constantly making 'sense and order from the world around us'. Humans organise information into categories as an 'efficient way of staying alive'. She gives the example of being able to differentiate berries that nourish us from berries that kill us, which helps us to survive. It is human nature to seek patterns and to see how things connect. Myatt suggests that the curriculum should be about creating coherence between subjects, topics and ideas.

Let us explore how this can be achieved through the teaching of vocabulary. In her 2017 blog, Clare Sealy talks about the 3D curriculum that promotes learning. She describes the curriculum as being 'the means by which we ensure that all our children get their fair share of the rich cultural inheritance our world affords'. Sealy goes on to say that a good curriculum will arm children with the wealth of knowledge they require to take part in society.

One of the most important aspect of teaching the curriculum is to ensure that what is taught is remembered: 'Knowledge can't empower if it is forgotten'. Sealy (2017) goes on to advise that 'as well as thinking about what is the richest, best material to put into our curriculum, we also have to structure our curriculum in a way that makes remembering almost inevitable'.

Although schools rightly think about how children learn, schools should also consider what children learn. According to Sealy (2017) one aspect which is overlooked in schools is how to plan the curriculum systematically and 'build their curriculum so that children remember it'.

Sealy started the blog by explaining that there was no national curriculum when she started teaching and although teachers endeavoured to link topics together, sometimes certain topics were not taught and were missed out altogether. The idea was that by linking topics together not only would it be fun but it would be memorable to pupils, rather than having separate topics with no common thread or with tenuous links.

Topic webs (showing links between subjects) have been used in schools, particularly in primary schools, for years, however, the topic web itself needs revamping and suggests that 'we need to build in those links in a far more systematic and structural way than the "topic web" approach ever imagined'? (Sealy, 2017).

Sealy (2017) advises that the curriculum across the years and across subjects needs to link in a 'well thought out way, so that knowledge taught in one subject is explicitly reinforced and revisited ... not only in other subjects, but in subsequent years'. The reason for this is to reinforce new vocabulary and key concepts through 'meaningful contexts'; this is what Sealy refers to as the 3D curriculum.

Sealy's (2017) 3D curriculum consists of three types of links: 'vertical, horizontal and diagonal links'.

Vertical links are 'deliberately constructed' within subjects, 'so that over the years, key "high yield" concepts are encountered again and again'. The idea is that not only are the key concepts revisited throughout the 'unit of work' but also in 'subsequent years'.

Sealy (2017) explores the word 'tyrant' and related words 'tyranny' and 'tyrannical' when teaching history. The word 'tyrant' is first taught in Year 1, where they learn about King John being a tyrant. Tyrants are not studied again until Year 5, when Dionysius of Syracuse is introduced, and 'his tyranny is counterpoised with the democracy of Ancient Greek city states'. Although it would have been four years since learning the word tyrant back in Year 1, it is a chance to refresh pupils' minds about the limited power in Britain and the Magna Carta. The understanding of the word tyranny can be further developed in Year 6, by learning about the adjective 'tyrannical', where pupils, for example, can compare Churchill with Hitler.

As well as the vertical links mentioned above, Sealy (2017) explains the importance of developing 'horizontal links between subjects in a year'. Horizontal links were the ones found in topic webs back in the days. One way to teach nominalisation (crucial for academic writing) is through horizontal links. The example offered is in Year 4, where pupils are taught about the 'invasion' of England by the Vikings, the invasion of the body by microbes and 'invasion games in PE'.

> For example, children are taught that rather than writing that the Nazi's invaded Poland ... it is more effective to write about the invasion. Instead of saying the French were defeated we write about the defeat of the French and later about the opposition and resistance of the French. (Sealy, 2017)

The final dimension of the 3D curriculum is 'diagonal links'. These are links which connect concepts across years groups and across subjects.

The diagonal link for the word 'tyrant' is in Year 3, where they encounter it in Religious Education through the story of the Exodus and they learn about how brutal the pharaoh was. This is the second time they encounter the word tyrant since Year 1.

Each time a concept is revisited in a different context, it is 'more likely to be remembered' and 'the understanding of that concept becomes more nuanced' (Sealy, 2017). It is a way of developing the schema.

Sealy (2017) advises that this is planned into the curriculum deliberately and pupils should be explicitly reminded, possibly in the form of retrieval practice. Prior learning should be built upon, not only within lessons but throughout the curriculum. This will help with memory development. The curriculum should be seen 'as the progression model'.

In Sealy's experience, 'most primary schools are only just beginning to map out the kind of knowledge they think children should be learning, let alone thinking about the route map of key concepts within and across years and subjects'.

There has been much research to show that there is a huge vocabulary gap, which affects those for whom English is an additional language and for those from lower socio-economic backgrounds. It has been suggested that by three years of age there is a 30-million-word gap between the richest and poorest families (Hart and Risley, 2003). However, there are many ways educators can help close this gap.

Sealy (2017) refers to teaching tiers of vocabulary through the curriculum and focuses on linking vocabulary in her 3D curriculum in a structured way. This is taken from the book entitled *Bringing Words to Life* by Beck, Mckeown and Kucan (2013). They state that not only does a rich vocabulary help with the understanding of the world but it also helps us to appreciate the 'beauty of language'. Understanding vocabulary is key to developing reading comprehension, however, pupils come with a range of understanding.

Beck et al. (2013) agree that although there are too many words to learn, they do not all need to be taught by instruction; they can be taught in 'tiers'. Tier 1 words consists of conversational words. These are the 'most basic words' and include the words: warm, dog, tired, run, walk and so on. Pupils would have been exposed to these words frequently.

Tier 3 words are encountered rarely and are more domain specific. These include words such as evolution, immunisation, organism and so on. These words would be learned when studying a particular topic or subject domain.

In comparison, words in the second tier are used frequently by 'mature language users', and are found across more than one domain. Words in this tier include: contradict, circumstance, precede and so on. Tier 2 words play a significant role on the 'impact of verbal functioning'. According to Beck et al. (2013) it is therefore important to pay more attention to tier 2 words. The case study below highlights how sequencing of vocabulary and developing memory can be incorporated into the curriculum.

Case study: Developing vocabulary within the curriculum

In her blog, 'Curriculum decisions – Using knowledge to create moments of joy', Victoria Morris (2020) discusses memory development through school trips. This is one of the reasons why Morris plans school trips at the end of a topic rather than at the beginning. Children can apply vocabulary and knowledge already learned and apply it to the context.

The first example given is prior to studying Charles Darwin, Year 6 had learned about the Victorians. When they visited Down House, they were able to apply the knowledge they had learned to the house of Charles Darwin. They were able to apply the knowledge about Darwin's life to the house.

Morris (2020) explains that it was Clare Sealy's blogs which helped develop her understanding of learning.

> To learn something is to be changed in some way that lasts beyond the immediate. If we encounter momentary joy or fleeting pleasure along the way, so much the better. But it is the lasting change that makes learning purposeful. Learning enables us to see the world in a new way. Whereas before we only saw trees, now we see elms, oaks and sycamores. Whereas before we only saw rocks, we now see granite, limestone and sandstone. Whereas before we only saw shopping, we now see profit, loss and externalities. (Morris, 2020)

The second example that Morris refers to is a residential trip which she planned so that children could make the most of the experience. The trip was planned for November, however, prior to this in September, Year 5 were taught the 'science unit on lifecycles of animals and plants'. Firstly, pupils recapped how to group plants and animals, which included woodland plants and animals. Morris carefully included the types of trees pupils would encounter on the trip, and 'mosses lichens and ferns, as well as stinging nettles and dock leaves' (2020).

Urban and rural vocabulary was then introduced through a range of texts 'with contrasting city and country settings'. Morris planned reading *The Town Mouse and the Country Mouse* and extracts from the stories of Brambly Hedge. In contrast the class novel *Varjak Paw* was used amongst other texts focusing not only on setting descriptions but also a continuation of developing vocabulary of rural and urban environments.

After that, in October, a geography unit was taught contrasting urban and rural settings and populations. In addition to this, 'UK locational knowledge and physical and human features' were studied (Morris, 2020). As the school where Morris taught was in East London, this was compared to Kent, where Morris grew up. Using her own 'story of growing up in the country was really powerful for the children, and using the photos helped to build their vocabulary relating to the countryside even further' (Morris, 2020). This helped children share their own stories, some of which were from around England and some as far afield as Bangladesh. This embedded the language further.

The children also did map work, comparing surrounding areas of the school with the area of the visit, and studied population densities and the advantages and disadvantages of living in each area. Misconceptions were identified and rectified. The children were excited about spending the week together but also about seeing what they had learned in real life.

Apart from 'jumping in muddy puddles', there was rich discussion of different plants encountered on the trip. Pupils also questioned 'whether different plants were dock leaves, whether what they could see on trees was moss or lichen, whether different bushes were brambles, and which trees were oak trees. There was a lot of excitement in particular about the different types of fungus growing in the woods. And this year no one got stung because they could all recognise the stinging nettles!' (Morris, 2020).

Without pre-teaching the vocabulary, pupils would not have had the language to describe what they were seeing on their trip, they may not have been able to question what they were seeing and the rich discussion may not have taken place.

Morris concludes by saying: 'If we can structure the curriculum to ensure children feel that joy on every visit, we are creating truly powerful

(Continued)

learning experiences by providing them with the knowledge they need to appreciate the experience more fully'.

- What preparations did Morris make for a 3D curriculum?
- How was vocabulary developed within the 3D curriculum for learning about urban and rural environments?
- What experiences were planned for?
- Why were personal experiences retrieved?
- How was this beneficial for all pupils?

Summary

- If new ideas do not fit our existing schemas, our schemas need to be changed.
- Prejudice can hinder the development of schemas.
- The new knowledge and experience needs to be close to our existing schemas, to better integrate new and old ideas.
- One way of doing this is by mapping out vocabulary throughout the curriculum, to develop schemas.

Think!

- How can memory be developed throughout the curriculum?
- Why is it important for learning to take place in a variety of different contexts?
- How can reading texts be used to pre-teach, develop and embed language and vocabulary?
- Why are external experiences and personal experiences necessary for vocabulary development?
- What role does vocabulary play in schema development?
- What experiences can be planned for each topic?
- How can a 3D curriculum be designed, which would provide the language pupils would need to navigate their way through it?
- How can higher order thinking skills be developed within the curriculum?

Teacher metacognition

- What is the big idea, schema or skill you want pupils to learn at the end of a key stage or school?
- How could the knowledge and/or skills for the schema be broken down for learning in the curriculum?
- Why is activating prior knowledge important in both vocabulary and schema development?
- Does the frequency of retrieval practice vary depending on subject or topic?
- Will it be easy or a challenge to retrieve knowledge/skills required?
- What needs to be planned in to retrieve knowledge/skills?

Pupil metacognition

- What do pupils already know about the topic?
- How much knowledge is easy to retrieve?
- How much experience have pupils had about using the vocabulary of the topic?
- What experiences have pupils had linked to the topic?

References

Beck, I.L., McKeown, M.G. and Kucan, L. (2013) Bringing Words To Life. New York: The Guilford Press.

Cherry, K. (2019) *The role of a schema in psychology* [online]. Available at: www.verywellmind.com/what-is-a-schema-2795873 (accessed 28 January 2021).

Hart, B. and Risley, T.R. (2003) The early catastrophe: The 30 million word gap by age 3. *American Educator*, Spring: 4–9. Available at: www.aft.org//sites/default/files/periodicals/TheEarlyCatastrophe.pdf (accessed 16 March 2021).

Mannion, J. and Mercer, N. (2020) Teaching listening: The gateway to understanding. *Impact: Journal of the Chartered College of Teaching* [online]. Available at: https://impact.chartered.college/article/teaching-listening-gateway-understanding/ (accessed 16 March 2021).

Mercer, N. and Hodgkinson, S. (eds) (2008) *Exploring Talk in School*. London: Sage.

Morris, V. (2020) Curriculum decisions – Using knowledge to create moments of joy [online]. Available at: https://mrssteaches.school.blog/2020/06/16/curriculum-decisions-using-knowledge-to-create-moments-of-joy/ (accessed 3 February 2021).

Myatt, M. (2018) *The Curriculum: Gallimaufry to Coherence*. John Catt Educational Ltd.

Nutbrown, C. (2011) Threads of Thinking: Schemas and Young Children's Learning (4th edn). London: Sage.

Sealy, C. (2017) The 3D curriculum that promotes remembering [online]. Available at: https://primarytimery.com/2017/10/28/the-3d-curriculum-that-promotes-remembering/ (accessed 28 January 2021).

14

METACOGNITION AND FORMATIVE ASSESSMENTS

Contents

In this chapter we will explore

- how our biases can affect assessment
- why we tend to use cognitive shortcuts and follow our stereotypes when it comes to assessment
- emotional intelligence and its role in self-regulation
- using other forms of assessment, in the classroom, as a way of assessing pupil potential.

The problems with assessment

Society has always used cognitive assessment as a measure of success and intelligence, which is prioritised over all other forms of assessment.

If you can remember more and recall more and prove it in a test, then you are perceived to be highly intelligent. Usually, passing tests gives you freedom of choice over what you study and how your career progresses. However, there are issues associated with tests.

Christodoulou (2015a), in 'Tests are inhuman – and that is what is so good about them', describes tests as 'dehumanising', in the way that older pupils are 'herded' into exam halls and all required to answer the same questions in formats devoid of real-life contexts. When it comes to formal testing, there is no let up: it does not matter what happened the night before or even if they are ill, they still have to take the test or fail! In addition to this, 'exams offer a highly artificial snapshot of a pupil's grasp of atomised knowledge at just one moment in time'.

Christodoulou (2015b) compares formal testing to teacher assessment, which is considered to be a much fairer way of assessing pupils and is much more pleasant for all concerned. There are a number of reasons why teacher assessment is seen as favourable: teachers have in-depth knowledge and long-term understanding of where pupils are with their subjects and topics. This also takes away the time pressure in exam halls.

Tests are designed to override human flaws and therefore 'dehumanise' them by treating all pupils in exactly the same way and they are sent away to be marked by someone who does not know your pupils. This impersonalisation makes the test results reliable and fairly accurate. Pupils do not get an opportunity to draft out answers, edit and redraft. There are not many people who can write something perfectly from scratch.

Although some believe that formal testing is not the way forward, there seems to be evidence to indicate that summative testing can be beneficial for disadvantaged pupils. Burgess (2015) states that when it comes to gender, there are stereotypical beliefs about the academic areas of strength and weakness. Burgess also found that pupils on free school meals were frequently underassessed in comparison with outcomes in national tests: 'Another way of saying the same thing is that poor pupils systematically and significantly outperformed what their teachers thought they would achieve' (Burgess, 2015).

Christodoulou (2015a) highlights the important work of Professor Rob Coe (2014) who tackles the issue of teacher trust. He invariably agrees that teachers should be trusted as professionals but that this comes with a number of caveats, the main one being biases, which are more reflective of natural human biases as opposed to trust in teachers. There are a number of barriers to consistent assessments, including: the order of doing assessments, the types of assessments used, the impression teachers have of pupils, leniency of professionals and the neatness of handwriting.

Unconscious biases

According to Christodoulou (2015b), 'teacher assessment is biased against disadvantaged pupils'. However, this is not conscious or even something that educators are aware of; it forms part of human nature and judgement. Coe (2014) states that teacher bias exists against pupils with SEN, those with challenging behaviour, EAL, FSM pupils, ethnicity and pupils with a different personality type than themselves.

Another important point to consider is that teacher assessment can lead to reinforcement of stereotypes, for example that boys are better at maths, and those from ethnic backgrounds are not able to access learning.

Campbell (2015) also backs up the idea of bias. Evidence suggests that there is systemic bias within teacher assessments which are based on 'income-level, gender, special educational needs status, ethnicity and spoken language', particularly in the area of 'reading and maths ability and attainment'. Due to these 'attainment inequalities' learning gaps can appear, which need to be realised and narrowed. Even when disadvantaged children (from low-income families) had similar cognitive scores to their richer peers, they were seen as being less able.

Cognitive shortcuts

We all use cognitive shortcuts - we would not be human otherwise! Christodoulou (2015b) explains that it is not only teachers who experience these biases but that this is something prevalent amongst other professions too as it is part of human nature. It is natural to use 'cognitive shortcuts'.

When we are presented with challenging decisions to make and are faced with cognitive overload, we naturally take cognitive shortcuts; it 'limits human cognitive capacity' (Christodoulou, 2015b). It is perfectly natural to assume that the reason why biases happen in teacher assessment is because it is so onerous:

> When faced with such a difficult challenge, defaulting to stereotypes is in many ways a sensible attempt by our unconscious minds to reduce our workload. (Christodoulou, 2015b)

She uses an example of what we know about certain pupils to illustrate this further:

> We know that *on average* pupils on free school meals do not attain as well, we know that the essay we are marking isn't great, but it isn't terrible, we know it sort of meets some of the criteria on the mark scheme, we need some more evidence in order to reach a final judgment, we could reread the essay and mark scheme but the mark scheme is hard to interpret ... we also know that the pupil who wrote the essay is from the wrong side of the tracks.

> Done: it's a below average essay. None of us want to admit that this is how our minds work, and for most of us, our minds don't consciously work like this, but there is plenty of evidence that this is how our reasoning goes. (Christodoulou, 2015b)

Assessment of thinking processes

How do we, therefore, counteract human biases and the way they can impact on teacher assessments? As mentioned earlier in the chapter, disadvantaged pupils can benefit from testing, as society mainly relies on test data to determine potential, however, teachers are aware that test data needs to be used with caution and used in combination with other non-formal classroom assessments.

When we think of learning potential it is not only gaps in subject knowledge that teachers look for. If pupils do not have thinking skills, they will be prevented from learning subject knowledge.

By assessing the thinking skills gap aswell as the subject knowledge gap, cognition could be accelerated.

Assessing self-regulation and self-regulated learning

The EEF guidance on *Metacognition and Self-regulated Learning* (2018) recognises that some form of assessment other than high stakes tests and teacher assessments are required in the classroom. Although due to the reasons stated earlier in the chapter, it is a challenge to conduct reliable assessments, it is still important to assess self-regulated learning and self-regulation in the classroom. This would provide educators with more reliable assessments of potential to learn as opposed to solely focusing on cognitive ability and strategies.

In addition to this, due to better understanding of the mechanisms at work of self-regulated learning, self-regulation and the role metacognition plays in it, these can be utilised to develop measures of assessment which would be beneficial, not only to disadvantaged pupils but to all pupils.

What we now know about metacognition and self-regulated learning is that it is specific to the task (Dent and Koenka, 2016).

The EEF (2018) suggests some assessments to use in the classroom. These include: traces, observations, talk aloud procedures, self-report questionnaires and structured interviews. Let us explore each type in a little more detail.

When pupils are completing tasks, traces can be used to observe metacognitive strategies. Examples of traces include underlining key words or phrases in a piece of text or making notes.

Educators can observe how much time pupils spend on tasks to give an indication of where they are with self-regulated learning. Another observable characteristic is 'homework completion rates' (EEF, 2018).

Talk aloud procedures can also be used to assess metacognition. This is when pupils verbalise 'their thought processes while doing a particular task' (EEF, 2018). It is important to note that this may be self-limited due to lack of language and ability to verbalise their thought processes.

Another way to assess metacognition and self-regulated learning is through the completion of self-reported questionnaires, although these need to be used with caution as it is very challenging to recall metacognitive strategies. This would be better used with older students.

A challenging method of assessment is conducting structured interviews, where pupils answer questions such as how they would use self-regulated learning strategies and whether or not that would allow them to access more during learning, thus allowing them to access 'more context-specific strategies'. Again, these would suit older students better.

Levels of independence

As mentioned in Chapter 2, there are five main elements which develop self-regulated learning and independence; these are cognition, metacognition, motivation, emotional control and the kindness factor. In Chapter 6 we explored the social and emotional aspect of metacognition and in particular emotional language. In the paragraph above, we have explored how to assess metacognition too. Let us now focus on cognition, motivation, emotional control and the kindness factor.

In conjunction with using summative assessments in subject knowledge through testing and formative assessments during lessons, teachers continuously assess the factors shown in Figure 14.1 The following 'Level of independence' document could be used as a guide to the gaps which need closing.

HUNTINGTON RESEARCH SCHOOL

Level of independence (teacher assessment)

RAG rating of current practice	Learners currently don't do this...	Learners do some of this...	Learners are competent in this.
Emotional			
• Can speak about own and others behaviour & consequences			
• Tackles new tasks confidently			
• Can control attention and resist distraction			
• Persists in the face of difficulties			
ProSocial			
• Negotiates when and how to carry out tasks			
• Can resolve social problems with peers			
• Is aware of feelings & others and helps and comforts			
• Engages in independent cooperative activities with peers			
• Shares and takes turns independently			
Cognitive			
• Is aware of own strengths & weaknesses			
• Can speak about how they have done something or what they have learnt			
• Can speak about planned activities			
• Can make reasoned choices and decisions			
• Asks questions and suggests answers			
Motivation			
• Initiates activities			
• Finds own resources without adult help			
• Develops own ways of carrying out tasks			
•Plans own tasks, targets & goals			
• Enjoys solving problems			

Figure 14.1 Level of independence from Huntington Research School (Huntington RSN/EEF training materials)

Let us now explore each component of independence.

They say there is no cognition without metacognition, but this does not only relate to subject knowledge. Cognition also includes self-awareness and understanding ones' own strengths and weaknesses, which crosses over to metacognition. Cognition also includes the ability to verbally communicate. Another factor of cognition is understanding reasoning and being able to ask questions. These are all important skills in the development of metacognition.

Motivation includes initiation of tasks and activities, having the ability to find your own resources, the ability to carry out activities and planning your own tasks. Which crosses with metacognition.

Emotional control is about recognising behaviour and how it affects others. It is also concerned with the ability to start new tasks independently, the ability to stay attentive and remain persistent during challenges.

The kindness factor includes the ability to negotiate with others, the ability to resolve conflict with others and empathising with others.

A pupil who is independent will have high levels of cognition, motivation, emotional control and kindness factor.

Assessing cognitive ability using Piaget's stages of development

Jean Piaget developed the theory of cognitive ability and intelligence by observing relationships between people, and created a four stage developmental processes to help us understand how knowledge is acquired and intelligence developed.

Piaget's four stages of child development are as follows:

> During the first stage, the sensorimotor stage, children learn through sensory experiences and the 'manipulation of objects' (Cherry, 2020). Children learn through their senses, basic reflexes and motor responses. Knowledge about how the world works is learned by interacting with their environment and the people around them. Physical changes such as crawling and walking also take place as well as language development and the first thought processes begin.

> The second stage is the preoperational stage between the ages of two and seven. This is where language begins to emerge and children start learning through 'pretend play'. However, at this stage of cognitive development, they do not have logical thought or understand the viewpoint of others. They are also not very perceptive and remain egocentric.

> The third stage of cognitive development is the concrete operational stage between the ages of seven and eleven. Learning through objects continues at this stage and children are still very

literal in their thought processes, however, they become less egocentric and they begin to understand and appreciate how others might be feeling. They also begin to realise that not everyone thinks in the same way.

The final stage is the formal operational stage from the age of twelve upwards. At this stage, there is an increase in logical thinking, deduction, reasoning and abstract ideas begin to develop. Understanding of problem solving also develops and children begin to see multiple solutions. Scientific understanding also improves. Piaget also thought that how children think changes as they get older as opposed to an increase in what they know. This is called qualitative change.

It is important to consider that these are not concrete stages, where children move from one stage to the next, as each stage is fully completed. Rather, some learning at age twelve may still require concrete resources, due to the fact that learning is not linear and due to learning being so complex, learning gaps can appear at any stage of the learning process.

In his book *Visible Learning for Teachers* (2012), Hattie has taken Piaget's four stages of development and suggests that teachers need to be aware of where pupils are with their thinking, so they can challenge pupils and accelerate their cognitive learning.

Case study: Using assessment of thinking skills to identify gaps and accelerate cognition

Kim was not classified as a disadvantaged child. He had never been an FSM or pupil premium child. He was not EAL and neither did he have an obvious SEN needs but his teacher classified him as being disadvantaged. The disadvantage was that although he was from an affluent family, he found it challenging to control his emotions. He would get upset and angry easily and would start swearing and crying.

(Continued)

His behaviour was related to high expectations of the family. His handwriting was poor and his mother would set him handwriting tasks every weekend. If his handwriting contained any errors, the work would be torn up and he would have to start all over again.

At the start of the academic year, at the beginning of every literacy lesson, he would start swearing at his teacher.

His teacher did not react but would calmly ask him to leave the classroom and wash his face and return when he had calmed down. She used Piaget's four stages of cognitive development and found that he had high cognitive ability and that he had the potential to reach end of Year 6, if not achieve greater depth; he clearly had the potential to do so. She also assessed his level of independence and realised that he would initially require one-to-one support with his writing but after about three months this support could be removed. Her assessments indicated that there were issues with Kim's fine motor skills. These were all his learning gaps. There were no subject knowledge gaps.

Realising that there was something deeper affecting his emotional state, his teacher called his parents to find out more. That was when she discovered that his emotional state was linked to the act of writing. She thanked his parents for wanting him to improve but to leave the development of handwriting to the school.

She set about building up his confidence in the composition of writing skills first, as she knew that he had excellent use of vocabulary and sentence structure. She explicitly taught metacognitive strategies and regulation and focused on giving Kim more immediate feedback but used the language of feedback carefully. She also developed the language of emotional expression (see Chapter 6 for more on this).

In addition to this, she planned in five minutes of handwriting practice for him during morning registration and encouraged him to attend Lego club and sewing club once per week to build up his fine motor skills.

After three months, he demonstrated cognitive acceleration and the swearing stopped and his handwriting began to improve. He was a much calmer and happier child, who looked forward to writing again.

- Which forms of teacher assessments were used?
- What action was taken to fill the thinking gaps?
- How was cognition accelerated?
- What improvements were made?

Summary

- Due to human cognitive shortcuts, incorrect assessments can be made.
- It is human nature to be biased about others and to stereotype people.
- Assessements of metacognition in conjunction with self-regulated learning, self-regulation could be a powerful way of assessing potential.

Think!

- Why is it important to conduct assessments in metacognition, cognition, motivation, emotional control and the kindness factor?
- How can we overcome our unconscious biases?

Teacher metacognition

- Do you have any gaps in your thinking skills?
- What are your thinking skills gaps?
- How could you use your knowledge of your own thinking skills to teach your pupils about their thinking skills?
- How do you assess thinking skills?
- How could you support pupils with any thinking skills gaps they have?
- How could you cognitively accelerate learning?

Pupil metacognition

- Which pupils have more thinking skills gaps than others?
- How could self-esteem be built up in pupils who have thinking skills gaps?
- Are there any pupils who could be targeted in a similar way to close these gaps?

References

Burgess, S. (2015) Gender, Teacher Assessments and Stereotypes. CMPO Viewpoint. A blog from The Centre for Market and Public Organisation. https://cmpo.wordpress.com/2015/03/

Campbell, T. (2015) Stereotyped at seven? Biases in teacher judgement of pupils' ability and attainment. *Journal of Social Policy*, 44 (3): 517–547. https://doi.org/10.1017/S0047279415000227

Cherry, K. (2020) The 4 stages of cognitive development: Background and key concepts of Piaget's theory [online]. Available at: www.verywell mind.com/piagets-stages-of-cognitive-development-2795457 (accessed 5 February 2021).

Christodoulou, D. (2015a) Tests are inhuman – and that is what is so good about them [online]. Available at: https://daisychristodoulou.com/2015/10/tests-are-inhuman-and-that-is-what-so-good-about-them/ (accessed 5 February 2021).

Christodoulou, D. (2015b) Why is teacher assessment biased? Available at: https://daisychristodoulou.com/2015/11/why-is-teacher-assessment-biased/

Coe, R. (2014) Teacher Assessment: Trust, professionalism, Balance, Equality. Centre for Evaluating and Monitoring (part 3 on Vimeo).

Dent, A. and Koenka, A. (2016) The relation between self-regulated learning and academic achievement across childhood and adolescence: A meta-analysis. *Educational Psychology Review*, 28 (4): 425–474.

EEF (2018) *Metacognition and Self-regulated Learning: Guidance Report* [online]. Available at: https://educationendowmentfoundation.org.uk/public/files/Publications/Metacognition/EEF_Metacognition_and_self-regulated_learning.pdf (accessed 4 February 2021).

Hattie, J. (2012) Visible Learning for Teachers: Maximising Impact on Learning. London: Routledge.

INDEX